天福元年中元日
書于觀音導利院

規繩遍通少林之消息莫勞
拂耳之風更驚擊石之響耶
但能正開自寶藏受用使如意

普勸坐禪儀

Zen Master Dōgen

ZEN

MASTER DŌGEN

An Introduction with Selected Writings

by Yūhō Yokoi

with the assistance of Daizen Victoria

and with a foreword by Minoru Kiyota

New York • WEATHERHILL • *Tokyo*

The endpaper design reproduces a portion of a scroll of "A Universal Recommendation for Zazen" (*Fukan Zazen-gi*) believed to be in Dōgen's own hand. This scroll is in the possession of Eihei-ji temple, Fukui Prefecture, and is reproduced here with permission. The design on the title page is the official crest of Eihei-ji, consisting of a stylized arrangement of five gentian (*rindō*) blossoms. The resemblance of one of the design elements to a cross is coincidental.

First edition, 1976

Published by John Weatherhill, Inc., 149 Madison Avenue, New York, New York 10016, with editorial offices at 7-6-13 Roppongi, Minato-ku, Tokyo 106, Japan. Printed in the Republic of Korea and first published in Japan.

Library of Congress Cataloging in Publication Data: Yokoi, Yūhō, 1918–/Zen Master Dōgen./1. Sōtōshū—Collected works. 2. Dōgen, 1200–1253./ I. Dōgen, 1200–1253. Selected works. 1976. II. Victoria, Daizen, 1939– joint author. III. Title./BQ9449.D652Y63/294.3'927/75-33200/ISBN 0-8348-0112-4/ISBN 0-8348-0116-7 pbk.

In memory of my late master
Eigan Kiyū-rōshi
chief monk of Tōyō-ji
to whom I am deeply indebted
for his guidance and encouragement
in my study of Zen Buddhism

To study the Way is to study the self.
To study the self is to forget the self.
To forget the self is to be enlightened by all things.
To be enlightened by all things is to remove the barriers between one's self and others.

Dōgen
from "The Manifestation of the *Kōan*"
(*Genjō Kōan*), *Shōbō-genzō*

Contents

PART ONE: ZEN MASTER DŌGEN

PART TWO: INDEPENDENT WORKS

PART THREE: TWELVE SECTIONS OF THE SHŌBŌ-GENZŌ

Foreword

This book is written by a Japanese practitioner of the Sōtō tradition of Zen Buddhism, with the aid of an American practitioner of the same tradition. It is intended for the nonspecialist reader whose interest lies in investigating the thought and practice of that tradition directly. Translations of selected works of Zen Master Dōgen constitute the main body of the book, prefaced by a brief history of early Japanese Buddhism and a short biography of Dōgen. The translations of Dōgen's works, though not literal, are intended to convey the essence of his thought and are faithfully accomplished.

The purpose of this book is to describe the Sōtō Zen tradition within the historical context of Japanese Buddhism and to articulate the principle of nonduality. In view of the relative scarcity of English-language materials on Sōtō Zen, this book is most valuable, providing an insight into the thought and practice of Dōgen, who transmitted the Sōtō tradition from China to Japan and shaped it to the practical needs of the Japanese.

The Sōtō school of Zen Buddhism was introduced to Japan in the early part of the Kamakura period (1185–1336), a time characterized by the emergence of a new breed of leaders who rebelled against the aristocratic culture of the preceding Heian period (794–1185): the political corruption of the powerful Fujiwara family, who had long held the reins of actual power; the socioeconomic system of the *shōen*, or feudal manor, which was designed for the exploitation of the peasantry by the aristocracy; and the Buddhism of the late Heian period, which catered to the establishment. Sōtō Zen articulates the individuality of man, cultivated by meditative discipline, making no distinction whatsoever between classes; and it identifies that individuality as one that is completely integrated with the Law of the Buddha, though in the Zen tradition the integration of man and the Law is specifically referred to as the awakening of man's inherent quality of Buddha-nature. This is the point of departure from which the author considers the principle of nonduality.

The principle of nonduality is found in the school of Buddhist philosophy known as Mādhyamika, which claims that systems of thought based on duality—such as the subject-object split, the whole and the part, being and nonbeing, enlightenment and nonenlightenment—cannot produce insight into the true nature of existence, which Mādhyamika terms the "middle." The middle-path (*madhyamā-pratipad*) doctrine establishes two levels of truth, the "supreme" (*paramārtha-satya*) and the "conventional" (*samvṛtti-satya*), and claims that the raison d'être of each is contingent on the other. "Supreme" means insight into the transcendental (specifically, this refers to *śūnyatā*, a realm in which all opposites are dissolved), while "conventional" means insight into the phenomenal (specifically, this refers to *pratītya-samutpāda*, the realm of dependent causation). The middle-path principle does not consider opposites as forms of dichotomy. They are complementary entities constituting an organic world of existential progression. The author has translated a number of sections of the *Shōbō-genzō* in order to indicate the central idea underlying Dōgen's thought: the practical implementation of the principle of nonduality, based on Mādhyamika philosophy, in the development of a Zen personality.

Shōbō-genzō literally means "Eye Storehouse of the True Law." "True Law" refers to the middle-path principle, and "Eye Storehouse" to the quality of mind capable of realizing that principle—specifically, Buddha-nature. Because Sōtō Zen considers that Buddha-nature is inherent in all beings and is a universal quality, not something that is to be acquired by selected individuals, the practice of Zen is not a means to enlightenment. Practice in itself is the goal. Hence Sōtō Zen claims the identity of man and the Buddha, and the identity of enlightenment and practice. The theory of the identity of man and the Buddha presupposes the inherent quality of Buddha-nature; the theory of the identity of enlightenment and practice presupposes that practice is the embodiment of the state of enlightenment, while enlightenment is conceived as the implementation of insight into the middle-path principle in empirical matters.

Because Zen presupposes the universal quality of Buddha-nature, it makes no distinction among human beings. Because it presupposes that man is inherently enlightened, its logic flows from the whole to the part, not the other way around as in traditional Western philosophy. ("Whole" in the Zen context refers to Buddha-nature, and "part" to the individual practitioner.) And because it emphasizes the implementation of insight into empirical matters, Zen values human labor.

As must now be apparent, Zen is not a system of analytic philosophy. It is an experiential philosophy based on the premise of the inherent and universal quality of Buddha-nature, and emphasizes work. Zen meditation has meaning only to those who have understood the nature of self—that it is endowed with Buddha-nature and that Buddha-nature is inherent and universal—and who value work.

A Zen monastery, referred to as *zen-rin,* meaning meditation grove, symbolizes harmony with its environment, both natural and man-made, through the discipline of meditation and work. It is a microcosm of human social organization dedicated to the practice of the Bodhisattva path. A Bodhisattva is one who willingly renounces the possibility of realizing enlightenment for himself alone, identifies himself with the problems of the world of sentient beings, and improvises skill in means to alleviate the suffering of others. Zen does not permit the life of a hermit, isolated from the reality of social organization and the complexity of the problems associated with it.

This book is an attempt to describe the experiential aspect of Dōgen's Sōtō Zen, by actual practitioners of that tradition, for the general English-reading public, with the implicit message that Zen provides a solution to the problems of the alienation of modern man and of the complexity of modern social organization that he is responsible for having created.

MINORU KIYOTA
Professor of Buddhist Studies
University of Wisconsin

Preface

Zen Buddhism is a universal religion that is to be practiced in one's daily life. The Zen of Dōgen (1200–1253), the founder of the Sōtō Zen sect in Japan, in particular is quite concrete and detailed in its expression, yet at the same time profoundly philosophic. The two main points of his teachings are: (1) there is no gap between practice and enlightenment, and (2) our right daily behavior is Buddhism itself. In emphasizing these two points his teachings are quite different from those of the Rinzai Zen sect, which stresses the achievement of enlightenment through the use of the Zen riddles known as *kōan.*

Having entered the Sōtō Zen monkhood at the age of twenty and trained at Sōji-ji, one of the sect's two head monasteries, I realized that without an understanding of Dōgen's Zen it is impossible to talk of Zen Buddhism in its entirety. I therefore decided to embark on a lifelong effort to introduce to the English-speaking world the life and unique thought of this Zen master as recorded in his numerous works, particularly his masterwork, the *Shōbō-genzō.*

In 1960 I began a detailed study of the *Shōbō-genzō* in preparation for its translation. At the same time I also studied the grammatical structure of the Japanese language of the Kamakura period (1185–1336) in order to grasp more fully the linguistic meaning of the original and wrote a thesis concerning my findings. It was not until 1965, however, that I actually began to translate the *Shōbō-genzō* into English as well as modern Japanese.

Acting on the advice of senior colleagues, I decided first to publish in English a minor work by Dōgen, the *Shōbō-genzō Zuimonki,* which consists of a collection of Dōgen's discourses compiled by his leading disciple, Koun Ejō (1198–1280). Because of its easy, literary style, this collection may be said to form the gateway to the Sōtō sect in Japan. The Sankibō Buddhist Bookstore, Tokyo, published my translation of this work in 1972, and in 1973 the same publisher issued my translation of Dōgen's *Eihei Genzenji Shingi* (Regulations for Zen Monasteries). This work, composed of six sections, is a detailed statement of the rules to be followed by Zen trainees during their monastic life.

With the publication of the present book I have at last brought to at least partial fruition my long-cherished desire to introduce the *Shōbō-genzō* to the Western world. Rather than introduce the whole work, consisting of ninety-two sections in all, many parts of which are difficult even for advanced students of Buddhism to understand, I have decided to introduce first its twelve most readily understood, and in many ways most important, sections. At the same time I have included three of Dōgen's important independent works: "A Universal Recommendation for Zazen" (*Fukan Zazen-gi*), "Points to Watch in Buddhist Training" (*Gakudō Yōjin-shū*), and "The Meaning of Practice-Enlightenment" (*Shushō-gi*). These I believe will give the reader a more comprehensive understanding of Dōgen's thought. It is my hope that these translations, coupled with the short biography of Dōgen in the first part of this book, will serve as an introduction to a man who is considered by many Japanese to be one of the most profound, fecund, and deeply spiritual products of Japanese Buddhism in its more than fourteen-hundred-year history.

In translating Dōgen's works I have been guided by three general principles. The first, which of course holds true for any translation, is to render as faithful a translation of the original as possible. However, a translation cannot avoid being interpretive in the sense that one language can never be rendered exactly into another; consequently, the translator must constantly choose what he believes to be the word or phrase in the new language corresponding most closely to the original. The problems involved in making such choices are greatly increased when the subject matter deals with religious and philosophical concepts, particularly those of Zen, which are inevitably cryptic and pithy. Even at the risk of somewhat stilted English and sentences bursting at the seams with dependent clauses, adverbial phrases, and so on, I have tried to convey the spirit of the original as faithfully as possible. I have done this not only to provide a better insight into Dōgen's teachings but also to help Western readers become more familiar with Oriental thought and modes of expression.

At the same time, I have inserted material in brackets where I felt that a literal rendering of the text alone failed to give full expression to Dōgen's intended meaning or when something had been abbreviated in the original text which, if left unexplained, would make the passage more difficult for the reader to understand. I have also enclosed in brackets English translations of the titles of Buddhist works as well as brief supplementary information on Buddhist terminology and personages. Notes, based primarily on Dr. Hakuju Ui's *Concise Bukkyō Jiten* (Concise Buddhist Dictionary), have been provided where lengthier explanations were required.

The second principle guiding this translation has been to use English words to express Buddhist terminology as far as possible. Some readers familiar with Buddhist terminology may be surprised to see common Buddhist Sanskrit terms, such as *Dharma* or *Saṃgha,* rendered into English instead of being preserved in their transliterated Sanskrit forms. It is my belief, however, that if Buddhism is to take firm root in the West and lose, in the process, its foreign "smell," it must attempt to express itself in a way that allows for the greatest possible understanding on the part of the general populace rather than limit itself to an exclusive "in-group."

One of the characteristics of early Chinese Zen, which undoubtedly helped it to gain wide support and influence, was that its leaders, the Chinese patriarchs, expressed Buddhist Truth in the vernacular Chinese of the day. Dōgen, too, broke with tradition when he used Japanese, rather than classical Buddhist Chinese, to record the majority of his teachings. The general reader should be forewarned, however, that the meanings of the English words used to express Buddhist terms are often quite different from their ordinary English usage, and he would be well advised to study either the notes provided when these terms are first introduced or the glossary at the back of this book.

In spite of this second principle, even a cursory glance at the text will reveal many foreign words and phrases. A closer examination will disclose that many are the titles of various Buddhist works or personal and place names in Sanskrit, Chinese, or Japanese. There are also numerous Buddhist technical terms that are presented, unless otherwise noted, in their original Sanskrit forms, for in the case of terms like *samādhi* and *karma* there are, I feel, no English equivalents that can adequately express their full meaning. The reader is asked to realize that these transliterated terms are used reluctantly, not to obfuscate but, with the aid of the notes, to clarify the original meaning.

Terms generally known in the West through their Japanese pronunciations, such as *zazen, kōan,* and *gasshō,* are used in that form in the text, their original forms to be found in the accompanying notes or in the glossary. As an aid to the correct pronunciation of all non-English words, I have consistently used the diacritical marks appropriate to the various languages throughout the book. In a book of this length, there may well be some mistakes or omissions in these marks, and I would be deeply appreciative if readers would point these out to me so that they may be corrected in future editions. Any other comments, criticisms, and suggestions concerning this book are also welcome, of course.

The third general principle used in this translation has been to present a traditional interpretation of Dōgen's teachings, taking into account the best of present-day Sōtō Zen scholarship. To Westerners, obsessed as they often seem to be with "newer," "better," and "unique" ideas as well as things, such a traditional interpretation may not be so appealing, particularly when it becomes clear that it necessitates the revision of many of their ego-centered and self-indulgent conceptions of Zen.

I am also aware that there are some Sōtō Zen–related masters and trainees, both in Japan and abroad, who are critical of some aspects of this traditional interpretation as well as of the actual practice to which it leads. Although it is beyond the scope of the present book to discuss these criticisms in detail, I would be among the first to admit that the present state of the Sōtō sect in Japan leaves much to be desired. It is my belief, however, that the root of the problem lies in the question of practice, or in this instance lack of practice, not interpretation. It may seem strange for me, as a Buddhist scholar and translator, to say this, but it is far easier to talk and write about Zen than to live and practice it! How important such practice is to Dōgen's Zen, as well as what the nature of that practice is, will become abundantly clear through this book; and for this practice, I am confident, the traditional interpretation will prove more than sufficient.

Finally, I would like to express my deep appreciation to the Venerable Daizen Victoria for the tireless assistance he rendered in the translations in this book. Due to his many years of training in the Sōtō Zen monkhood, as well as his high level of Japanese-language comprehension, he was able not only to improve the general level of my English translation but, by being able to check the translations with the original texts, to correct errors that might otherwise have gone undetected. Without his cooperation this book could not have been published. Needless to say, however, I take ultimate responsibility for the accuracy of the translated material. Special thanks also go to Ronald Bell, formerly of Weatherhill in Tokyo, for his helpful suggestions in the initial stages of the preparation of this book. Suzanne Trumbull has served as a most understanding and cooperative editor, and I wish to express my appreciation to her, as well as to all those at Weatherhill who have made the publication of this book possible. Last, but not least, I would like to express my sincere appreciation to Professor Minoru Kiyota of the University of Wisconsin for having kindly consented to write the foreword to this book. His emphasis on the doctrinal origins of Zen thought offers a valuable insight into an area that is all too often neglected in works on Zen.

YŪHŌ YOKOI
Associate Professor of English
Aichi-gakuin University

Nagoya, B.E. 2519 (A.D. 1975)

Part One

Zen Master Dōgen

ONE

Introduction

ZEN BUDDHISM IS STILL, I think, relatively little understood in the West. It is also true, however, that recently many Westerners have shown an increasing interest in Zen, an interest that has been greatly stimulated by the late Daisetz T. Suzuki, who published numerous works on Zen Buddhism during his lifetime. Thanks largely to his prodigious efforts, Zen Buddhism is no longer a monopoly of the East. At the same time, it cannot be denied that Zen, which originated in India and came to Japan by way of China, has a unique Oriental character composed of such qualities as simplicity, straightforwardness, and paradoxical expression.

Although Zen is a religion centering on the practice of zazen,[1] it is not limited to this practice alone. Rather, it is to be expressed in all our daily actions—coming, going, sitting, and lying down. Zen emphasizes that "Mind itself is the Buddha."[2] In other words, our mind is originally one with the Buddha's. However, our Buddha-mind will not reveal itself until strenuous efforts have been made in the practice of the Way. Without such devout and wholehearted practice, we cannot realize our Buddha-mind. In this sense it may be said that Zen is a religion that must be expressed in our daily lives.

The essence of Zen is, of course, to realize this mind of the Buddha. This realization is known as *satori,* or enlightenment, in Japanese Zen. But such enlightenment is not the goal of our training. For in essence there is no difference between practice and enlightenment. Practice is, as it is, enlightenment, and vice versa. According to Dōgen, a little training is already shallow enlightenment, just as thorough training is deep enlightenment.

Though the practice of zazen was an important form of Buddhist discipline in India, Zen first became established as an independent school in China. Similarly, although this same practice had been introduced to Japan as early as the Nara period (A.D. 646–794), it was not until the twelfth century, when the Sung tradition of Zen was imported from China, that this form of Buddhism established an independent existence in Japan. Initially Zen was used to train samurai (feudal warriors), as it provided them with a standard for their daily actions. Later, Zen also had a strong influence on many other aspects of Japanese culture, such as architecture, sculpture, garden design, and the tea ceremony.

In Japan, Zen became divided into three major sects, these being further divided into a total of twenty-four subsects. The three major sects are the Sōtō, Rinzai,[3] and Ōbaku. Eisai-*zenji*[4] (1141–1215), the founder of the Rinzai sect in Japan, went to China to study Zen at the age of twenty-eight but was unsuccessful in his efforts to realize enlightenment. At the age of forty-nine he went there once again; this time he was successful, with the result that he was able to transmit the essence of the Lin-chi (Rinzai) sect to Japan. He was persecuted tenaciously by the older, established Buddhist sects, however, and in order to propagate this new form of Buddhism throughout the country he was often forced to seek the protection of the feudal government.

The Zen that Eisai introduced is somewhat mixed with the teachings of other sects, for he taught that strict adherence to the rules of discipline (*vinaya*) that the historical Buddha set forth for monks and nuns was of the first importance, ascribing the practice of zazen to a secondary though still important role. He further taught that the Buddhist teachings, or Law (*Dharma*),[5] were identical with the Buddha-mind, not with the *sūtras,* the latter being but the temporary expression of the Buddha's own enlightened mind. For him the Buddha-mind came first and the *sūtras* second. However fine and profound the *sūtras* might be, they were of no value unless one had directly realized the Buddha-mind. In short, Eisai taught that the Buddha-mind is directly transmitted from Buddha to Buddha apart from the *sūtras*.

Monks of Eisai's sect are said to realize enlightenment step by step through thinking, during zazen, of the essence of each progressively more difficult *kōan*[6] that is assigned to them by their Zen masters. Their efforts are made solely for the purpose of realizing enlightenment through the use of *kōan*. They are quite unaware of the fact that, from the Sōtō Zen point of view, the practice of zazen itself is the manifestation of the *kōan* and of enlightenment.

Finally, in regard to the relationship between Zen and the state, Eisai wrote in his famous treatise on the subject, *Kōzen Gokoku-ron* (Protecting the Nation through the Establishment of Zen), that both have the common objective of ensuring peace and happiness for the people. Eisai stressed, however, that it was only by the state's support of Zen that this common objective could be realized. He actively sought the support of, and was willing to align himself with, the secular powers of his day.

Contrary to Eisai, Dōgen-*zenji* ascribed first importance to the practice of zazen, which, he taught, was identical with adherence to the rules of discipline. He also stressed the importance of those *sūtras* that were at one with the Truth, believing them to be identical with the Buddhist Law. Opposing the use of *kōan* as objects of meditation, as well as the concept of step-by-step enlightenment, Dōgen taught that Buddhist training itself was the only true *kōan,* the manifestation of enlightenment.

Dōgen, like Eisai, believed that the peace and prosperity of the people could be ensured through the state's support of Zen. Later, however, when he discovered that the state did not share his ideals, he refused to give it his support, criticizing its leaders for their lack of virtue. Although Dōgen was also subjected to persecution by other sects, he did not ask the feudal government for protection. Refusing to be dependent on the state authorities, he devoted himself completely to the propagation of Buddhism through the spoken and written word.

The Ōbaku (Hwang-po) sect, the smallest of the three Zen sects of Japan, was introduced by the Chinese monk Yin-yüan (J., Ingen; 1592–1673), who went to Japan in 1654 and subsequently founded Mampuku-ji monastery at Uji, near Kyoto. His teachings were very much like those of the Rinzai sect, except that he emphasized that zazen is one with the Jōdo sect's practice of *nembutsu,* the repeated invocation of the Buddha Amitābha in order to be reborn in the Pure Land.[7]

TWO

Japanese Buddhism before Dōgen

ALTHOUGH BUDDHISM IS RECORDED as having been introduced to Japan from China and Korea as early as A.D. 522, it was the prince-regent Shōtoku, who ruled Japan from 593 to 622, to whom credit goes for having made the greatest contribution to the establishment of Buddhism in Japan. He is one of the many political rulers in ancient Buddhist Asia who actively tried to incorporate Buddhist teachings into the political and social life of his country.

One of Prince Shōtoku's first acts upon assuming power was to proclaim Buddhism the state religion. He called for the foundation of a grand Buddhist institution composed of a temple, an asylum, a hospital, and a dispensary. In 604 he promulgated what is known as the first Japanese constitution (the content of which consisted of moral instructions), in which he stated that the rulership of a single monarch implied the equality of all people, just as faith in the unique personality of the Buddha as savior of all mankind presupposed the intrinsic value and destiny of every individual who was in communion with him. The high aims of the prince can be seen in the opening statements of his constitution's first article: "Harmony is to be valued, and discord is to be deprecated. . . . All men are influenced by partisanship, and there are few who have wide vision."

In the second article, the prince enunciated his vision of spiritual harmony based on Buddhism: "Simply revere the Three Treasures. The Three Treasures are the Buddha, the Law, and the Buddhist community [*Saṃgha*],[1] the final resort of all beings and the supreme object of faith for all peoples. Should any age or any people fail to revere this truth? There are few men who are utterly vicious. Everyone will realize it [this truth] if duly instructed. Can any wickedness be corrected without having resort to the Three Treasures?"

Prince Shōtoku employed Buddhism as an instrument to bring about national unity. Buddhism was effective in this enterprise because it was a universal religion, transcending the native Japanese religion of Shintō, whose deities were identified with clans. But it should be noted here that the ideal principles enumerated by Prince Shōtoku were not realized during his lifetime.

The founding of a permanent capital in the new city of Nara in 710 not only marked an important step in the establishment of national unity but also represented the culmination of two centuries of growth in Buddhist influence in nearly every branch of social life. Numerous temples and monasteries had been built, and in addition to their religious functions, these institutions served to develop the national resources of the nation and to establish communications. These circumstances led to a steady accumulation of wealth in such ecclesiastical establishments, and while in the beginning this wealth was freely spent on social and educational work, by the latter half of the eighth century it had become a cause of corruption of the monkhood.

Before discussing this problem in detail, however, we must take note of what is often referred to as the most brilliant event in Japanese history, the dedication in 752 of the Central Cathedral, later known as Tōdai-ji, in Nara. The erection of this magnificent temple dedicated to the Buddha Vairocana (Dainichi), a symbolic representation of the eternal Law, marked a still closer relationship between Buddhism and the central government. Emperor Shōmu (r. 724–49) had conceived the foundation of a central cathedral as a symbolic display of the Buddhist ideal of universal spiritual communion centered on the person of the Buddha, parallel to the political unity of national life centered on the monarch.

It was also during the Nara period that another significant event occurred that was to have a lasting effect on Japanese Buddhism. This was the merging of the three dominant schools of spiritual teachings then existing in Japan, Shintō, Buddhism, and Confucianism. Although Shintō was the indigenous religion of the Japanese people, it was primarily a tribal cult combining local rituals with belief in clan-protecting deities.

Since Buddhism with its universal message, which justified a centralized government, was the dominant force of the eighth century, Shintō decided to raise its prestige by identifying itself closely with Buddhism and thereby with the central government. To this end it proclaimed that the sun goddess of Shintō, Amaterasu Ōmikami, was identical with the Buddha Vairocana enshrined in Tōdai-ji, and that the Shintō god Hachiman, the "God of Eight Banners," was the symbol of the Eightfold Noble Path of Buddhist morality. Through an oracle the god Hachiman even made known his desire to act as a guardian for the Central Cathedral.

The relationship between Confucianism and Buddhism was a more natural one. Confucianism was able to supply Japanese Buddhism with its practical ethical teachings, especially its emphasis on "virtue." Furthermore, the Hindu-influenced Buddhist exercise of religious veneration of the dead was easily combined with the practice of ancestor worship and filial piety as taught by Confucianism. The populace came to regard Confucianism as the teaching for the present life and Buddhism as the way to spiritual bliss in the future life.

However, it was not long after the grand dedication ceremonies of the Central Cathedral that signs of corruption began to appear. The accumulation of wealth and power, both in the government and in the Buddhist hierarchy, led to degeneracy in every phase of aristocratic life. Land newly opened to cultivation was granted to the cultivators as their private property, with much of it falling into the hands of Buddhist temples and monasteries through donation, or by virtue of their own enterprise, or even as mortgage forfeits. The resultant accumulation of wealth in Buddhist institutions tempted the clergy to strive for worldly power, one high monk reportedly even aiming at the throne. Shintō priests became servile followers and servants of the Buddhist clergy, who by this time had divided themselves along Chinese lines into six competing scholastically oriented schools or "sects."[2] The need for both political and religious reform was great.

The impetus for this reformation occurred with the transfer of the capital from Nara to Heian (present-day Kyoto) in 794. Through this change of capital, political regeneration became possible as a result of the freedom gained from the interference of the ecclesiastic dignitaries entrenched in the former capital. Two little-known but brilliant monks, Saichō (767–822) and Kūkai (774–835), were also to develop two new centers of the Buddhist hierarchy, which were to dominate the religious and social life of the coming centuries. Although a strong rivalry developed between the two schools of Buddhism that they founded, both men shared the aims of establishing a new unified center of Japanese Buddhism with the support of the state, deriving new materials from Chinese Buddhism, and emphasizing symbolic practices to represent doctrinal content. While neither monk was successful in establishing such a center of Buddhism, due in no small degree to their rivalry, this goal proved to be the strongest force in social and religious control during the four centuries of the Heian period (794–1185).

It is to Saichō, better known by his posthumous title of Dengyō-*daishi,* that Japanese Buddhism owes the foundation and development of its greatest seat of learning, Mount Hiei, located not far from Kyoto. Here, in the forerunner of the modern university, Saichō introduced the scriptures and treatises of the Tendai (T'ien-t'ai) school of Chinese Buddhism. This emphasized the universality of salvation or attainment of Buddhahood, embracing even the lowest of beings, such as beasts and infernal beings.

Saichō's stress on universality won him wide support among the general populace, and the performance of special Tendai-inspired grand and mystical ceremonies on Mount Hiei gained him governmental support as well, with the whole institution officially declared to be the "Chief Seat of the Buddhist Religion for Ensuring the Security of the Country" (*Chingo-kokka no Dōjō*). Before its decay in the twelfth and thirteenth centuries, Mount Hiei had become the most powerful center of the Buddhist hierarchy, and had even come to control state affairs.

Kūkai, also better known by his posthumous title, Kōbō-*daishi,* like Saichō had visited China and brought back a new Chinese form of Buddhism known as Shingon (Chên-yen), a combination of mysticism and occultism. The headquarters of the sect was on Mount Kōya, about fifty miles from Kyoto, and it was here that Kūkai repeated deeply mystic formulas, which on a popular level were thought to evoke divine powers able to fulfill any desire, religious or otherwise. Herein lay the secret of its ability to attract all kinds of people, influencing ambitious nobles and simple folk alike. Eventually Shingon succeeded in overshadowing all other forms of Buddhism; even Saichō's followers found it expedient to emphasize more and more the esoteric aspects of their master's teachings.

After Kūkai's death the superstitious and ritualistic elements in Shingon Buddhism came to play an ever more central role, setting the stage for degeneration and corruption. The temples and their rich properties fell prey to avaricious monks, and the relaxation of the official registration of the clergy from the last part of the ninth century onward aggravated the evil. The corruption of the Buddhist hierarchy vied with the irregularities of the monkhood in the provinces. The great Buddhist centers increased their influence in proportion to their exercise of occult ceremonies, and the power thus acquired became the weapon of ambitious prelates and degenerate monks. The increase in their lands and other property gradually induced such monks to organized armed defense. The monk-soldiers (*sōhei*) proceeded from defensive to offensive acts in asserting their rights and claims, attacking their rivals and even intimidating the national government.

The power and outrages of the monk-soldiers grew so alarming in the course of the eleventh century that the powerful Fujiwara clan, which had been the creator of this force, finding itself unable to control the monks, had to resort to the help of military men from the provinces to suppress their riots. This was of great significance because when the provincial warriors were called to the capital to combat the monk-soldiers, they began to realize their potential power. From this time on their self-assertion grew until they controlled the seat of power, supplanting the Fujiwara oligarchy and finally establishing a military government (*bakufu*) in Kamakura, near present-day Tokyo, in 1185.

The establishment of an austere military government under the dictatorship of the Minamoto clan, far removed from the luxurious life and lax administration of the court nobles in Kyoto, signaled an epochal change for Japan in almost all areas of life, not least the religious. The Buddhist hierarchies lost much of their prestige, together with their political supporters at court; ceremonies and mysteries were discredited, while various new combinations of ideas and practices began to appear in religious belief and moral teaching. Confucianism, while still providing the basis for morality in daily life, was altered in that the object of one's fidelity now became the chief of the clan, engendering an acute sense of honor coupled with adherence to family tradition and obedience to the will of one's superior.

Buddhism, on the other hand, furnished the fighters with training in self-control and fortitude. The three new forms of Buddhism (Jōdo and its later branch Jōdo Shin, Zen, and Nichiren) that were established in the thirteenth century were characterized not by ceremony and mystery but by simple piety and spiritual exercises. Dogma gave way to personal experience, ritual and sacerdotalism to piety and intuition. Moreover, these new sects exerted their influence across class bounds, exhibiting a growing concern for the common people.

Two of the new Buddhist schools—Jōdo, founded by Hōnen, and Nichiren, founded by a monk of the same name—although different in many respects were basically alike in their emphasis on simple faith and piety, particularly faith in the continual recitation of short formulas as the basis for salvation.[3] This development represented a drastic change from the scholastic type of Buddhism that had originally entered Japan, as well as from its later ritualized, mystical forms. Especially as taught by Shinran, founder of the Jōdo Shin sect, who advocated a family life even for monks, this meant that Buddhist salvation was no longer the prerogative of monks or those "men of leisure" who had ample time to devote to religious pursuits. Its attainment was now possible for anyone, layman or monk, man or woman, young or old, who followed the greatly simplified tenets and practices of the various sects' founders. Buddhism for the common man had been born.

THREE

Dōgen's Life and Thought

Dōgen was born into an aristocratic family in Kyoto in 1200, his father, Kuga Michichika, being a high-ranking government minister. Even as a child Dōgen's brilliant mind was apparent; it is said that by the age of four he was able to read Chinese poetry and by the age of nine a Chinese translation of a treatise on the *Abhidharma*.[1] His childhood, however, was not a happy one; for at the age of two he lost his father, and his mother died when he was seven. The loss of both his parents deeply impressed Dōgen's sensitive mind with the transient nature of life, so much so that he became determined to enter the Buddhist monkhood to seek the answer to life's ultimate question—the meaning of life and death.

Concerning the transient nature of life and the merit of becoming a monk, Dōgen was later to write in the first part of the "Merit of Becoming a Monk" (*Shukke Kudoku*) section of the *Shōbō-genzō*, "Life is as transient as a dewdrop, and so, having been fortunate enough to be born as a human being, we should not waste our lives. If we lead the life of a monk in our successive existences, much merit will be accumulated." In the latter part of the same section he says, "When death suddenly comes, neither the king nor his ministers, relatives, servants, wife or children, or rare jewels can save us. We are obliged to enter the realm of the dead alone, accompanied only by our good and bad karma.[2] How desperately we cling to our body at death's door! Therefore while we still retain our human body we should quickly enter the monkhood. This is indeed the true teaching of the various Buddhas in the three stages of time [the past, present, and future]."

At the age of thirteen Dōgen was formally initiated into the monkhood on Mount Hiei, the center of Tendai Buddhist learning in Japan. For the next several years he studied the Mahāyāna, or "Great Vehicle," and Hīnayāna, or "Lesser Vehicle,"[3] versions of Buddhism under the guidance of his master, Abbot Kōen. By the time he was fourteen, however, he had become troubled by a deep doubt concerning one aspect of the Buddhist teaching: if, as the *sūtras* say, all human beings are endowed with the Buddha-nature, why is it that one must train oneself so strenuously to realize that Buddha-nature, that is, to attain enlightenment? Dōgen hoped that Abbot Kōen would be able to help rid him of his doubt, but when he put this problem before Kōen, the abbot was unable to give him an answer. Deeply disappointed, Dōgen decided to leave Mount Hiei in search of someone who could set his mind at rest. One of those he visited was Abbot Kōin, the chief monk of Mii-dera monastery in present-day Shiga Prefecture; but he too was unable to give Dōgen a clear answer. He only suggested that Dōgen seek the answer to his question from Eisai-*zenji*, who was then residing at Kennin-ji temple in Kyoto.

Following the abbot's advice, Dōgen journeyed to Kennin-ji; and when he asked Eisai the same question, the Zen master replied, "All the Buddhas in the three stages of time are unaware that they are endowed with the Buddha-nature, but cats and oxen are well aware of it indeed!" In other words, the Buddhas, precisely because they are Buddhas themselves, no longer think of having or not having the Buddha-nature; only the animallike (that is, the grossly deluded) think in such terms. Upon hearing this reply, Dōgen experienced an inner realization that partially dissolved his deep-seated doubt and, believing deeply in Eisai's understanding of Buddhism, decided to study the teachings of the Rinzai Zen sect under Eisai's guidance. Unfortunately, however, Eisai died the following year.

How different Eisai was from the other masters of his day can be seen in the collection of Dōgen's sayings entitled the *Shōbō-genzō Zuimonki*. Speaking of the masters he had visited before meeting Eisai, he says, "The masters I had seen all advised me to study until I was as learned as those who had preceded me. I was told to make myself known to the state and gain fame in the world."

Eisai transmitted the Law to seven of his disciples. It was under one of this number, Myōzen (1184–1225), that Dōgen continued his study of Zen for nine more years. The "Practice of the Way" (*Bendō-wa*) section of the *Shōbō-genzō* contains the following reference to Myōzen: "Ever since I awakened to the Bodhi-mind[4] and sought the supreme Truth I made many visits to Buddhist masters throughout the country. It was thus that I happened to meet the Venerable Myōzen at Kennin-ji. Nine years quickly passed as I studied the Way under him. During that period I had the opportunity to learn from him, to some extent, the training methods of the Rinzai Zen sect. To the Venerable Myōzen, leading disciple of my late master Eisai, was rightly transmitted the highest supreme Law and he was unparalleled among his fellow disciples in learning and virtue."

Another episode concerning Myōzen, which describes how earnest he was in the pursuit of the Buddhist Truth, is contained in the *Shōbō-genzō Zuimonki*. This passage concerns a criticism of Myōzen that was raised by his fellow monks because of his determination to leave the dying Myōyu, his original master, to go to China to continue his training in spite of the latter's request that Myōzen remain by his side. In answer to their criticism Myōzen is quoted as saying, "You have all advised me to stay, but I cannot agree. Even if I stay here in Japan now, I cannot protect him [Myōyu] from death if he is to die. Even if I stay here and nurse him, I cannot relieve him of his pain.

Even though I treat his body with due ceremony at his death, I cannot detach him from the transmigration of birth and death. To stay here is merely to obey his orders. It may be of great solace to him, but it is all useless in realizing enlightenment. If he should mistakenly hinder my earnest desire for the supreme Truth, he will have committed a sin."

In spite of his long years of training under Myōzen, Dōgen still felt spiritually unfulfilled. Thus, at the age of twenty-three, he decided to make the hazardous journey to China with Myōzen in order to study Zen Buddhism further. Leaving Japan at the end of March in 1223, they arrived at the Chinese port of Mingchou in the first part of April. To feel out the actual circumstances of Zen Buddhist temples in China, Dōgen stayed on board ship for some time after its arrival in port. In his *Tenzo Kyōkun* (Instructions to the Kitchen Supervisor), Dōgen records an interesting meeting he had with an elderly *tenzo*-monk (the senior monk in charge of cooking) from Ayuwan-shan monastery, who happened to visit his ship one day to buy some Japanese mushrooms.

"I said to him [the *tenzo*-monk], 'When did you leave Ayuwan-shan monastery?'

" 'After lunch.'

" 'How far is it from here?'

" 'About thirty-five *li*.'[5]

" 'When are you going back?'

" 'As soon as I've purchased some mushrooms.'

" 'I am very glad to have this unexpected chance to meet and chat with you for a while here on board ship. Please allow me to serve you, Zen Master *tenzo*.'

" 'I'm sorry, but without my supervision tomorrow's meals will not go well.'

" 'In such a large monastery as Ayuwan-shan there must be enough other cooking monks to prepare the meals. They can surely get along without a single *tenzo*-monk.'

" 'Old as I am, I hold the office of *tenzo*. This is my training during my old age. How can I leave this duty to others? Moreover, I didn't get permission to stay out overnight when I left.'

" 'Venerable sir! Why don't you do zazen or study the *kōan* of ancient masters? What is the use of working so hard as a *tenzo*-monk?'

"On hearing my remarks, he broke into laughter and said, 'Good foreigner! You seem to be ignorant of the true training and meaning of Buddhism.' In a moment, ashamed and surprised at his remark, I said to him, 'What are they?'

" 'If you understand the true meaning of your question, you will have already realized the true meaning of Buddhism,' he answered. At that time, however, I was unable to understand what he meant."

The preceding episode clearly shows that at that time Dōgen was still unable to understand the essence of Zen. He had not yet realized that Zen is and must be expressed through our daily actions, be they cooking, cleaning, or whatever. His belief that the practice of zazen or the study of *kōan* were the most important aspects of Zen training showed that he was still deeply attached to the doctrine of the Rinzai Zen sect.

After leaving the ship Dōgen first went to T'ien-t'ung monastery, where he trained under Abbot Wu-chi. It was here that he first encountered discrimination based on the fact that he was a foreign monk. The *Kenzei-ki,* a biography of Dōgen by Kenzei, relates that Dōgen was assigned a low rank because he was not Chinese. Dōgen protested this discrimination, saying that monks should be ranked by the length of time that had elapsed since their entrance into the monkhood, regardless of their nationality. At first, however, his protests went unheard. It is said that it was not until he made a final appeal to the emperor that his rank was determined on the same basis as that of the Chinese monks.

In spite of this experience, Dōgen significantly deepened his understanding of Zen during his training at T'ien-t'ung. The importance of the office of *tenzo* finally struck home to him as a result of an incident there, which is also recorded in the *Tenzo Kyōkun.* It happened one day when Dōgen was going to the abbot's living quarters, located along the eastern corridor of the monastery. On the way he came across an old, bare-headed *tenzo*-monk with a bamboo stick in his hand, earnestly drying some mushrooms in front of the Buddha hall. The sun's rays beat down upon him, causing him to perspire profusely. Still he continued to move here and there, drying the mushrooms. Moved by this sight, Dōgen drew near him and asked, "What is your Buddhist age?"

"Sixty-eight," the *tenzo*-monk answered.

"Why don't you make the other cooking monks under your supervision do it?"

"They are not me."

"You are really one with Buddhism, but I wonder why you work so hard in the burning sun."

"When else can I do it but now?"

Dōgen said nothing. As he continued to walk along the corridor, he thought to himself how important the office of *tenzo* was.

A second significant event during Dōgen's training at T'ien-t'ung took place one day at the conclusion of the zazen period. At that time the monk seated beside him put a folded *kaśāya*[6] on top of his head and reverently recited a *sūtra* passage concerning its wearing. Deeply moved by this practice, Dōgen states in the "Merit of a *Kaśāya*" (*Kesa Kudoku*) section of the *Shōbōgenzō:*

"At that time I was filled with the deepest emotion and joy that I had ever experienced. Unknowingly I shed so many tears of gratitude that my collar became wet. Why? Although I had opened the *Āgama-sūtras* before and read the verse concerning the placing of the *kaśāya* on one's head, I did not know the details of the manner in which it was to be done. Seeing it at that time before my very eyes filled me with great joy. I said to myself, 'Alas! When I was in Japan, no teacher told me about this, nor were there any fine friends to recommend this practice to me. How much time, sorry to say, I uselessly idled away! How fortunate it is that, owing to my good deeds in the past, I have now been able to see this! If I had remained in Japan, how could I have ever seen the monk next to me wearing the Buddha's *kaśāya?*' Filled with these mixed feelings of happiness and sorrow, I cried copiously. Then I vowed to myself, 'With compassion for my fellow countrymen I will, unworthy though I am, become an heir to Buddhism, a right receiver of the true Way, and teach them the Law that was correctly transmitted by the Buddhas and patriarchs together with the *kaśāya.*' "

In spite of the deeper understanding of Zen that Dōgen realized during his training at T'ien-t'ung, he still felt spiritually incomplete. Hence he decided to leave that monastery in search of a master under whose guidance he might realize total liberation. For the next several months he visited numerous monasteries, but to no avail. Just as he was about to give up his search and return to Japan, he happened to hear that the former abbot of T'ien-t'ung had died and that his successor, Ju-ching (1163–1228), was said to be one of China's finest Zen masters. Upon returning to that monastery, Dōgen found that Ju-ching was indeed a Zen master in whom he could place his full confidence. In the "Ceaseless Training" (*Gyōji*) section of the *Shōbō-genzō* Dōgen writes:

"My late master, Abbot Ju-ching, was from Yüeh. At the age of nineteen he quit scholastic Buddhism to train himself in the Way. Even in his sixties he continued to practice strenuously. Though given a purple robe and the title of Zen Master [*Ch'an-shih*] by Emperor Ning-tsung in the Chia-ting era [1208–25], he would not accept them and sent a letter of refusal to the emperor. This excellent deed of his was respected by monks everywhere and admired by knowledgeable men far and near. The emperor, too, was deeply impressed, and honored him with tea. Those who heard about his action praised it as being unprecedented."

With respect to Ju-ching's severe training, Dōgen continues in the same section: "My late master used to say, 'Ever since I was nineteen years old I made numerous visits to monasteries in search of Buddhism, but without finding a true teacher. During this period, not a day or a night passed without my doing zazen seated on a meditation cushion. Even before I became head monk of this temple [T'ien-t'ung] I did not talk with those in my home village for fear that I would waste a single moment. I always lived in the meditation hall of the temple in which I resided, never entering anyone else's hermitage or dormitory, not to mention going on pleasure trips to the mountains, lakes, and so on. Not only did I practice zazen at the appointed times in the meditation hall, but wherever and whenever it was possible to practice it I did so—in the upper stories of temple buildings, beneath cliffs, or in other solitary places, always carrying a cushion concealed in the sleeve of my robe. It was my intention to sit so hard as to make this cushion fall into tatters. This was my only wish. As a result, my buttocks sometimes became inflamed, causing hemorrhoids; but I liked zazen so much the better.' "

Following the example of his master, Dōgen devoted himself to the practice of zazen day and night. Early one morning, as he was making his usual round of inspection at the beginning of the formal zazen period, Ju-ching discovered one of the monks dozing. Scolding the monk, he said, "The practice of zazen is the dropping away of body and mind. What do you expect to accomplish by dozing?" Upon hearing these words, Dōgen suddenly realized enlightenment, his Mind's eye opening fully. Going to Ju-ching's room to have his enlightenment confirmed as genuine, Dōgen burned some incense and prostrated himself before his master.

"What do you mean by this?" Ju-ching asked.

"I have experienced the dropping away of body and mind," Dōgen replied.

Ju-ching, realizing that Dōgen's enlightenment was genuine, then said, "You have indeed dropped body and mind!"

Dōgen, however, remonstrated, "I have only just realized enlightenment. Don't sanction me so easily."

"I'm not sanctioning you easily."

Dōgen, still unsatisfied, persisted: "What is the basis for your saying that you haven't sanctioned me easily?"

Ju-ching replied, "Body and mind dropped away!"

Hearing this, Dōgen prostrated himself before his master in deep respect and gratitude, showing that he had indeed transcended his discriminating mind.

Even after his enlightenment Dōgen continued his training at T'ien-t'ung under Ju-ching's guidance for approximately two years, for as has been previously mentioned, there is in Zen Buddhism no gap between practice and enlightenment. Thus, practice after having realized enlightenment is just as important as that preceding it. Just how important a role Dōgen felt a true master like Ju-ching plays in the enlightenment process can be seen in his "Points to Watch in Buddhist Training" (*Gakudō Yōjin-shū*). He writes: "The Buddhist trainee can be compared to a fine piece of timber, and a true master to a good carpenter. Even quality wood will not show its fine grain unless it is worked on by a good carpenter. Even a warped piece of wood will, if handled by a good carpenter, soon show the results of good craftsmanship. The truth or falsity of enlightenment depends upon whether or not one has a true master. This should be well understood."

In 1227 Dōgen decided to return to Japan to propagate his teaching among the many people in his homeland who were ignorant of true Buddhism. When he asked for Ju-ching's permission to return, the latter readily granted it, for he highly evaluated the necessity and importance of Dōgen's coming work. As a symbol of the transference of the Law to Dōgen, Ju-ching presented him with a *kaśāya* that had originally belonged to Fu-jung Tao-ch'üeh (1043–1118). He also presented Dōgen with copies of the famous Ts'ao-tung (Sōtō) Zen texts *Pao-ching San-mei* (*Hōkyō Zammai*) and *Wu-wei Hsien-chüeh* (*Goi Kenketsu*) by Liang-chieh of Mount Tung (807–69), as well as a portrait of himself. In parting he said, "With all sincerity I gave these to you, a foreign monk. I hope you will propagate true Buddhism throughout your country, thereby saving deluded people. You should not live in cities or other places of human habitation. Rather, staying clear of kings and ministers, make your home in deep mountains and remote valleys, transmitting the essence of Zen Buddhism forever, if even only to a single true Bodhi-seeker."

After his return to Japan, Dōgen once more took up residence at Kennin-ji. He stayed there for three years, but to his great disappointment he found that the quality of the training at this temple had deteriorated considerably from what it had been in the past. In the *Shōbō-genzō Zuimonki* Dōgen is recorded as saying, "It is an obvious fact that Buddhism is now on the decline. I witnessed the gradual changes that had taken place between the first time I resided at Kennin-ji and the time I returned there seven or eight years later. At that time every room of the temple was furnished with a lacquered case, and every monk had his own furniture, liked fine clothes, and stored away treasures. Not only that, but they loved to utter licentious words, neglecting the correct manner of salutation and worship."

As a result of his disappointment in life at Kennin-ji, Dōgen decided to move to An'yō-in temple, though not before he had written his first treatise on Zen Buddhism, "A Universal Recommendation for Zazen" (*Fukan Zazen-gi*). This work not only contained a detailed description of the correct method of doing zazen but also expressed the essence of Zen Buddhism. At An'yō-in, Dōgen continued his writing; and it was here that he wrote "The Practice of the Way," which was to form the first section of his great masterwork, the *Shōbō-genzō*, in the Eihei-ji edition.

It was not until Dōgen moved to Kōshō-ji temple, where he had a *sōdō* (meditation hall) built, that he began in earnest to give practical guidance in zazen to monks as well as devout laymen. Although he approved of the construction of a simple and suitable meditation hall in order that Buddhist trainees might pursue their practice single-mindedly, Dōgen stringently warned against the building of magnificent temples or the making of Buddha images for their own sake. In the *Shōbō-genzō Zuimonki* he says:

"Nowadays most people think that making Buddha images or constructing temples is an index of the spread of Buddhism. This is quite wrong. No magnificent temple, though commanding a fine view and decorated with jewels or gold leaf, can be a medium of our enlightenment. It is true that laymen receive a sense of happiness when they have committed beneficial deeds by introducing their riches into the Buddha world, but such actions are not those of monks. Such actions by monks have nothing to do with the spread of Buddhism. We should think of the Buddha's words and practice zazen for even a short time in a humble cottage or under a tree; then Buddhism will really flourish. In order to build a meditation hall I am now exerting my utmost efforts to find benefactors willing to make contributions. However, I do not necessarily think this will contribute to the spread of Buddhism. Not having many trainees and having much to do, I am now forced to waste much time. Therefore, I sincerely hope to have the hall built in order that it may help deluded people to come into contact with Buddhism, and present Buddhist trainees to practice zazen. Even if my plan is not realized, I shall not be disappointed. If only I can set up even a single pillar, it will remind my descendants of my unattained hope. But what happens later on is no concern of mine."

At the opening ceremony of the meditation hall, Dōgen talked about what he had "gained" as a result of his training in China. He said, "I realized clearly that my eyes are set horizontally and my nose vertically. I returned to Japan without carrying a single *sūtra*. So I have no Buddhism [I am completely at one with Buddhism]."

As Dōgen became known for his virtuous character and severe training, an ever increasing number of people gathered around him until finally the hall he had built was unable to hold them all. Obliged to build a new hall, Dōgen decided to codify the regulations to be followed therein in a work entitled the *Jū Undō-shiki* (Rules of the Newly Built Meditation Hall). Concrete and minutely detailed, yet profoundly spiritual, these regulations give concrete expression to Dōgen's belief that Zen is a religion to be practiced in one's daily life. They are included here in their entirety in order that this unique aspect of Dōgen's teaching may be better understood.

"1. No monk shall be admitted to this meditation hall unless he has an earnest desire for the Way and a strong determination not to seek fame and profit. Neither should anyone enter here merely expecting to gain enlightenment. If you come to realize that your entrance was a mistake, you should leave. Once aspiration for the Way arises, your deep-rooted desire for fame and profit will disappear in a moment. In the whole world there are, I dare say, very few true transmitters of the Buddhist Law. With the building of this meditation hall at Kōshō-ji, I intend to lay the foundation for a Zen training institute in our country because I feel compassion for people in this age of degenerate Buddhism and attach more importance to what happens in the present than to what occurred in the past.

"2. All monks in this hall should try to live in harmony with one another, just as milk blends well with water, and should try to open their eyes to the supreme Wisdom together with others. Then your present position of 'guest' will afterward become that of 'master,' that is, of the Buddhas and patriarchs. For this reason we may say that here you are able to meet a friend ordinarily hard to meet and do things ordinarily hard to do. Always try to be of single purpose; then you will be identical with the Buddhas and patriarchs—nay, with their body and mind. Already separated from your homes and other human habitations, resting as with the floating clouds or running water, take good care of yourselves and pursue the Way to enlightenment—in all this you owe a great deal to the benefaction of other monks, above even that which you owe to your parents. Parents are those in the transient world, while other monks will long be your fellow trainees in the Way.

"3. You should not walk about in the outside world; but if unavoidable, it is permissible to do so once a month. In times past, some, I hear, lived in distant mountains or woods, aloof from worldly relations as well as from troublesome human affairs. You should realize they followed the Way without being attached to it. Now is the best time to save your head from a burning fire. How deplorable it is that even in this time of urgency you should be concerned with worldly troubles! Everything is too transient to be relied upon, and it is impossible to foretell when this transient life will come to an end. You should not read books here—not even books on Zen—but pursue the truth of Buddhism through strict training. Facing the wall, reflect on yourselves using the teachings of the ancient Buddhas and patriarchs as if looking into an old mirror, studying the Way wholeheartedly without wasting a single moment.

"4. Keep the supervisor of this hall informed of your whereabouts at all times. Do not idle away your time uselessly. Follow the rules for all monks here. Who can assert that your present body is not the last you will ever have? How sorry you would feel in the future if you should have lived to no purpose!

"5. Never speak ill of others, nor find fault with them. As the old saying goes, 'If you neither find fault with others nor take pride in your own merits, you will naturally be respectful to your seniors and harmonious with your juniors.' Never imitate others' faults but try to cultivate your own moral character. Śākyamuni did not teach [us] to hate others for their faults, but rather warned us to guard against our own faults.

"6. Never fail to do what is required of you, whether it be large or small, always taking care to keep the hall supervisor informed of your actions. If you fail to do so, you will be made to leave the hall. If the signs of courtesy between those of 'high' and 'low' position are not observed, it is impossible to tell right from wrong.

"7. In or about the hall, never speak loudly or in a group. If this occurs, it is the hall supervisor's responsibility to warn you.

"8. Never loiter in the hall.

"9. Never carry a rosary here, nor go in or out with your hands hanging down.

"10. Never invoke or read any *sūtra* here unless you have been earnestly requested to do so by a lay supporter.

"11. Never blow your nose, nor spit loudly in the hall. Realizing that time is too short for your lifelong training—just as a fish cannot live long in a pool where the water is insufficient—be regretful that you have not yet realized final enlightenment.

"12. Wear only robes made of plain material. Those who have hitherto sought Buddhism have always done so.

"13. Never enter the hall drunk with wine, but if by mistake you do so, bow to the Mañjuśrī image[7] and make repentance. Never bring wine into the hall, nor enter here emitting its smell.

"14. Never quarrel with one another here. If you do, both of you will be ordered to leave, because it will prevent others, as well as the parties concerned, from practicing the Way. Also to be censured is he who sees them quarreling without warning them.

"15. He who does not abide by the rules of this hall must be expelled by all the monks here; so must he who remains indifferent to such a monk.

"16. Never disturb the training of other monks by inviting outsiders, lay or clerical, into the hall. Never be desirous of offerings from lay supporters, thinking yourselves worthy of such gifts because of your long training. It should be noted, however, that this hall is open to any earnest and long-time seeker of the Way, though the hall supervisor's permission is necessary.

"17. Do zazen here as befits a meditation hall, and listen attentively to the head monk's lectures on Buddhism.

"18. Should you drop one of your bowls on the floor during breakfast or lunch, you must keep the oil lamp in front of the Mañjuśrī image burning for twenty-four hours running as a penalty.

"19. Observe these regulations of the Buddhas and patriarchs, keeping them in your mind and heart.

"20. During your lifelong pursuit of the Way, seek calmness and freedom.

"The articles mentioned above are all the body and mind of the ancient Zen masters. This is why you should observe them."

During his residence at Kōshō-ji, Dōgen acquired numerous dedicated disciples, among whom Ejō, Sōkai, Sen'e, Ekan, Gikai, Giin, Gien, Gijun, Gizen, and Giun were the most notable. Ejō (1198–1280) in particular was very close to Dōgen, even though he was two years older than his master. It was he who was responsible for compiling the collection of Dōgen's sayings known as the *Shōbō-genzō Zuimonki*. Later he was also to assist his master in founding the monastery of Eihei-ji on the Japan Sea coast, and still later would become its second head monk.

Dōgen, for his part, was busily engaged at Kōshō-ji in continuing his written introduction to Zen, completing not only forty more sections of the *Shōbō-genzō* but also several other works. Yet the now middle-aged Dōgen was encountering more and more problems. Not only did his growing fame attract an increasing number of visitors, who tended to disturb his training and study, but also he became the target of persecution by the older, more established Buddhist sects. The clerical leaders of Mount Hiei, affiliated with the then almighty and increasingly degenerate Tendai sect, were especially vociferous in their condemnation of Dōgen, jealous of his widening influence. There is even a tradition to the effect that they ordered Kōshō-ji to be destroyed, forcing Dōgen to move once again.

Dōgen, accompanied by a small number of his closest disciples, did at any rate leave Kōshō-ji, first finding temporary haven at a small temple, Yoshimine-dera, located on the Japan Sea coast in what was then known as Echizen province (present-day Fukui Prefecture). Here, with the support and protection of Hatano Yoshishige, a powerful district clan leader and devout Buddhist, Dōgen wrote twenty-four more sections of the *Shōbō-genzō* before moving on to Yamashibu-dera temple for three months, where he completed five more sections. At least Dōgen found a permanent home at Daibutsu-ji, a temple that had been built for him by Yoshishige, who requested that he become its founder. Two years later the name of this temple was changed to Eihei-ji (Temple of Eternal Peace), the name that it has kept to the present, when it is one of the two head temples of the Sōtō Zen sect[8] and the largest Zen monastery in Japan.

According to the traditional history of the Japanese Sōtō Zen sect, the primary motivation for Dōgen's having gone to such an extremely remote area as Echizen was his desire to act in accordance with the instructions of his Chinese master Ju-ching to stay "clear of kings and ministers" and "make your home in deep mountains and remote valleys, transmitting the essence of Zen Buddhism forever, if even only to a single true Bodhi-seeker." Although these instructions did no doubt play an important part in Dōgen's decision to move, not to mention persecution by the other sects, the traditional historical view does not adequately explain why Dōgen chose to live for nearly sixteen years in the vicinity of Kyoto, the home of the emperor, upon his return from China. Nor does it explain why, during his residence near Kyoto, he presented the cloistered emperor Gosaga with a treatise entitled *Gokoku Shōbō-gi* (The Method of Pacifying the State by the True Law).

The actual content of the treatise is now unknown, but from Dōgen's other writings it may be fairly assumed that he proposed that the state should be governed by the spirit of Zen Buddhism, that is, the spirit of the equality and identity of all things and all people: a view that was not likely to please the leadership of the older established sects, denying as it must have their privileged position. In the first section of the *Shōbō-genzō*, "The Practice of the Way," Dōgen describes the relationship of Buddhism to the state as follows: "When the true Way is widely practiced in the nation, the various Buddhas and heavenly deities will continuously protect it and the virtue of the emperor will exert a good influence on the people, thereby bringing peace. When the nation is thus pacified by such a wise and virtuous emperor, then the Way, being strengthened by these circumstances, can be truly practiced."

It was this view, no doubt, that led Dōgen in 1247 to accept the invitation of Hōjō Tokiyori, head of the feudal military government in the new capital of Kamakura near present-day Tokyo, to give him instruction in the Buddhist precepts. After making the long trip from Eihei-ji, Dōgen eventually conferred the Bodhisattva precepts[9] on Tokiyori; but, perhaps being disappointed in the ruler, he refused the latter's request to remain in the capital for a longer period of time.

From these various attempts by Dōgen to influence national policy, it is clear that while he exerted his greatest efforts in giving practical instruction and guidance to individual seekers of the Way, he was also interested in establishing an entire society based on Zen Buddhist thought and practice. Underlying all his efforts was his fundamental belief that in essence there is no difference between so-called worldly affairs and the Way. In another passage from "The Practice of the Way" he states, "He who regards worldly affairs as an obstacle to his training only knows there is no Way in worldly affairs, not knowing that there is nothing such as worldly affairs to be distinguished from the Way."

In line with his statement that there is no Way in worldly affairs, Dōgen severely warned Buddhist initiates against the pursuit of fame and profit, regarding them as great obstacles to the realization of the Way. His thought in this regard is clearly shown in the first article of the *Jū Undō-shiki,* in which one of the conditions placed on those entering the meditation hall was that they have "a strong determination not to seek fame and profit." Dōgen himself refused to accept an honorary purple *kaśāya* sent to him at Eihei-ji by the cloistered emperor Gosaga. The cloistered emperor, however, continued to beseech Dōgen to accept his gift; and after having twice refused it, he finally accepted it the third time. Vowing never to wear it during his lifetime, however, Dōgen composed the following poem:

Shallow is the valley of Eihei-ji temple,
But grave is the edict of the emperor.
If an old monk here wore a purple *kaśāya*
He would be laughed at by monkeys and cranes.

At the comparatively early age of fifty-two, Dōgen became seriously ill. Realizing that his illness was beyond medical treatment, he presented his disciples with his last treatise on Buddhism, "The Eight Aspects of Enlightenment" (*Hachi Dainin-gaku*). This treatise was later incorporated as the last section of the *Shōbō-genzō.* At the urging of his disciples, Dōgen returned to Kyoto to receive medical treatment; but this was of no avail and he died soon after his arrival, on August 28, 1253, at Seido-in temple in Takatsuji, Kyoto.

Dōgen delivered a great many discourses on Buddhism during his lifetime of fifty-three years. Those that have been preserved were copied down either directly by him or by his disciples, and form a total of eight separate works with more than 120 sections in all. Broadly speaking, they can be divided into the following five categories: (1) the essence of Zen, (2) instructions, (3) regulations for a Zen monastery, (4) precepts, and (5) poetry. His principal works are "A Universal Recommendation for Zazen," "Points to Watch in Buddhist Training," *Eihei Genzenji Shingi,* a collection of Ju-ching's sayings known as the *Hōkyō-ki,* a collection of Dōgen's teachings and verse called the *Eihei Kōroku,* the *Shōbō-genzō,* and the *Shōbō-genzō Zuimonki.*

Dōgen's numerous writings make it clear that the teachings of Sōtō Zen Buddhism are quite different from those of the Rinzai sect. As has been mentioned, Japanese Zen is divided into three main sects. Of these the Ōbaku is the smallest. The Rinzai sect is much larger, though still lacking in wide support among the general populace. Due to the numerous English works on Zen Buddhism by Daisetz Suzuki, however, it is undoubtedly the best known of the Zen sects outside Japan. By comparison, although still relatively unknown abroad, the Sōtō sect is spread throughout the Japanese countryside, having approximately one hundred thousand affiliated monks and nuns and five million lay devotees. This means that the Sōtō sect is equal in size to Japan's other most popular Buddhist sect, the Jōdo Shin or True Pure Land sect.

There are many different ways of extracting the essence of Dōgen's thought. Perhaps the most useful and readily understood method is that in which the essential characteristics of his thought are expressed as identities of what are ordinarily considered to be mutually opposing or exclusive concepts. In Dōgen's case there are eleven such identities, which form the basis of his thought.

1. *Identity of self and others.* The original spirit of Dōgen's Zen is, of course, to do zazen. Zazen is the complete realization of self—self identified with others. Self identified with others is the universal or true Self. To realize this it is necessary to realize non-ego through the practice of zazen—thinking beyond conceptual thought. By way of explanation, Dōgen says in the "Manifestation of the *Kōan*" (*Genjō Kōan*) section of the *Shōbō-genzō:* "To study the Way is to study the self. To study the self is to forget the self. To forget the self is to be enlightened by all things. To be enlightened by all things is to remove the barriers between one's self and others."

2. *Identity of practice and enlightenment.* As mentioned earlier, Dōgen emphasized that there is no gap between practice and enlightenment. Ordinarily, man works in order to obtain something he desires. Therefore, once he has obtained that object he often becomes satisfied and makes no further effort. On the other hand, if he fails to obtain his object he tends to become too discouraged to continue his task. As long as one is attached in this manner to the results achieved, it is impossible to make constant effort. It is necessary to understand that, originally, there is no difference between first and last, cause and effect.

3. *Identity of the precepts and Zen Buddhism.* Novice monks must not enter the monkhood without having received the sixteen Bodhisattva precepts. In this sense, these precepts are the first gate through which monks must pass in their search for Zen. In the eyes of Dōgen, however, there is no difference between the precepts and Zen itself. The precepts are simply the function of the inner Buddha-mind. In other words, when one has realized his Buddha-mind, he is already endowed with the precepts.

4. *Identity of life and death.* The most important problem for Buddhist trainees is to realize the meaning of life and death. Ordinary people love life and hate death. But however hard they may try to avoid this hateful death, they find it impossible to do so. However, once one faces death courageously, one finds that there is no gap between life and death. In other words, life is life itself and death is death itself. Life is no other than life; death is no other than death. There is no death opposed to life, no life opposed to death. Thus, Dōgen says in the "Birth and Death" (*Shōji*) section of the *Shōbō-genzō,* "There is no life or death to love or hate." Both, in fact, are the life of the Buddha.

5. *Identity of* kōan *and enlightenment.* The 1,700 *kōan* are an important aid to the realization of enlightenment. Monks of the Rinzai sect are said to be

unable to realize enlightenment unless they are able to find a "solution" to their *kōan* during zazen. Dōgen, however, stresses that the *kōan* themselves are enlightenment, and vice versa. As already mentioned, enlightenment is practice. Therefore single-hearted practice of zazen is already the undisguised manifestation of the *kōan* themselves. The "solution" to the *kōan,* as well as enlightenment itself, should not be sought intentionally but should be realized naturally through strenuous practice of the Way.

6. *Identity of time and being.* Dōgen writes in the "Being-Time" (*Uji*) section of the *Shōbō-genzō,* "Time is being and vice versa," and "Each thing is one time." Time is not the object of our cognition, for it can be understood only when it is experienced directly. When time is time itself, being can be being itself. In this sense Dōgen's viewpoint is similar to that expressed by the German philosopher Martin Heidegger in *Sein und Zeit* (Being and Time). Spring becomes summer. But spring is spring, and summer is summer, each including the other. "Now" is "now," including the past, present, and future. Without "now" there is none of the others. "Now" is absolute and eternal. "Now" once lost never returns. So there is every need to apply oneself to the present practice of the Way.

7. *Identity of being and nonbeing.* In Dōgen's Zen, nonbeing is far from "nothing," for nonbeing is being, and vice versa. Both are absolutes beyond the dualistic viewpoint. From the absolute viewpoint, Dōgen taught, it is equally correct to say "We have the Buddha-nature" and "We do not have the Buddha-nature." This may sound like a paradoxical statement, opposed to common sense, but it can be verified through Buddhist practice. In this sense, nonbeing in Zen is never the "nothing" of nihilism but is a lively and creative function of the Way.

8. *Identity of Zen Buddhism and the state.* Dogen believed that ideally, the state should be based on the spirit of Zen Buddhism. The fact that he presented the cloistered emperor Gosaga with the treatise *Gokoku Shōbō-gi* shows how eagerly he tried to teach the national authorities the universality of Zen. As previously stated, his viewpoint of the state was that the citizens thereof should be governed by the spirit of Zen, that is, the equality and identity of all things and all people.

9. *Identity of men and women.* Śākyamuni, the historical Buddha, said, "All creatures have the Buddha-nature." Therefore they are all originally equal. With regard to the ability to realize Buddhahood, there is no difference between clever and foolish, high and low social status, or men and women. Dōgen states in the "Realization of the Way through Venerating the Buddhas" (*Raihai Tokuzui*) section of the *Shōbō-genzō,* "There is no gap between right and wrong, or between men and women." One is not respected as a true Buddhist by others because of one's sex but according to whether or not one has realized the Way. Although women may appear weaker than men, this has nothing to do with their realization of the Way. The Way is open to men and women equally.

10. *Identity of monks and lay people.* Monks can apply themselves to Buddhist practice, freed from worldly affairs. However, lay people are often too oc-

cupied with securing their livelihood to pursue the Way. Is there no gap in the realization of the Way between the two? About this Dōgen says in the "Practice of the Way" section of the *Shōbō-genzō,* "It depends upon the intensity of their Bodhi-seeking mind whether they [laymen] can realize the Way." It should be noted, however, that although Dōgen admits that it is theoretically possible for laymen to realize the Way, he states in the "Merit of Becoming a Monk" section of the *Shōbō-genzō,* "Laymen should definitely enter the monkhood and follow the precepts for monks." Contradictory? Yes, but it is necessary to remember that, in Dōgen's Zen, practice takes precedence over theory.

11. *Identity of the* sūtras *and Zen Buddhism.* In Zen, the Way of the Buddha-mind is often said to be beyond letters and *sūtras.* This is because attachment to letters can easily become a hindrance to realizing the Buddha-mind. But this does not mean that letters and *sūtras* are less valuable than the Buddha-mind. From the viewpoint of enlightenment there is no gap between the two. Letters are the Way itself, and vice versa; *sūtras* are the Buddha-mind, and vice versa. About this Dōgen states in the "Buddhist Teachings" (*Bukkyō*) section of the *Shōbō-genzō:* "If you say that the Buddha-mind is transmitted beyond the *sūtras,* it follows that the *sūtras* are transmitted beyond the Buddha-mind. If this were true, not a syllable of the *sūtras* could have been transmitted." It is the attachment to letters, not letters themselves, that must be cast away.

The preceding "identities" show that Dōgen regarded the essence of the Way as equality. But equality is closely connected with the state of absolute freedom that exists beyond such dualistic ideas as right and wrong, life and death, time and being, men and women, and so on. The equality of self and others, in particular, promotes altruistic love for all things and people. Dōgen's words in the "Four Practices of Bodhisattvas" (*Bodaisatta Shi-shōbō*) section of the *Shōbō-genzō*—"Save others before you realize your own enlightenment"—express the essence of his Zen, sustained as it was by his single-hearted practice of zazen. This feature of Dōgen's Zen is based on the identity (equality) of all things, which includes absolute freedom and altruistic love for all beings.

As already mentioned, Dōgen negated the use of *kōan* as objects of meditation to be used in the course of realizing enlightenment and stressed, instead, practice identified with enlightenment and the precepts, based on the firm belief that one is already united with the Buddha. Because the basic premise of Buddhism regarding sentient beings is that they are inherently in possession of the Buddha-nature, having the innate quality of enlightenment, Dōgen's Zen may be said to have a common standpoint with the other new sects of the Kamakura period, such as Jōdo, Jōdo Shin, Rinzai, and Nichiren. However, in his teaching that the practice of zazen embodies both practice and enlightenment he may be said to have made a unique contribution to Japanese Buddhism. Through the emphasis he placed on the Bodhisattva precepts and the ceaseless practice of zazen, he developed Zen Buddhism to new heights, making it a truly universal religion.

Part Two

Independent Works

ONE

A Universal Recommendation for Zazen

(Fukan Zazen-gi)

The original version of the Fukan Zazen-gi *was written by Dōgen at Kennin-ji temple in Kyoto between October 5 and December 10 in 1277. He was twenty-eight years old and had just returned from China. At that time the Rinzai sect's method of zazen, emphasizing the use of* kōan, *was prevalent in Japan, having been previously introduced by Eisai. Contrary to this method, however, Dōgen taught: "There is no gap between practice and enlightenment," and "We do zazen for its own sake."*

In the final twenty or so years of his life Dōgen revised his original version of "A Universal Recommendation for Zazen" into what has come to be known as the "popular edition." Although this is a relatively short work, the fact that Dōgen devoted so much time to its writing is indicative of the importance that he placed on the practice of zazen with a "nonseeking mind." It also expresses his earnest desire that this method of zazen be disseminated to as large an audience as possible. This translation is based on the popular edition.

Now, WHEN YOU TRACE THE SOURCE of the Way, you find that it is universal and absolute. It is unnecessary to distinguish between "practice" and "enlightenment." The supreme teaching is free, so why study the means to attain it? The Way is, needless to say, very far from delusion. Why, then, be concerned about the means of eliminating the latter?

The Way is completely present where you are, so of what use is practice or enlightenment? However, if there is the slightest difference in the beginning between you and the Way, the result will be a greater separation than between heaven and earth. If the slightest dualistic thinking arises, you will lose your Buddha-mind. For example, some people are proud of their understanding, and think that they are richly endowed with the Buddha's Wisdom.[1] They think that they have attained the Way, illuminated their minds, and gained the power to touch the heavens. They imagine that they are wandering about in the realm of enlightenment. But in fact they have almost lost the absolute Way, which is beyond enlightenment itself.

You should pay attention to the fact that even the Buddha Śākyamuni had to practice zazen for six years.[2] It is also said that Bodhidharma had to do zazen at Shao-lin temple for nine years in order to transmit the Buddha-mind.[3] Since these ancient sages were so diligent, how can present-day trainees do without the practice of zazen? You should stop pursuing words and letters and learn to withdraw and reflect on yourself. When you do so, your body and mind will naturally fall away, and your original Buddha-nature will appear. If you wish to realize the Buddha's Wisdom, you should begin training immediately.

Now, in doing zazen it is desirable to have a quiet room. You should be temperate in eating and drinking, forsaking all delusive relationships. Setting everything aside, think of neither good nor evil, right nor wrong. Thus, having stopped the various functions of your mind, give up even the idea of becoming a Buddha. This holds true not only for zazen but for all your daily actions.

Usually a thick square mat is put on the floor where you sit and a round cushion on top of that. You may sit in either the full or half lotus position. In the former, first put your right foot on your left thigh and then your left foot on your right thigh. In the latter, only put your left foot on the right thigh. Your clothing should be worn loosely but neatly. Next, put your right hand on your left foot and your left palm on the right palm, the tips of the thumbs lightly touching. Sit upright, leaning to neither left nor right, front nor back. Your ears should be on the same plane as your shoulders and your nose in line with your navel. Your tongue should be placed against the roof of your mouth and your lips and teeth closed firmly. With your eyes kept continuously open, breathe quietly through your nostrils. Finally, having regulated your body and mind in this way, take a deep breath, sway your body to left and right, then sit firmly as a rock. Think of nonthinking. How is this done? By thinking beyond thinking and nonthinking. This is the very basis of zazen.[4]

Zazen is not "step-by-step meditation." Rather it is simply the easy and pleasant practice of a Buddha, the realization of the Buddha's Wisdom. The Truth appears, there being no delusion. If you understand this, you are completely free, like a dragon that has obtained water or a tiger that reclines on a mountain. The supreme Law will then appear of itself, and you will be free of weariness and confusion.

At the completion of zazen move your body slowly and stand up calmly. Do not move violently.

By virtue of zazen it is possible to transcend the difference between "common" and "sacred" and attain the ability to die while doing zazen or while standing up. Moreover, it is impossible for our discriminating mind to understand either how the Buddhas and patriarchs expressed the essence of Zen to their disciples with finger, pole, needle, or mallet,[5] or how they passed on enlightenment with a *hossu,* fist, staff, or shout.[6] Neither can this be understood through supernatural power or a dualistic view of practice and enlightenment. Zazen is a practice beyond the subjective and objective worlds, beyond discriminating thinking. Therefore, no distinction should be made between the clever and the stupid. To practice the Way single-heartedly is, in itself, enlightenment. There is no gap between practice and enlightenment or zazen and daily life.

The Buddhas and patriarchs, both in this world and that, in India and in China, have all preserved the Buddha-mind and enhanced Zen training. You should therefore devote yourself exclusively to and be completely absorbed in the practice of zazen. Although it is said that there are innumerable ways of understanding Buddhism, you should do zazen alone. There is no reason to forsake your own sitting place and make futile trips to other countries. If your first step is mistaken, you will stumble immediately.

You have already had the good fortune to be born with a precious [human] body, so do not waste your time meaninglessly. Now that you know what is the most important thing in Buddhism, how can you be satisfied with the transient world? Our bodies are like dew on the grass, and our lives like a flash of lightning, vanishing in a moment.

Earnest Zen trainees, do not be surprised by a real dragon[7] or spend a long time rubbing only one part of an elephant.[8] Exert yourself in the Way that points directly to your original [Buddha] nature. Respect those who have realized full knowledge and have nothing more to do. Become one with the Wisdom of the Buddhas and succeed to the enlightenment of the patriarchs. If you do zazen for some time, you will realize all this. The treasure house will then open of itself, and you will be able to enjoy it to your heart's content.

TWO

Points to Watch in Buddhist Training

(*Gakudō Yōjin-shū*)

Dōgen completed this treatise for his disciples at Kōshō-ji in 1234, seven years after he had returned from China. Whereas in the Fukan Zazen-gi *the primary emphasis is on a practical explanation of how to do zazen, in this later work Dōgen gives a more thorough explanation of the spirit in which not only zazen but all of one's actions are to be done.*

Beginning with an exhortation to awaken to the Bodhi-mind, Dōgen goes on to discuss the importance of training under a true master, as well as such topics as the relationship of training to enlightenment and the significance of the practice of zazen. Although the content of the Shōbō-genzō *is philosophically more profound, the* Gakudō Yōjin-shū *is highly esteemed as a training guide in the Sōtō Zen sect by those who are actually engaged in daily practice of the Way. Among Dōgen's numerous works this one in particular deserves repeated reading, ideally in conjunction with the deepening of one's own practice; for although relatively short, it presents nothing less than the blueprint of enlightenment.*

1. THE NEED TO AWAKEN TO THE BODHI-MIND The Bodhi-mind is known by many names; but they all refer to the One Mind of the Buddha. The Venerable Nāgārjuna[1] said, "The mind that sees into the flux of arising and decaying and recognizes the transient nature of the world is also known as the Bodhi-mind." Why, then, is temporary dependence on this mind called the Bodhi-mind? When the transient nature of the world is recognized, the ordinary selfish mind does not arise; neither does the mind that seeks for fame and profit.

Aware that time waits for no man, train as though you were attempting to save your head from being enveloped in flames. Reflecting on the transient nature of body and life, exert yourself just as the Buddha Śākyamuni did when he raised his foot.[2]

Although you hear the flattering call of the god Kiṃnara and the *kalavinka* bird,[3] pay no heed, regarding them as merely the evening breeze blowing in your ears. Even though you see a face as beautiful as that of Mao-ch'ang or Hsi-shih,[4] think of them as merely the morning dew blocking your vision.

When freed from the bondage of sound, color, and shape, you will naturally become one with the true Bodhi-mind. Since ancient times there have been those who have heard little of true Buddhism and others who have seen little of the *sūtras*. Most of them have fallen into the pitfall of fame and profit, losing the essence of the Way forever. What a pity! How regrettable! This should be well understood.

Even though you have read the expedient or true teachings[5] of excellent *sūtras* or transmitted the esoteric and exoteric teachings,[6] unless you forsake fame and profit you cannot be said to have awakened to the Bodhi-mind.

There are some who say that the Bodhi-mind is the highest supreme enlightenment of the Buddha, free from fame and profit. Others say that it is that which embraces the one billion worlds[7] in a single moment of thought, or that it is the teaching that not a single delusion arises. Still others [say] that it is the mind that directly enters into the realm of the Buddha. These people, not yet understanding what the Bodhi-mind is, wantonly slander it. They are indeed far from the Way.

Reflect on your ordinary mind, selfishly attached as it is to fame and profit. Is it endowed with the essence and appearance of the three thousand worlds in a single moment of thought? Has it experienced the teaching that not a single delusion arises? No, there is nothing there but the delusion of fame and profit, nothing worthy of being called the Bodhi-mind.

Although there have been patriarchs since ancient times who have used secular means to realize enlightenment, none of them has been attached to fame and profit, or even Buddhism, let alone the ordinary world.

The Bodhi-mind is, as previously mentioned, that which recognizes the transient nature of the world—one of the four insights.[8] It is utterly different from that referred to by madmen.

The nonarising mind and the appearance of the one billion worlds are fine practices *after* having awakened to the Bodhi-mind. "Before" and "after," however, should not be confused. Simply forget the self and quietly practice the Way. This is truly the Bodhi-mind.

The sixty-two viewpoints are based on self; so when egoistic views arise, just do zazen quietly, observing them. What is the basis of your body, its inner and outer possessions? You received your body, hair, and skin from your parents. The two droplets, red and white,[9] of your parents, however, are empty from beginning to end; hence there is no self here. Mind, discriminating consciousness, knowledge, and dualistic thought bind life. What, ultimately, are exhaling and inhaling? They are not self. There is no self to be attached to. The deluded, however, are attached to self, while the enlightened are unattached. But still you seek to measure the self that is no self, and attach yourselves to arisings that are nonarising, neglecting to practice the Way. By failing to sever your ties with the world, you shun the true teaching and run after the false. Dare you say you are not acting mistakenly?

2. THE NEED FOR TRAINING UPON ENCOUNTERING THE TRUE LAW A king's

mind can often be changed as the result of advice given by a loyal retainer. If the Buddhas and patriarchs offer even a single word, there will be none who will remain unconverted. Only wise kings, however, heed the advice of their retainers, and only exceptional trainees listen to the Buddha's words.

It is impossible to sever the source of transmigration without casting away the delusive mind. In the same way, if a king fails to heed the advice of his retainers, virtuous policy will not prevail, and he will be unable to govern the country well.

3. THE NEED TO REALIZE THE WAY THROUGH CONSTANT TRAINING Lay people believe that government office can be acquired as a result of study. The Buddha Śākyamuni teaches, however, that training encompasses enlightenment. I have never heard of anyone who became a government official without study or realized enlightenment without training.

Although it is true that different training methods exist—those based on faith or the Law, the sudden or gradual realization of enlightenment[10]—still one realizes enlightenment as a result of training. In the same way, although the depth of people's learning differs, as does their speed of comprehension, government office is acquired through accumulated study. None of these things depends on whether the rulers are superior or not, or whether one's luck is good or bad.

If government office could be acquired without study, who could transmit the method by which the former king successfully ruled the nation? If enlightenment could be realized without training, who could understand the teaching of the Tathāgata,[11] distinguishing, as it does, the difference between delusion and enlightenment? Understand that although you train in the world of delusion, enlightenment is already there. Then, for the first time, you will realize that boats and rafts [the *sūtras*] are but yesterday's dream and will be able to sever forever the old views that bound you to them.

The Buddha does not force this understanding on you. Rather it comes naturally from your training in the Way, for training invites enlightenment. Your own treasure does not come from the outside. Since enlightenment is one with training, enlightened action leaves no traces. Therefore, when looking back on training with enlightened eyes, you will find there is no illusion to be seen, just as white clouds extending for ten thousand *ri* cover the whole sky.

When enlightenment is harmonized with training, you cannot step on even a single particle of dust. Should you be able to do so, you will be as far removed from enlightenment as heaven is from earth. If you return to your true Self, you can transcend even the status of the Buddha. *(Written on March 9, the second year of Tempuku [1234])*

4. THE NEED FOR SELFLESS PRACTICE OF THE WAY In the practice of the Way it is necessary to accept the true teachings of our predecessors, setting aside our own preconceived notions. The Way cannot be realized with mind or without it. Unless the mind of constant practice is one with the Way,

neither body nor mind will know peace. When the body and mind are not at peace, they become obstacles to enlightenment.

How are constant practice and the Way to be harmonized? To do so the mind must neither be attached to nor reject anything; it must be completely free from [attachment to] fame and profit. One does not undergo Buddhist training for the sake of others. The minds of Buddhist trainees, like those of most people these days, however, are far from understanding the Way. They do that which others praise even though they know it to be false. On the other hand, they do not practice that which others scorn even though they know it to be the true Way. How regrettable!

Reflect quietly on whether your mind and actions are one with Buddhism or not. If you do so, you will realize how shameful they are. The penetrating eyes of the Buddhas and patriarchs are constantly illuminating the entire universe.

Since Buddhist trainees do not do anything for the sake of themselves, how could they do anything for the sake of fame and profit? You should train for the sake of Buddhism alone. The various Buddhas do not show deep compassion for all sentient beings for either their own or others' sakes. This is the Buddhist tradition.

Observe how even animals and insects nurture their young, enduring various hardships in the process. The parents stand to gain nothing by their actions, even after their offspring have reached maturity. Yet, though they are only small creatures, they have deep compassion for their young. This is also the case with regard to the various Buddhas' compassion for all sentient beings. The excellent teachings of these various Buddhas, however, are not limited to compassion alone; rather, they appear in countless ways throughout the universe. This is the essence of Buddhism.

We are already the children of the Buddha; therefore we should follow in his footsteps. Trainees, do not practice Buddhism for your own benefit, for fame and profit, or for rewards and miraculous powers. Simply practice Buddhism for the sake of Buddhism; this is the true Way.

5. THE NEED TO SEEK A TRUE MASTER A former patriarch once said, "If the Bodhi-mind is untrue, all one's training will come to nothing." This saying is indeed true. Furthermore, the quality of the disciple's training depends upon the truth or falsity of his master.

The Buddhist trainee can be compared to a fine piece of timber, and a true master to a good carpenter. Even quality wood will not show its fine grain unless it is worked on by a good carpenter. Even a warped piece of wood will, if handled by a good carpenter, soon show the results of good craftsmanship. The truth or falsity of enlightenment depends upon whether or not one has a true master. This should be well understood.

In our country, however, there have not been any true masters since ancient times. We can tell this by looking at their words, just as we can tell [the nature of] the source of a river by scooping up some of its water downstream.

For centuries, masters in this country have compiled books, taught disciples, and led both human and celestial beings. Their words, however, were still green, still unripe, for they had not yet reached the ultimate in training. They had not yet reached the sphere of enlightenment. Instead, they merely transmitted words and made others recite names and letters. Day and night they counted the treasure of others, without gaining anything for themselves.

These ancient masters must be held responsible for this state of affairs. Some of them taught that enlightenment should be sought outside the mind, others that rebirth in the Pure Land was the goal. Herein lies the source of both confusion and delusion.

Even if good medicine is given to someone, unless that person has also been given the proper directions for taking it the illness may be made worse; in fact, [taking medicine] may do more harm than taking poison. Since ancient times there have not been any good doctors in our country who were capable of making out the correct prescription or distinguishing between medicine and poison. For this reason it has been extremely difficult to eliminate life's suffering and disease. How, then, can we expect to escape from the sufferings of old age and death?

This situation is completely the fault of the masters, not of the disciples. Why? Because they guide their disciples along the branches of the tree, dispensing with its roots. Before they fully understand the Way themselves, they devote themselves solely to their own egoistic minds, luring others into the world of delusion. How regrettable it is that even these masters are unaware of their own delusion. How can their disciples be expected to know the difference between right and wrong?

Unfortunately, true Buddhism has not yet spread to this peripheral little country, and true masters have yet to be born. If you want to study the supreme Way, you have to visit masters in faraway Sung China, and reflect there on the true road that is far beyond the delusive mind. If you are unable to find a true master, it is best not to study Buddhism at all. True masters are those who have realized the true Law and received the seal of a genuine master. It has nothing to do with their age. For them neither learning nor knowledge is of primary importance. Possessing extraordinary power and influence, they do not rely on selfish views or cling to any obsession, for they have perfectly harmonized knowledge and practice. These are the characteristics of a true master.

6. Advice for the practice of Zen The study of the Way through the practice of zazen is of vital importance. You should not neglect it or treat it lightly. In China there are the excellent examples of former Zen masters who cut off their arms or fingers.[12] Long ago the Buddha Śākyamuni renounced both his home and his kingdom—another fine trace of the practice of the Way. Men of the present day, however, say that one need only practice that which is easily practiced. Their words are very mistaken and far removed from the Way. If you devote yourself to one thing exclusively and con-

sider it to be training, even lying down will become tedious. If one thing becomes tedious, all things become tedious. You should know that those who like easy things are, as a matter of course, unworthy of the practice of the Way.

Our great teacher, Śākyamuni, was unable to gain the teaching that prevails in the present world until after he had undergone severe training for countless ages in the past. Considering how dedicated the founder of Buddhism was, can his descendants be any less so? Those who seek the Way should not look for easy training. Should you do so, you will never be able to reach the true world of enlightenment or find the treasure house. Even the most gifted of the former patriarchs have said that the Way is difficult to practice. You should realize how deep and immense Buddhism is. If the Way were, originally, so easy to practice and understand, these former gifted patriarchs would not have stressed its difficulty. By comparison with the former patriarchs, people of today do not amount to even as much as a single hair in a herd of nine cows! That is to say, even if these moderns, lacking as they do both ability and knowledge, exert themselves to the utmost, their imagined difficult practice would still be incomparable to that of the former patriarchs.

What is the easily practiced and easily understood teaching of which present-day man is so fond? It is neither a secular teaching nor a Buddhist one. It is even inferior to the practice of demons and evil spirits, as well as to that of non-Buddhist religions and the two vehicles.[13] It may be said to be the great delusion of ordinary men and women. Although they imagine that they have escaped from the delusive world, they have, on the contrary, merely subjected themselves to endless transmigration.

Breaking one's bones and crushing the marrow to gain Buddhism are thought to be difficult practices. It is still more difficult, however, to control the mind, let alone undergo prolonged austerities and pure training, while controlling one's physical actions is most difficult of all.

If the crushing of one's bones were of value, the many who endured this training in the past should have realized enlightenment; but in fact, only a few did. If the practice of austerities were of value, the many who have done so since ancient times also should have become enlightened; but here, too, only a few did. This all stems from the great difficulty of controlling the mind. In Buddhism neither a brilliant mind nor scholastic understanding is of primary importance. The same holds true for mind, discriminating consciousness, thought, and insight. None of these are of any use, for the Way may be entered only through the harmonization of body and mind.

The Buddha Śākyamuni said, "Turning the sound-perceiving stream of the mind inward, forsake knowing and being known." Herein lies the meaning of the above. The two qualities of movement and nonmovement have not appeared at all; this is true harmony.

If it were possible to enter the Way on the basis of having a brilliant mind and wide knowledge, high-ranking Shên-hsiu[14] should certainly have been able to do so. If common birth were an obstacle to entering the Way, how did

Hui-nêng[15] become one of the Chinese patriarchs? These examples clearly show that the process of transmitting the Way does not depend on either a brilliant mind or wide knowledge. In seeking the Law, reflect on yourselves and train diligently.

Neither youth nor age is an obstacle to entering the Way. Chao-chou[16] was more than sixty years old when he first began to practice, yet he became an outstanding patriarch. Cheng's daughter,[17] on the other hand, was only thirteen years old, but she had already attained a deep understanding of the Way, so much so that she became one of the finest trainees in her monastery.

The majesty of Buddhism appears according to whether or not the effort is made, and differs according to whether or not training is involved.

Those who have long devoted themselves to the study of the *sūtras,* as well as those who are well versed in secular learning, should visit a Zen monastery. There are many examples of those who have done so. Hui-ssŭ[18] of Mount Nan-yüeh was a man of many talents, yet he trained under Bodhidharma. Hsüan-chüeh of Mount Yung-chia[19] was the finest of men; still he trained under Ta-chien [Hui-nêng]. The clarification of the Law and the realization of the Way are dependent upon the power gained from training under Zen masters.

When visiting a Zen master to seek instruction, listen to his teaching without trying to make it conform to your own self-centered viewpoint; otherwise you will be unable to understand what he is saying. Purifying your own body and mind, eyes and ears, simply listen to his teaching, expelling any other thought. Unify your body and mind and receive the master's teaching as if water were being poured from one vessel into another. If you do so, then for the first time you will be able to understand his teaching.

At present, there are some foolish people who either devote themselves to memorizing the words and phrases of the *sūtras* or attach themselves to that which they have heard before. Having done so, they try to equate these with the teachings of a master. In this case, however, there exist here only their own views and the words of ancient men. Consequently, the words of the master go unheeded. Still others, attaching primary importance to their own self-centered thinking, open the *sūtras* and memorize a word or two, imagining this to be Buddhism. Later when they are taught the Law by an enlightened Zen master, they regard his teaching as true if it corresponds with their own views; otherwise they regard it as false. Not knowing how to give up this mistaken way of thinking, they are unable to return to the true Way. They are to be pitied, for they will be subject to delusion for eternity. How regrettable!

Buddhist trainees should realize that Buddhism is beyond either thought, discrimination, and imagination, or insight, perception, and intellectual understanding. Were it not so, why is it that, having been endowed with these various faculties since birth, you have still not realized the Way?

Thought, discrimination, and so forth should be avoided in the practice of the Way. This will become clear if, using thought and so on, you examine yourself carefully.[20] The gateway to the Truth is known only to enlightened

Zen masters, not to their learned counterparts. *(Written on April 5, the second year of Tempuku [1234])*

7. THE NEED FOR ZEN TRAINING IN BUDDHIST PRACTICE AND ENLIGHTENMENT Buddhism is superior to any other teaching. It is for this reason that many people pursue it. During the Tathāgata's lifetime there was only one teaching and one teacher. The Great Master alone led all beings with his supreme Wisdom. Since the Venerable Mahākāśyapa transmitted the Eye Storehouse of the true Law, twenty-eight generations in India, six generations in China, and the various patriarchs of the five Zen schools[21] have transmitted it without interruption. Since the P'u-t'ung era [520–26] in the Chinese state of Liang all truly superior individuals—from monks to royal retainers—have taken refuge in Zen Buddhism.

Truly, excellence should be loved because of its excellence. One should not love dragons as Yeh-kung did.[22] In the various countries east of China the casting net of scholastic Buddhism has been spread over the seas and mountains. Even though spread over the mountains, however, it does not contain the heart of the clouds; even though spread over the seas, it lacks the heart of the waves. The foolish are fond of this kind of Buddhism. They are delighted by it like those who take the eye of a fish to be a pearl, or those who treasure a stone from Mount Yen in the belief that it is a precious jewel. Many such people fall into the pitfall of demons, thereby losing their true Self.

The situation in remote countries like this one is truly regrettable; for here, where the winds of false teachings blow freely, it is difficult to spread the true Law. China, however, has already taken refuge in the true Law of the Buddha. Why is it, then, that it has not yet spread to either our country or Korea? Although in Korea at least the name of the true Law can be heard, in our country even this is impossible. This is because the many teachers who went to study Buddhism in China in the past clung to the net of scholastic Buddhism. Although they transmitted various Buddhist texts, they seem to have forgotten the spirit of Buddhism. Of what value was this? In the end it came to nothing. This is all because they did not know the essence of studying the Way. How regrettable it is that they worked so hard their whole life to no purpose.

When you first enter the gateway of Buddhism and begin to study the Way, simply listen to the teaching of a Zen master and train accordingly. At that time you should know the following: the Law turns self, and self turns the Law. When self turns the Law, self is strong and the Law is weak. In the reverse case, the Law is strong and self is weak. Although Buddhism has had these two aspects since long ago, they have only been known by those who have received the true transmission. Without a true master, it is impossible to hear even the names of these two aspects.

Unless one knows the essence of studying the Way, it is impossible to practice it; for how, otherwise, could one determine what is right and what is wrong? Those who now study the Way through the practice of zazen naturally transmit this essence. This is why there have been no mistakes made in the transmission, something that cannot be said of the other Buddhist sects. Those who seek Buddhism cannot realize the true Way without the practice of zazen.

8. THE CONDUCT OF ZEN MONKS Since the time of the Buddha the twenty-eight patriarchs in India and the six in China have directly transmitted the true Law, adding not even so much as a thread or hair, nor allowing even a particle of dust to penetrate it. With the transmission of the Buddha's *kaśāya* to Hui-nêng, Buddhism spread throughout the world. At present the Tathāgata's treasury of the true Law is flourishing in China. It is impossible to realize what the Law is by groping or searching for it. Those who have seen the Way forget their knowledge of it, transcending relative consciousness.

Hui-nêng lost his face [his deluded self] while training on Mount Huang-mei. Hui-k'o showed his earnestness by cutting off his arm in front of Bodhidharma's cave, realizing, through this action, the essence of Buddhism and turning his delusive mind into enlightenment. Thereafter he prostrated himself before Bodhidharma in deep respect before returning to his original position. Thus did he realize absolute freedom, dwelling in neither body nor mind, nonattached, unlimited.

A monk asked Chao-chou, "Does a dog have the Buddha-nature?"[23] Chao-chou replied, "Wu."[24] This word *wu* can be neither measured nor grasped, for there is nothing to grab hold of. I would suggest that you try letting go! Then ask yourself these questions: What are body and mind? What is Zen conduct? What are birth and death? What is Buddhism? What are worldly affairs? And what, ultimately, are mountains, rivers, and earth, or men, animals, and houses?

If you continue to ask these questions, the two aspects—movement and nonmovement—will clearly not appear. This nonappearance, however, does not mean inflexibility. Unfortunately, however, very few people realize this, while many are deluded thereby. Zen trainees can realize this after they have trained for some time. It is my sincere hope, however, that you will not stop training even after you have become fully enlightened.

9. THE NEED TO PRACTICE IN ACCORDANCE WITH THE WAY Buddhist trainees should first determine whether or not their practice is headed toward the Way. Śākyamuni, who was able to harmonize and control his body, speech, and mind, sat beneath a bo tree doing zazen. Suddenly, upon seeing the morning star, he became enlightened, realizing the highest supreme Way, which is far beyond that of the Śrāvakas and Pratyekabuddhas. The enlightenment that the Buddha realized through his own efforts has been transmitted from Buddha to Buddha without interruption to the present day. How, then, can those who have realized this enlightenment not have become Buddhas? To be headed toward the Way is to know its appearance and how far it extends. The Way lies under the foot of every man. When you become one with the Way you find that it is right where you are, thus realizing per-

fect enlightenment. If, however, you take pride in your enlightenment, even though it be very deep, it will be no more than partial enlightenment. These are the essential elements of being headed toward the Way.

Present-day trainees strongly desire to see miracles, even though they do not understand how the Way functions. Who of these is not mistaken? They are like a child who, forsaking both his father and his father's wealth, runs away from home. Even though his father is rich, and he, as an only son, would someday inherit it all, he becomes a beggar, searching for his fortune in faraway places. This is truly the case.

To study the Way is to try to become one with it—to forget even a trace of enlightenment. Those who would practice the Way should first of all believe in it. Those who believe in the Way should believe that they have been in the Way from the very beginning, subject to neither delusion, illusive thoughts, and confused ideas nor increase, decrease, and mistaken understanding. Engendering belief like this, clarify the Way and practice it accordingly—this is the essence of studying the Way.

The second method of Buddhist training is to cut off the function of discriminating consciousness and turn away from the road of intellectual understanding. This is the manner in which novices should be guided. Thereafter they will be able to let body and mind fall away, freeing themselves from the dualistic ideas of delusion and enlightenment.

In general there are only a very few who believe they are in the Way. If only you believe that you are truly in the Way, you will naturally be able to understand how it functions, as well as the true meaning of delusion and enlightenment. Make an attempt at cutting off the function of discriminating consciousness; then, suddenly, you will have almost realized the Way.

10. THE DIRECT REALIZATION OF THE WAY There are two ways to realize enlightenment. One is to train under a true Zen master, listening to his teaching; the other is to do zazen single-mindedly. In the former case you give full play to the discriminating mind, while through the latter, practice and enlightenment are unified. To enter the Way neither of these two methods can be dispensed with.

Everyone is endowed with body and mind, though their actions inevitably vary, being either strong or weak, brave or cowardly. It is through the daily actions of our body and mind, however, that we directly become enlightened. This is known as the realization of the Way.

There is no need to change our existing body and mind, for the direct realization of the Way simply means to become enlightened through training under a true Zen master. To do this is neither to be bound by old viewpoints nor to create new ones; it is simply to realize the Way.

THREE

The Meaning of Practice-Enlightenment

(Shushō-gi)

As has been often stated, the essence of Dōgen's Zen is that there is no gap between practice and enlightenment, and therefore, that neither precedes or follows the other. That is to say, enlightenment is not something that is attained as the result *of practice; it is embodied in practice from the very beginning. It is only through the single-minded practice of the Way, however, that this truth can be fully understood.*

The Shushō-gi, *consisting of five sections, deals primarily with this identity of practice and enlightenment. Although this work did not come into existence until 1890, when Takashū Takiya-*zenji *of Eihei-ji and Baisen Azegami-*zenji *of Sōji-ji issued an edict that prescribed it as the standard of faith for both laymen and monks, the contents are based on key passages from all ninety-two sections of the* Shōbō-genzō. *For this reason it may be said to be an even more refined storehouse of the true Law than Dōgen's original work. It should be noted, however, that since it was compiled primarily with laymen in mind, many of Dōgen's most important teachings, such as the need to practice zazen and to train under a true master, have been omitted. Nevertheless, with its emphasis on the importance of a thorough understanding of life and death, the need for repentance, and acceptance of the sixteen Bodhisattva precepts, it serves as possibly the best introduction to the* Shōbō-genzō *presently available. Furthermore, its presentation of the meaning and expression of compassion, as well as of gratitude, is undoubtedly one of the finest in all Buddhist literature.*

1. General introduction The thorough clarification of the meaning of birth and death—this is the most important problem of all for Buddhists. Since the Buddha [enlightenment] dwells within birth and death [delusion], the latter do not exist. Simply understand that birth and death are in themselves Nirvāṇa, there being no birth-death to be hated nor Nirvāṇa to be desired. Then, for the first time, you will be freed from birth and death. Realize that this problem is of supreme importance.

It is difficult to be born as a human being, let alone come into contact with Buddhism. By virtue of our good deeds in the past, however, we have been able not only to be born as human beings but to encounter Buddhism as well. Within the realm of birth-death, then, our present life should be considered to be the best and most excellent of all. Do not waste your precious human body meaninglessly, abandoning it to the winds of impermanence.

Impermanence cannot be depended upon. We know neither when nor where our transient life will end. This body is already beyond our control; and life, at the mercy of time, moves on without stopping for even an instant. Once the ruddy face of youth has disappeared, it is impossible to find even its traces. When we think about time carefully, we find that time, once lost, never returns. Faced suddenly with the prospect of death, kings, state ministers, relatives, servants, wife and children, and rare jewels are of no use. We must enter the realm of death alone, accompanied only by our good and bad karma.

You should avoid associating with those deluded people in this present world who are ignorant of the law of causality and karmic retribution. They are unaware of the existence of the three stages of time and unable to distinguish good from evil.

The law of causality, however, is both clear and impersonal: those who do evil inevitably fall [into hell]; those who do good inevitably ascend [into heaven]. If this were not so, the various Buddhas would not have appeared in this world, nor would Bodhidharma have come to China.

The karmic retribution of good and evil occurs at three different periods in time: (1) retribution experienced in one's present life, (2) retribution experienced in the life following this one, and (3) retribution experienced in subsequent lives. This is the first thing that should be studied and understood when practicing the Way. Otherwise many of you will make mistakes and come to hold wrong views. Not only that, you will fall into evil worlds,[1] undergoing a long period of suffering.

Understand that in this life you have only one life, not two or three. How regrettable it is if, fruitlessly holding false views, you vainly do wrong, thinking that you are not doing bad when, in fact, you are. You cannot avoid the karmic retribution of your evil acts even though you mistakenly assume that because you do not recognize its existence you are not subject to it.

2. Release through repentance The Buddhas and patriarchs, because of their great mercy, have left open the vast gates of compassion in order that all beings—both human and celestial—may thereby realize enlightenment. Although karmic retribution for evil acts must come in one of the three stages of time, repentance lessens the effects, bringing release and purity. Therefore, let us repent before the Buddha in all sincerity.

The merit-power of repentance before the Buddha not only saves and purifies us; it also encourages the growth within us of pure, doubt-free faith and earnest effort. When pure faith appears it changes others just as it changes us, its benefits extending to all things, both animate and inanimate.

The essence of the act of repentance is as follows: "Even though the accumulation of our past bad karma is so great that it forms an obstacle to practicing the Way, we beseech the various enlightened and compassionate Buddhas and patriarchs to free us from karmic retribution, eliminate all obstacles to the practice of the Way, and share with us their compassion, for it is through this compassion that their merit and teachings fill the entire universe.

"In the past the Buddhas and patriarchs were originally just like us; in the future we shall become like them. 'All our past evil deeds were the result of beginningless greed, anger, and ignorance: products of our body, speech, and mind. Of all these do we now repent.' "

If we repent in this way, we shall certainly receive the invisible help of the Buddhas and patriarchs. Keeping this in mind and acting in the proper manner, make your repentance. The power derived thereby will wipe out your wrongdoings at their roots.

3. Ordination and enlightenment Next, you should deeply venerate the Three Treasures. They deserve our veneration and respect no matter how much our life and body may change. The Buddhas and patriarchs, in both India and China, correctly transmitted this reverent veneration of the Buddha, the Law, and the Buddhist community.

Unfortunate and virtueless people are unable to hear even the name of the Three Treasures, let alone take refuge in them. Do not act like those who, awe-struck, vainly take refuge in mountain deities and ghosts or worship at non-Buddhist shrines, for it is impossible to gain release from suffering in this way. Instead, quickly take refuge in the Buddha, the Law, and the Buddhist community, seeking not only release from suffering but complete enlighten ment as well.

Taking refuge in the Three Treasures means, first of all, to come with a pure faith. Whether during the Tathāgata's lifetime or after it, people should place their hands together in *gasshō*[2] and, with lowered heads, chant the following: "We take refuge in the Buddha. We take refuge in the Law. We take refuge in the Buddhist community. We take refuge in the Buddha because he is our great teacher. We take refuge in the Law because it is good medicine. We take refuge in the Buddhist community because it is composed of excellent friends." It is only by taking refuge in the Three Treasures that one can become a disciple of the Buddha and become qualified to receive all the other precepts.

The merit of having taken refuge in the Three Treasures inevitably appears when there is spiritual communion between the trainee and the Buddha. Those who experience this communion inevitably take this refuge whether they find themselves existing as celestial or human beings, dwellers in hell, hungry ghosts, or animals. As a result, the merit that is accumulated thereby inevitably increases through the various stages of existence, leading ultimately to the highest supreme enlightenment. Know that the Bhagavat[3] himself has already borne witness to the fact that this merit is of unsurpassed value and unfathomable profundity. Therefore all living creatures should take this refuge.

Next we should receive the three pure precepts. The first of them is to do no evil, the second to do good, and the third to confer abundant benefits on all living creatures.

We should then accept the ten grave prohibitions: (1) do not kill, (2) do not steal, (3) do not engage in improper sexual conduct,[4] (4) do not lie, (5) do not deal in intoxicating beverages, (6) do not speak of the faults of others, (7) do not be too proud to praise others, (8) do not covet either the Law or property, (9) do not give way to anger, and (10) do not disparage the Three Treasures.

The various Buddhas have all received and observed the three refuges, the three pure precepts, and the ten grave prohibitions. By receiving these precepts one realizes the supreme Bodhi-wisdom,[5] the adamantine, indestructible enlightenment of the various Buddhas in the three stages of time. Is there any wise person who would not gladly seek this goal? The Bhagavat has clearly shown to all sentient beings that when they receive the Buddha's precepts, they enter into the realm of the various Buddhas—truly becoming their children and realizing the same great enlightenment.

All the Buddhas dwell in this realm, perceiving everything clearly without leaving any traces. When ordinary beings make this their dwelling place, they no longer distinguish between subject and object. At that time everything in the universe—whether earth, grass, tree, fence, tile, or pebble—functions as a manifestation of enlightenment; and those who receive the effects of this manifestation realize enlightenment without being aware of it. This is the merit of nondoing and nonstriving—awakening to the Bodhi-mind.

4. MAKING THE ALTRUISTIC VOW To awaken to the Bodhi-mind means to vow not to cross over to the other shore [of enlightenment] before all sentient beings have done so. Whether layman or monk, living in the world of celestial beings or of humans, subject to pain or to pleasure, all should quickly make this vow.

Though of humble appearance, a person who has awakened to the Bodhi-mind is already the teacher of all mankind. Even a little girl of seven can become the teacher of the four classes of Buddhists[6] and the compassionate mother of all beings; for [in Buddhism] men and women are completely equal. This is one of the highest principles of the Way.

After having awakened to the Bodhi-mind, even wandering in the six realms of existence and the four forms of life[7] becomes an opportunity to practice the altruistic vow. Therefore even though up to now you may have vainly idled your time away, you should quickly make this vow while there is still time. Though you have acquired sufficient merit to realize Buddhahood, you should place it at the disposal of all beings in order that they may realize the Way. From time immemorial there have been those who have sacrificed their own enlightenment in order that they might be of benefit to all beings, helping them to cross over first to the other shore.

There are four kinds of Wisdom that benefit others: offerings, loving words, benevolence, and identification, all of which are the practices of a

Bodhisattva. Giving offerings means not to covet. Although it is true that, in essence, nothing belongs to self, this does not prevent us from giving offerings. The size of the offering is of no concern; it is the sincerity with which it is given [that is important]. Therefore one should be willing to share even a phrase or a verse of the Law, for this becomes the seed of good in both this life and the next. This is also the case when giving of one's material treasure, whether it be a single coin or a blade of grass, for the Law is the treasure and the treasure is the Law. There have been those who, seeking no reward, willingly gave their help to others. Supplying a ferry and building a bridge are both acts of giving offerings, as are earning a living and producing goods.

The meaning of loving words is that when beholding all beings one is filled with compassion for them, addressing them affectionately. That is to say, one regards them as if they were his own children. The virtuous should be praised and the virtueless pitied. Loving words are the source of overcoming your bitter enemy's hatred and establishing friendship with others. Directly hearing loving words spoken brightens the countenance and warms the heart. An even deeper impression is made, however, by hearing about loving words spoken about oneself in one's absence. You should know that loving words have a revolutionary impact on others.

Benevolence means to devise ways of benefiting others, no matter what their social position. Those who aided the helpless tortoise[8] or the injured sparrow[9] did not expect any reward for their assistance; they simply acted out of their feelings of benevolence. The foolish believe that their own interests will suffer if they put the benefit of others first. They are wrong, however. Benevolence is all-encompassing, equally benefiting oneself and others.

Identification means nondifferentiation—to make no distinction between self and others. For example, it is like the human Tathāgata who led the same life as that of us human beings. Others can be identified with self, and thereafter, self with others. With the passage of time both self and others become one. Identification is like the sea, which does not decline any water no matter what its source, all waters gathering, therefore, to form the sea.

Quietly reflect on the fact that the preceding teachings are the practices of a Bodhisattva. Do not treat them lightly. Venerate and respect their merit, which is able to save all beings, enabling them to cross over to the other shore.

5. Constant practice and gratitude The opportunity to awaken to the Bodhi-mind is, in general, reserved to human beings living in this world. Now that we have had the good fortune not only to be born in this world but also to come into contact with the Buddha Śākyamuni, how can we be anything but overjoyed!

Quietly consider the fact that if this were a time when the true Law had not yet spread throughout the world, it would be impossible for us to come into contact with it, even if we were willing to sacrifice our lives to do so. How fortunate to have been born in the present day, when we are able to make this encounter! Listen to what the Buddha said: "When you meet a master who expounds the supreme Bodhi-wisdom, do not consider his birth, look at his appearance, dislike his faults, or worry about his behavior. Rather, out of respect for his great Wisdom, reverently prostrate yourself before him three times a day—morning, noon, and evening—giving him no cause for worry."

We are now able to come into contact with the Buddha Śākyamuni and hear his teachings due to the compassionate kindness that has resulted from the constant practice of each of the Buddhas and patriarchs. If the Buddhas and patriarchs had not directly transmitted the Law, how could it have come down to us today? We should be grateful for even a single phrase or portion of the Law, still more for the great benefit accruing from the highest supreme teaching—the Eye Storehouse of the True Law. The injured sparrow did not forget the kindness shown to it, rewarding its benefactor with four silver rings. Neither did the helpless tortoise, who rewarded its benefactor with the seal of Yün-pu-t'ing. If even animals show their gratitude for kindness rendered to them, how can human beings fail to do the same?

The true way of expressing this gratitude is not to be found in anything other than our daily Buddhist practice itself. That is to say, we should practice selflessly, esteeming each day of life.

Time flies faster than an arrow; life is more transient than the dew. No matter how skillful you may be, it is impossible to bring back even a single day of the past. To have lived to be a hundred years old to no purpose is to eat of the bitter fruit of time, to become a pitiable bag of bones. Even though you have allowed yourself to be a slave to your senses for a hundred years, if you give yourself over to Buddhist training for even one day, you will gain a hundred years of life in this world as well as in the next. Each day's life should be esteemed; the body should be respected. It is through our body and mind that we are able to practice the Way; this is why they should be loved and respected. It is through our own practice that the practice of the various Buddhas appears and their great Way reaches us. Therefore each day of our practice is the same as theirs, the seed of realizing Buddhahood.

All the various Buddhas are none other than the Buddha Śākyamuni himself. The Buddha Śākyamuni is nothing other than the fact that the Mind itself is the Buddha. When the Buddhas of the past, present, and future realize enlightenment, they never fail to become the Buddha Śākyamuni. This is the meaning of the Mind itself being the Buddha. Study this question carefully, for it is in this way that you can express your gratitude to the Buddhas.

Part Three

Twelve Sections of the *Shōbō-genzō*

Introduction to the *Shōbō-genzō*

Dōgen intended his masterwork, the *Shōbō-genzō,* to be composed of one hundred sections in all. Death prevented him from completing his original plan, though not before he had written ninety-two sections.[1] These ninety-two sections, discussing the regulations for a Zen monastery, standards of daily conduct, explanations of various *kōan,* historical anecdotes concerning past Zen masters, and many other topics, provide one of the finest descriptions of Zen Buddhism available today. They make it abundantly clear that Dōgen is not only one of Zen's leading exponents but also one of the major figures in the religious and philosophical history of Japan, if not the world.

The twelve sections of the *Shōbō-genzō* included here are known collectively as Dōgen's "later writings" (*shinsō-bon*).[2] They were given this name because Dōgen wrote them as a distinctive group shortly before his death, for the most part while in residence at Eihei-ji. Actually, most of these sections did not take on their final form until after his death, when they were edited by Ejō and other leading disciples.

In many ways Dōgen's thought can be said to have reached its fullest fruition in these twelve sections. Nearly half the doctrinally important "Meaning of Practice-Enlightenment" was selected from their contents, particularly from those sections dealing with the Bodhi-mind and the nature of causation and karma. The great importance Dōgen attached to the latter two closely related concepts can be seen in his allocation of three full sections ("Deep Belief in Causality," "Karmic Retribution in the Three Stages of Time," and "A Monk at the Fourth Stage of Meditation") to their explanation.

The reader may be surprised to find quite fanciful or even seemingly superstitious language in some parts of these twelve sections. It should be kept in mind, however, that Dōgen is not trying to present a scientific analysis of man or society. Instead he, like the Buddha himself, hopes to provide the catalyst for the spiritual awakening of each individual, which is the beginning and end of all Buddhist teachings. Although fanciful language is sometimes used, it always contains an important spiritual message. In order truly to understand these twelve sections, it is necessary for the reader to ask himself continually what that message is.

The repetitive nature of much of the content of these sections may also surprise the reader. As previously stated, one of the distinguishing characteristics of the *Shōbō-genzō* is that it was written in Japanese rather than Chinese, the clerical language of Japanese Buddhism in Dōgen's time. This does not mean, however, that Dōgen did not employ Chinese at all; although many sections of this work are either entirely or almost entirely in Japanese, the twelve sections translated here contain many passages in Chinese. The material Dōgen quotes, consisting primarily of passages from various *sūtras,* is in fact almost all in Chinese. Only Dōgen's own comments and explanations are in Japanese.

It may seem to the modern reader that Dōgen is unnecessarily tedious in his explanations of the Chinese texts. It should be remembered, however, that although the Japanese language uses some of the same ideographs as Chinese, there is a vast difference between the two languages. Chinese was almost completely unintelligible to all but the most highly educated Japanese of that day. The first part of Dōgen's comments, therefore, might be better viewed as a translation rather than an explanation of the preceding quotation. Nevertheless, a close comparison of the first part of his comments with the quoted material preceding them discloses significant differences between the two, revealing on the one hand the inherent structural differences of the two languages, and on the other hand the often unique interpretation that Dōgen gives to the material he presents. This English translation has attempted to preserve these differences, particularly of the latter type, as faithfully as possible.

Finally, a word about the suggested order for reading these twelve sections. For those who have an extensive knowledge of Buddhism or have actually undergone Zen training for some time, there is no reason not to read these sections in the traditional order, which is retained here. Because of the strong monastic orientation of the first three sections, however, newcomers to Buddhism may find it more helpful to leave these sections until last, beginning instead with "Awakening to the Bodhi-mind." This section and the following four deal with the basic elements of Buddhist belief, and in themselves constitute an excellent introduction to Buddhism. Though beguilingly simple in content, their mastery, which according to Dōgen necessarily involves monastic training, is far from easy.

The final section, "The Eight Aspects of Enlightenment," is also of fundamental importance to an understanding of Buddhism, for it deals with no less a topic than the nature of enlightenment. It is certainly not coincidental that when Dōgen fell ill and realized death was near, he chose this theme for his last writing. Like all his work, it expresses his vow as a Bodhisattva "to help all sentient beings cross over to the other shore [of enlightenment] before doing so oneself."

ONE

The Merit of Becoming a Monk

(Shukke Kudoku)

THE BODHISATTVA NĀGĀRJUNA asked himself, "If we follow even the [Buddhist] precepts for laymen[1] we can be born in the celestial world, attain the way of Bodhisattvas, and realize enlightenment. Why, then, is there any need to follow the precepts for monks?"[2] In answer to his own question he replied, "Although it is true that both laymen and monks can realize enlightenment, there is a difference in the relative difficulty each encounters. Because laymen have to make a living, it is difficult for them to devote themselves completely to Buddhist training. If they attempt to do so, their livelihood will be endangered, while if they do the opposite, they must necessarily neglect their practice of the Way. To attempt to do both at the same time is not an easy matter. On the other hand, it is much easier for monks, being free of worldly responsibilities, anger, and various distractions, to devote themselves to the practice of Buddhism. The same thing is true in regard to the realization of enlightenment.

"Laymen find it difficult to realize enlightenment because of the great amount of work they must do, the disorder and clamor in their lives, and the fact that they must live among worldly desires. Monks, on the other hand, are able to go out and meditate in deserted fields, thereby controlling their minds and realizing the essential emptiness of all things. When they pass beyond the realm of discriminative thinking they leave the world of outer causation behind them as well.

"The following verse describes the monk's life:

Monks sit peacefully among the trees,
Ridding themselves of illusion with a calm mind.
Quietly realizing enlightenment,
They experience a joy that is beyond that of heaven.
Laymen seek fame and profit,
Or fine robes, seats, and bedding.
Though the joy in getting them is only fleeting,
They are untiring in their quest.
Monks, however, beg for food in humble robes,

Their daily actions being one with the Way.
With their Wisdom-eye opened
They realize the essence of the Law.
Gathering all together to listen
To the countless Buddhist teachings,
They leave behind the world of illusion,
Quietly enveloped in enlightenment's Wisdom.

"As this verse shows, it is much easier to observe the Buddhist precepts and practice the Way if one enters the monkhood. Furthermore, by entering the monkhood and observing the precepts it is possible to fully make these noble precepts a part of oneself. For this reason laymen should definitely enter the monkhood and follow the precepts.

"At the same time, it must be said that following the precepts for monks is not an easy task. The following conversation between a Brāhman[3] named Jambukṣadaka and Śāriputra[4] concerns this problem. Jambukṣadaka asked, 'What is the most difficult thing in Buddhism?' Śāriputra answered, 'It is to follow the way of monks.' 'Why is it difficult to do so?' Jambukṣadaka then asked. 'Because it is not easy to attain true happiness,' Śāriputra answered. 'If one has attained it,' Jambukṣadaka continued, 'what is the next most difficult thing?' 'To do good. Therefore, one should by all means enter the monkhood,' Śāriputra answered in conclusion.

"Whenever someone enters the monkhood, Pāpīyas[5] says in surprise and sorrow, 'This person will gradually free himself from illusion, realize enlightenment, and become a true monk.'

"Even if a monk fails to observe the precepts and commits a crime, he may still realize enlightenment after he redeems himself. In regard to this the *Utpalavarṇā-jātaka-sūtra* relates the story of a nun by the name of Utpala[6] who lived during the Buddha's lifetime. It was the custom of this nun, who had herself realized Arhathood[7] and was endowed with the six powers for saving sentient beings,[8] to visit the homes of noblewomen. At such times she would praise the act of entering the nunhood, saying, 'You should all become nuns.' They would answer, 'We are still young and healthy and have attractive features. We are afraid it would be difficult for us to observe the precepts for nuns. Perhaps we would break the precepts.' 'Perhaps you would,' Utpala answered, 'but even so it would be better for you to enter the nunhood.' 'But if we break the precepts,' they replied, 'we will inevitably fall into hell. How could we dare to break the precepts?' 'If that's what it takes, it's better to fall into hell,' she continued. Laughing at her, the noblewomen said, 'How can you say that it's all right for us to fall into hell when, if we were to do so, we would be punished there?'

"Speaking from her own experience, the nun replied, 'In a previous existence I was a prostitute and often uttered licentious words while dressed improperly. One day, however, I put on a nun's robes as a joke. Owing to this good deed, I was reborn a nun in the time of the Buddha Kāśyapa.[9] My problems did not end then, however. Because of my noble birth and good looks, I became proud and conceited, and consequently I broke the precepts, falling into hell, where I was severely punished. After having redeemed myself and been born in the human world once more, I was finally able to meet the Buddha Śākyamuni and reenter the nunhood. As a result I was able to realize Arhathood and become endowed with the six powers for saving sentient beings. Therefore, based on my own experience, I can tell you that even if you break the precepts after having entered the nunhood, you will still be able to realize Arhathood. On the other hand, if you do wrong without having entered the nunhood, you will be unable to realize the Way. In the past I fell into hell for two consecutive generations because of my wrongdoings. Each time I left hell, I became a bad woman and, upon dying, returned to hell without ever having realized enlightenment. This is why I know that even if you break the precepts after you have entered the nunhood, you will still be able to realize enlightenment.'

"Another story in this regard concerns a drunken Brāhman who, visiting the Buddha in Jetavana Garden,[10] asked for and received permission to enter the monkhood. After the Buddha had the Venerable Ānanda[11] shave his head and dress him in monk's clothing, however, he became sober and, startled to find himself a monk, ran away. The other monks asked the Buddha, 'Why did you allow him to become a monk?' The Buddha answered, 'For countless ages in the past this Brāhman had no desire to become a monk. However, when he became drunk there arose in him, to some extent at least, a desire to enter the monkhood. Though his present action is only a beginning, at some time in the future it will certainly result in his entering the monkhood again and awakening to the Way.' So immeasurable, then, is the merit of becoming a monk. Although Buddhist laymen observe the five precepts, their merit cannot be compared with that of monks."

The Bhagavat gave permission to a drunken Brāhman to enter the monkhood, thereby planting within him the first seed for his future awakening to the Way. This clearly shows that it is impossible for anyone to realize the Buddha's Wisdom without first having entered the monkhood. In the case of the Brāhman, he first decided to enter the monkhood, have his head shaved, and receive the precepts when he was somewhat intoxicated. Although it was not long before he became sober, the merit of his having entered the monkhood was preserved, thereby increasing his chances of awakening to the Way. The Bhagavat's truly excellent teaching concerning this incident expresses the original wish with which he entered this world. Therefore all sentient beings should believe in it and carry it out in the past, present, and future.

In actuality it takes only an instant to awaken to the Bodhi-mind and realize enlightenment. The Brāhman acquired merit even though he only entered the monkhood temporarily. Certainly the merit acquired by those who presently enter the monkhood and devote their whole life to the Way will not be less than that of this drunken Brāhman.

King Cakravarti[12] appears in this world when he has reached the human age of eighty thousand, ruling the four continents[13] and possessing all the seven treasures.[14] At that time the four continents are like the Pure Land, and his joy is so great as to be beyond description. It is said that sometimes he rules over the one billion worlds. The wheels that he possesses are of four kinds: gold, silver, copper, and iron. As the Gold-Wheel-Rolling King, he rules the four continents; as the Silver-Wheel-Rolling King, three; as the Copper-Wheel-Rolling King, two; and as the Iron-Wheel-Rolling King, one. He is also known never to have committed any of the ten wrong acts.[15] Although this king is filled with joy, as soon as he finds even a single white hair on his head he turns over the throne to the crown prince in order that he may enter the monkhood. Putting on a *kaśāya,* he goes into the forest to undergo training in the Way. When he dies he will undoubtedly be reborn in Brahma Heaven.[16] Furthermore, in order to ensure that the new king will follow in his footsteps, he puts his white hair in a silver case and places it in the palace for his successor. The new king repeats the same process when he in turn discovers his first white hair.

King Cakravarti's life after entering the monkhood is so long that it cannot be compared with that of present-day human beings, for as already stated, he does not appear in the human world until having reached an age equivalent to eighty thousand years. When he does appear he is endowed with the thirty-two distinguishing marks.[17] In this regard as well he is superior to the people of the present day. Nevertheless, when he discovers a white hair he awakens to the impermanence of life and, determining to do good and acquire merit, enters the monkhood to begin his training in the Way. Present-day kings cannot be considered his equals, for instead of entering the monkhood, they idle their time away in avarice. They will undoubtedly regret their actions in their coming existence. This is even truer in the case of this small country [Japan], which is far removed from China and India. Here there are kings in name, but they are without virtue. If they would only forsake their greed, enter the monkhood, and train in the Way, the various heavenly deities would rejoice, and the Dragon King[18] would respect and protect them. Those people who had already realized enlightenment and become Buddhas would also see what had happened and be filled with great joy.

In the past an irreligious prostitute[19] laughingly put on nun's clothing as a joke. Although she broke the precepts by this action that belittled the Law, because of the merit she gained from having worn nun's clothing, she was able to encounter the true Law in only two generations. The nun's clothing she wore was none other than a *kaśāya.* Through the merit of having worn a *kaśāya,* even though it was done laughingly as a joke, she was able to meet the Buddha Kāśyapa and enter the nunhood in her next existence. Later, because she violated the precepts, she once more fell into hell, where she was punished. In the end, however, due to the undying merit of having worn the sacred *kaśāya,* she was finally able to meet the Buddha Śākyamuni and listen to his teachings. As a result she awoke to the Bodhi-mind and trained herself in the Way, leaving the three worlds[20] behind her forever. In becoming an Arhat, she was endowed with the six powers to save sentient beings and the three types of superior wisdom.[21] She realized the excellent Way beyond all others.

This example shows that if one possesses deep faith in the unexcelled Wisdom of the Buddha and the sacred *kaśāya* from the very beginning, the merit he receives will be even greater than that gained by the former prostitute. Moreover, if while possessing this faith one enters the monkhood and receives the precepts, the merit to come will be immeasurable. Unless one has been born in human form, it is unusual to receive such merit.

Even though there are many lay and monk Bodhisattvas and patriarchs in India and China, none of them is equal to the Patriarch Nāgārjuna. Through the use of such stories as that of the drunken Brāhman and the prostitute, he strongly urged all people to enter the monkhood and follow the precepts. The words of this patriarch are none other than those of the Bhagavat himself. The Bhagavat said, "In this human world there are four unexcelled experiences: seeing the Buddha, hearing his teachings, becoming a monk, and realizing enlightenment." It should be clearly understood that these four things are superior to anything in either the continent of Uttarakuru[22] or the various heavenly worlds. Through the power of the good deeds and virtues accumulated in our previous lives, we have been fortunate enough to be born with a human form. Therefore, in deep rejoicing at our good fortune, we should enter the monkhood. Life is as transient as a dewdrop, and so, having been fortunate enough to be born as human beings, we should not waste our lives. If we lead the life of a monk in successive existences, much merit will be accumulated.

The Bhagavat said, "In Buddhism the merit of becoming a monk is immeasurable. Even if someone were to build a *stūpa*[23] decorated with the seven precious things[24] and equal in height to Mount Sumeru, the merit accumulated thereby would be less than that of becoming a monk. A *stūpa* decorated with the seven treasures can be destroyed by wrongdoers or foolish people, but the merit of entering the monkhood is indestructible. Therefore, if someone propagates this teaching, or allows his servants to enter the monkhood, or himself enters the monkhood, the resulting merit is beyond calculation."

The Bhagavat, because he realized clearly how much merit there was in becoming a monk, taught thus. Upon hearing this teaching, a rich man named Punyavadharna, though 120 years old, dared to enter the monkhood, practicing the Way in the lowest seat for boys.[25] He later became a great Arhat.

Our present body, we should realize, consists of a temporary union of the four elements[26] and the five aggregates.[27] Therefore we are always afflicted with the eight kinds of suffering.[28] Moreover, during each *kṣaṇa*[29] we are in the endless process of birth and decay. It is said that sixty-five *kṣaṇas* pass in the space of time it takes a man in the prime of life to snap his fingers, but we are too ignorant to realize it. There are 6,400,099,980 *kṣaṇas* in twenty-four hours, and we are unaware that during this time our body and mind are in a constant state of birth and decay. How deplorable it is that we are ignorant of this fact! Although there are many enlightened people, only the Buddha and Śāriputra among them know how much of our body and mind is subject to birth and decay each *kṣaṇa*. It is within this process of birth and decay that people perform good and bad deeds, and it is also within this same process that people seek the Buddha's Wisdom and realize the Way.

Since our human body is subject to birth and decay, no matter how ardently we may love it we cannot keep it from change. There has never been anyone, no matter how hard he tried, who has been successful in this regard. Thus it may be said that even our own body does not belong to us. Yet, though the body be transient, those who receive the precepts for monks and enter the monkhood are able to attain indestructible Buddhahood—the same supreme Bodhi-wisdom that all the Buddhas in the three stages of time have realized. Is there any wise man who would not seek this?

This is why the eight royal children of the Buddha Candrasūryapradīpa[30] forsook their future thrones and the opportunity to rule over the four continents in order to become monks. The sixteen royal children of the Buddha Mahābhijñājñānābhibhū[31] did the same. While their father was meditating, they expounded the *Saddharma-puṇḍarīka-sūtra*[32] for the sake of ordinary people, and are now the Tathāgatas of the whole world. When they saw the Buddha Mahabhijñājñānābhibhū's sixteen princely children enter the monkhood, the myriad celestial subjects of King Cakravarti asked for and quickly received the king's permission to follow their example. Śubhavyūharāja,[33] his wife, and their two royal children also entered the monk- and nunhood.

We should be aware that whenever a truly enlightened person appears in this world, he unfailingly teaches that entering the monkhood is in accordance with the true Law. It would be a mistake to assume that those who entered the monkhood did so out of ignorance; rather, we should realize that they were wise to become monks, and should try to be their equals. In the Buddha's lifetime, Rāhula,[34] Ānanda, and a few other disciples were among the first to become monks. They were followed by other disciples, numbering one thousand at first and eventually twenty thousand. What excellent exemplars! Without exception, all those who had faith in the Buddha, beginning with the first five monks[35] and ending with Subhadra,[36] entered the monkhood. The merit of their acts is immeasurable.

Thus, if one feels compassion for one's children and grandchildren or one's parents, one should urge them to enter the monkhood as soon as possible. The following verse states it in this way:

Without past time
No past Buddhas would have been;
Without the Buddhas of the past
No one could become a monk.

This verse was uttered by the various Buddhas in order to refute the non-Buddhist view that there is no past existence.

We may be certain, then, that entering the monkhood is in accordance with the teachings of the Buddhas of the past. Fortunately, we now have the opportunity to enter the monkhood in accordance with the excellent teachings of the various Buddhas. It is difficult to understand what could prevent us from doing so. Although we possess only the humblest of bodies, we may attain the most distinguished merit by entering the monkhood, so distinguished, in fact, as to be unexcelled either in this human world or in any of the three worlds. Before our body decays in this human world, we should definitely enter the monkhood and receive the precepts.

An ancient enlightened person has said, "Even though a monk breaks the ten grave prohibitions he is superior to a layman who observes the five lay precepts. For this reason the *sūtras* continuously advise us to enter the monkhood. It is difficult to repay the debt of gratitude that we owe to these *sūtras*. Furthermore, encouraging others to become monks is a most praiseworthy act. The merit thus acquired is superior to that of Kings Yama,[37] Cakravarti, or Śakrendra.[38] This is the reason the *sūtras* earnestly advise us to enter the monkhood, and also why it is difficult to repay the debt of gratitude we owe these *sūtras*. On the other hand, there is no such merit to be attained from encouraging others to receive the five precepts for laymen. Therefore no mention of it is made in the *sūtras*."

As has been stated, even though a monk breaks the ten grave prohibitions, he is still superior to a layman who observes the five lay precepts. Entering the monkhood is the most excellent way to express one's faith in the Buddha. The merit of encouraging others to enter the monkhood is superior to that of Kings Yama, Cakravarti, or Śakrendra. Even if a man is a commoner or a slave, once he enters the monkhood he is superior to the royal family and Kings Yama, Cakravarti, or Śakrendra. There is no such merit in observing the precepts for laymen; hence we should enter the monkhood.

It is important to realize that the words of the Bhagavat are beyond our conceptional grasp. That notwithstanding, the five hundred Arhats gathered the Bhagavat's teachings together, and it is due to their efforts that we can realize how great the merit of entering the monkhood is. The three types of knowledge and the six powers for saving sentient beings with which one Arhat is endowed, let alone the wisdom of five hundred Arhats, are beyond the reach of modern Law-masters. Even though these masters have realized, seen, or mastered something that others have not, there is still no comparison. Therefore one should not compare their dull words with those of an Arhat endowed with the three types of knowledge.

Section 120 of the *Mahāvibhāsa-śāstra* states, "Even a person who awakens to the Bodhi-mind and enters the monkhood is known as a sacred person, let alone one who is endowed with *ksānti*."[39] Thus, we should be aware that if we awaken to the Bodhi-mind and enter the monkhood we too will be known as sacred people.

Vow 137 of the Buddha Śākyamuni's 500 great vows states, "I vow that at the time of my future enlightenment I will not become enlightened if anyone wishing to enter the monkhood and follow my teaching is disturbed by such difficulties as mental weakness, forgetfulness, insanity, pride, lack of awe, ignorance, delusion, or distraction." Vow 138 states, "I vow that at the time of my future enlightenment I will not become enlightened if any woman who wishes to become a nun and follow my teaching attempts to receive the precepts for nuns[40] and is unable to do so." Vow 314 runs, "I vow that at the time of my future enlightenment if there is anyone who has good intentions, even though he has done few good deeds, I will assist him in his future existence to enter the monkhood, train in the Way, and observe the ten pure precepts. If I am unable to do so I will not become enlightened."

It should be clearly understood that it is with the help of these ancient great vows of the Bhagavat that faithful men and women of the present are able successfully to enter the monkhood. The Bhagavat, by having made these vows, is the one who has caused them to enter the monkhood. As has been made quite clear, entering the monkhood is a sacred act encompassing the highest merit.

The Buddha said, "Suppose there is a person who has not received the precepts for a monk, but yet shaves his head and wears even a piece of a sacred *kaśāya*. If someone makes an offering to him, that person will be able to realize enlightenment. Because this is so I have taught it to you." It is clear, then, that anyone who makes an offering to a person who has shaved his head and wears a sacred *kaśāya* will be able to realize enlightenment even though the person to whom the offering has been made has not received the precepts for monks.

The Buddha further said, "Suppose there is a person who has not received the precepts for a monk, yet becomes my disciple, shaves his head, and wears even a piece of a sacred *kaśāya*. If any should trouble him by their misconduct or do him harm, those people would be destroying the Law-body[41] and reward-body[42] of the Buddhas in the three stages of time. As a result, they would fall into the three evil worlds, to make these places still more populous. Entering the monkhood is so precious."

The Buddha said: "If people enter the monkhood as my disciples, shave their heads, and wear sacred *kaśāyas,* they have already realized enlightenment, even if they have not yet received the precepts for monks. Suppose someone enters the monkhood without having received the precepts. If any cause him anguish as a result of their misconduct, curse him, beat him with staves, stab him, cut off his hands or legs with a sword, or deprive him of his sacred *kaśāya,* eating bowls, or other daily living utensils, those people will be destroying the true reward-body of the Buddhas in the three stages of time and will be gouging out the eyeballs of all human and celestial beings. Such people are attempting to hide the Buddha's true Law and the essence of the Three Treasures with which enlightened people are endowed, in this way causing all human and celestial beings to lose their way and fall into hell. However, it is such people who will themselves fall into the three evil worlds and make them more populous."

We should understand that if a person shaves his head and wears a sacred *kaśāya,* he has realized the greatest enlightenment even though he has not received the precepts for a monk. Any who try to disturb him will be destroying the reward-body of the Buddhas in the three stages of time, thereby committing one of the five deadly wrongs.[43] It is clear that the merit of entering the monkhood is very near that of the Buddhas in the three stages of time.

The Buddha said, "A monk should do no wrong. If he does, he is not worthy of being a monk. A monk lives up to his word. If he does not, he is not a true monk. I left my parents, brothers and sisters, wife and son, relatives and acquaintances to become a monk and train myself in the Way. Now is the time to study what is truly enlightenment, not what is delusion. A truly enlightened person is one who has compassion for all sentient beings as if they were his own children. An unenlightened person is the opposite of this." The original nature of a monk is to have compassion for all sentient beings as if they were his own children. That is to say, he should do no wrong and, by his actions, should live up to his word. If he does this, the resulting merit will be great indeed.

The Buddha said, "Next, Śāriputra, if a Bodhisattva wishes to realize perfect enlightenment on the day he enters the monkhood, to turn the wheel of the Law[44] and thereby rid innumerable sentient beings of their delusive mind, enable them to realize the Truth of all things and grasp the Mind and Wisdom of the Buddha, dispel their illusion, and ensure that they pursue the supreme Bodhi-wisdom ceaselessly, then he should study the Buddha's Wisdom." That is to say, the Bodhisattvas studying the Buddha's Wisdom are the successive patriarchs. They were all able to realize perfect enlightenment at the same time that they became monks. Buddhist followers should realize that when they undergo training and realize enlightenment in the long and endless *kalpas*[45] of time, they are beyond "being" and "nonbeing."

The Buddha said, "A Bodhisattva should study the Buddha's Wisdom if he wishes to realize the highest supreme enlightenment at the same time that he gives up his future throne and enters the monkhood. He should do the same if he wishes to turn the wheel of the Law, rid innumerable sentient beings of their delusive mind, enable them to realize the Truth of all things and grasp the Mind and Wisdom of the Buddha, dispel their illusion eternally, and ensure that they pursue the supreme Bodhi-wisdom ceaselessly." The Buddha Śākyamuni is speaking here of the merit he achieved when, as a Bodhisattva in the last stage prior to becoming a Buddha, he was born in a palace, gave up his future throne, realized enlightenment, and turned the wheel of the Law in order to save all creatures.

Prince Siddhārtha[46] took Chandaka's[47] sharp-edged sword, whose hilt was decorated with *mani* jewels[48] and the seven precious things, unsheathed it with his right hand, grasped the topknot of his own deep-blue hair with his left hand, and, cutting [the topknot] off with the sharp-edged sword in his right hand, cast it up in the air with his left hand. King Śakrendra was overjoyed at seeing this unusual occurrence. He caught the prince's topknot in a fine celestial robe in order to prevent it from falling on the ground. After this the celestial beings made offerings to it with their finest venerative vessels.

Formerly, when the Buddha Śākyamuni was still a prince, he left his palace in the middle of the night, cut off his hair, and went into the mountains during the day. At that time a venerable personage of the Heaven of Pure Abode[49] came to help him shave his head, also presenting him with a sacred *kaśāya*. This was a good omen for the Tathāgata's appearance in this world. It is also the eternal teaching of the Buddha Śākyamuni and other Buddhas. Of all the Buddhas in the three stages of time and all directions there has never been even one who has achieved enlightenment as a layman. The only way for sentient beings to realize enlightenment is to enter the monkhood. It is due to the existence of past Buddhas that there is the present merit of entering the monkhood. Because entering the monkhood is the eternal teaching of all Buddhas, its merit is immeasurable. In some *sūtras* it is said that laymen can become Buddhas and that women can do the same. Such statements, however, are not the true transmission of the teachings of the Buddha and patriarchs. The true transmission is that Buddhahood can be realized only after having entered the monkhood.[50]

Dhītaka,[51] the son of a rich man, bowed before the fourth patriarch, the Venerable Upagupta,[52] requesting his permission to enter the monkhood. The Venerable One asked him, "Do you wish to enter the monkhood for the sake of your body or for the sake of your mind?" "For the sake of neither my body nor my mind," he answered. "Who is it, then," the Venerable One asked, "who now seeks to become a monk?" Dhītaka answered, "A monk is beyond self and what is possessed by self. Thus, his mind is beyond birth and decay. This is true of all Buddhas, whose bodies and minds are beyond form, and is nothing but the eternal Way itself." Hearing his answer, the Venerable Upagupta granted him permission to enter the monkhood, saying, "You should realize perfect enlightenment, free your mind, and cultivate the seed of your sacred Buddha-nature through reliance on the Three Treasures."

Coming into contact with the teachings of the Buddhas and entering the monkhood is an extremely fortunate occurrence. One should not enter the monkhood for self and what is possessed by self, nor for the sake of one's body or mind. It is neither our body nor our mind that becomes a monk. This is the teaching of all the Buddhas, the eternal Way of all the Buddhas. Because it is the eternal Way of all the Buddhas it is beyond self and what is possessed by self, beyond body and mind, and beyond the three delusive worlds.

It is for these reasons that entrance into the monkhood is the highest teaching of Buddhism. It is beyond "sudden" or "gradual," "eternal" or "temporary," "coming" or "going," "stationary" or "moving," "wide" or "narrow," "large" or "small," and "doing" or "nondoing." There has never been a patriarch who has directly transmitted the true Law who has not entered the monkhood and received the precepts. It was for this reason that Dhītaka asked the Venerable Upagupta's permission to enter the monkhood the first time he met him. After he became a monk he trained under the Venerable One and finally became the fifth patriarch.

The seventeenth patriarch, Saṃghanandi, was born in Śrāvasti Castle to King Ratnālaṃkāra. He was able to speak from birth and habitually praised the teachings of the Buddha. At the age of seven he lost interest in worldly pleasures and wrote the following verse to his parents:

> I bow respectfully to my compassionate Father
> And esteem the mother of my own flesh and blood.
> I now desire to become a monk.
> Pray be compassionate with your child.

His parents, however, firmly refused to grant his request. Their refusal caused the young prince to begin fasting, until finally his parents gave their consent, on the condition that he remain in the castle after becoming a monk. They gave him the Buddhist name of Saṃghanandi, and ordered the Buddhist monk Zenrita to become his teacher. During the following nineteen years he untiringly trained himself in the Way, though he continually thought to himself, "How can I be a monk when I remain in this castle?" One evening he saw a level road reflected in the sunlight. In spite of himself he began to walk slowly down the road, going about ten *ri*, until he passed in front of a huge rock. At the foot of this rock he discovered a cave and, entering it, began to practice zazen. When the king discovered his son was missing, he reproached Zenrita and ordered him to leave the country. Thereafter he searched for his son but was unable to find him. In the course of the following ten years the Venerable One realized enlightenment and, after having it verified as being genuine, went to the land of Madhi, where he gave instruction in the Way to its inhabitants.

This is the first time that the expressions "staying at home" and "leaving home"[53] were heard. With the help of his good deeds in his previous existences he was able to find a level road reflected in the sunlight. When at last he left the castle, he entered a cave. What a wonderful example! It is an enlightened person who loses interest in worldly pleasures and disdains worldly affairs, while it is a deluded person who aspires to the five desires,[54] forgetful of detachment from the delusive world.

The emperors Tai-tsung[55] and Su-tsung[56] often associated with monks, but they were too attached to their thrones to forsake them. Lay disciple Lu [Hui-nêng],[57] however, forsook his mother and eventually became a patriarch. Such is the merit of entering the monkhood. Lay disciple P'ang[58] was able to give up his treasures, but not his attachment to the delusive world. What a foolish man he was! There is no comparison between his attachment to the past and Lu's absorption in the Way. Those familiar with Buddhism inevitably enter the monkhood, while those unfamiliar with it, as a result of their bad deeds in the past, remain laymen their entire lives.

One day Abbot Huai-jang of Mount Nan-yüeh[59] said to himself admiringly, "There is nothing in the human and celestial worlds that is superior to entering the monkhood, for this act is beyond birth and decay." That which is beyond birth and decay is the true Law of the Tathāgata, and for this reason it is superior to anything in the human and celestial worlds. The celestial world is divided into the following parts: first, the world of desire, which includes the six lowest heavens;[60] second, the world of form, which includes eighteen heavens;[61] and third, the formless world, which has four heavens.[62] None of them, however, is superior in merit to becoming a monk.

Abbot Pao-chi of Mount Pan said, "Zen monks! The practice of the Way is like the earth holding up mountains, not knowing how high they soar, or a rock containing jewels, not knowing how flawless they are. A person such as this is called a monk. The true Law of the Buddhas and patriarchs does not necessarily depend on our knowledge of it. Since entering the monkhood is the true Law of the Buddhas and patriarchs, its merit is clear."

I-hsüan, the abbot of Lin-chi temple in Chinchou, said, "A monk should always be able to discern the correct view. He should be able to discriminate between the Buddhas and devils, between truth and falsehood, and between the common and the enlightened. If he is able to discriminate between these, he is called a true monk. If he is unable to tell the difference between them, then he has only left one house to enter another,[63] [in which case] he is to be called a producer of karma and can never be said to be a true monk."

The ever correct view means to have a deep belief in causation and the Three Treasures. Recognizing the Buddhas means to bear clearly in mind the merit of the Buddha's teaching of the unity of cause and effect and discern what is true and false, common and enlightened. If one is unable to tell the difference between Buddhas and devils, one's practice of the Way will suffer serious damage and will retrogress. If, however, one recognizes the acts of devils for what they are and has no part of them, then he will not retrogress in his practice of the Way. This is the true way of a monk. In recent times there have been many who mistook the acts of devils for those of the Way of the Buddha. This is very wrong. Trainees in Buddhism should quickly learn to distinguish the difference between Buddhas and devils and realize the Way through their practice.

When the Tathāgata was about to die, the Bodhisattva Kāśyapa[64] said to him, "Bhagavat! You are endowed with the powers to lead man to good conduct.[65] You undoubtedly knew that Sunakṣatra's[66] conduct would not be good, yet you allowed him to become a monk. Why did you do that?" The Buddha answered, "Virtuous men! In the past when I first became a monk, my half-brother Nanda,[67] cousins Ānanda and Devadatta,[68] and son Rāhula all followed me into the monkhood and practiced the Way. If I had not allowed Sunakṣatra to become a monk, he would have eventually ascended the throne. If this happened, he would have been able to use his power to destroy Buddhism. It was for this reason that I allowed him to enter the monkhood.

"Virtuous men! If the Bhikṣu[69] Sunakṣatra had not done any good and also had not become a monk, he would have been without merit for countless existences. Now, however, he has entered the monkhood, and although his conduct is not good, he has received the precepts and does respectfully pay reverence to senior monks as well as those monks who possess both learning and virtue. In addition he has practiced the first to fourth stages of meditation.[70] These actions are known as good causes and will surely produce good results. Such good results will, in turn, enable him to practice the Way, the end result of which will be the realization of perfect enlightenment. Virtuous men! It was for this reason that I allowed him to become a monk. If I had not allowed the Bhikṣu Sunakṣatra to enter the monkhood I would not be worthy of the name of Tathāgata with perfect comprehension in the ten fields of knowledge.[71] Virtuous men! I see that people are capable of doing both good and bad acts. Although they are capable of both, I am afraid that it will not be long before they stop doing good acts and only do bad ones. Why? Because they do not associate with good friends, nor listen to the true Law, nor think good thoughts, nor practice in accordance with the Way."

From this story we should understand that the Tathāgata, clearly knowing that people do bad acts, still allowed them to enter the monkhood in order that they be endowed with a good cause. What great compassion! It is because one does not associate with good friends, nor listen to the true Law, nor think good thoughts, nor practice in accordance with the Way that one is unable to do good. Present-day trainees of the Way should never fail to associate with good friends. A good friend is someone who states that enlightened human beings do exist, who teaches that there are such things as misconduct and happiness, and who does not ignore causality. Such a person is not only a good friend but an excellent leader as well, his words being the true Law. Thinking of these truths is what is meant by good thoughts, and using them as a basis for one's actions is what is known as practicing in accordance with the Way. Therefore, we should advise others, whether acquaintances or not, to enter the monkhood. There is no need to take into consideration or worry about whether or not they may backslide in their training or even stop training at some time in the future. This is the true teaching of the Buddha Śākyamuni.

The Buddha said to the assembled monks, "King Yama once spoke in the following way: 'Someday I will escape from this world of suffering and be reborn in the human world with a human body. Then I shall enter the monkhood, shave my head, wear the three kinds of sacred *kaśāya,* and practice the Way.' Since even King Yama cherished this idea, still more should you who have now been born with a human body and been able to enter the monkhood unfailingly lead the Buddhist life in body, speech, and mind. You should cast away the five delusions[72] and cultivate the five powers leading to good conduct. It is in this way that you monks should train yourselves." Having listened to the Buddha's words, the assembled monks gladly put them into practice.

As the preceding story makes clear, even King Yama wishes to be reborn in the human world. Those already born as human beings should quickly shave their heads, wear the three kinds of sacred *kaśāya,* and train in the Way. The merit of doing so in this human world is superior to that of any other world. Yet in spite of this, there are those who, although they have been born as human beings, vainly seek positions in government or worldly advancement. They spend their whole lives in an illusive dream world and think fruitlessly of service to their king or his ministers. Upon death they fall into hell with nothing to rely upon. How foolish they are!

Not only have we been fortunate enough to be born with a human body, which is hard to come by, but we have had the opportunity to come into contact with the true Law, which is difficult to encounter. Therefore, we should quickly cut off our relations with the outer world, enter the monkhood, and train ourselves in the Way. There is no question that one can meet the king or his ministers, one's wife or children at various times and places. Encountering the true Law, however, is as difficult to do as seeing an *uḍumbara* flower.[73] When death suddenly comes, neither the king nor his ministers, relatives, servants, wife or children, or rare jewels can save us. We are obliged to enter the realm of the dead alone, accompanied only by our good and bad karma. How desperately we cling to our body at death's door! Therefore while we still retain our human body we should quickly enter the monkhood. This is indeed the true teaching of the various Buddhas in the three stages of time.

There are four regulations that monks must observe in their practice: (1) to do zazen under a tree throughout life, (2) to wear robes made of discarded cloth throughout life, (3) to collect alms throughout life, and (4) to use discarded medicine in case of illness throughout life. Those who observe these four regulations may truly be said to have entered the monkhood and are worthy of being called monks. If they do not observe them, they cannot be called monks. It is for this reason that they are called the regulations that monks must observe in their practice.

Now, in India and China these regulations have been correctly transmitted by the Buddha and patriarchs. They are possessed by monks who have spent their entire lives in training. This is known as practicing the four regulations. There are those who have tried to establish five regulations[74] in opposition to them, but we should realize that this is false teaching. Who would believe such people or listen patiently to what they have to say? The true Law is that which has been correctly transmitted by the Buddha and patriarchs. Those who enter the monkhood in accordance with it enjoy the highest, most noble human happiness.

Hence, in India King Siṃhahanu's[75] grandsons, Nanda, Ānanda, Devadatta, Aniruddha,[76] Mahānāma,[77] and Bhadrika[78] all entered the monkhood even though they were still young and the most noble members of the royal family. They set an excellent example for later generations. Those who are not members of the royal family should not be so attached to their bodies. Those who are not princes—what do they have that they must take such great care of? It was entrance into the monkhood that resulted in the above-mentioned royalty becoming the most noble in the three worlds rather than in the human world alone. The kings of various small countries and other remote places have no desire to become monks; instead they love that which is unworthy of their love, take pride in that which is unworthy of their pride, and are attached to that which is unworthy of their attachment. Who would not say that they are unsuitable? Who would not say that they are extremely foolish?

The Venerable Rāhula was Śākyamuni's son and King Śuddhodana's grandson. King Śuddhodana tried to abdicate the throne in favor of his grandson, but the Bhagavat made Rāhula become a monk. We should realize that entrance into the monkhood is exalted above all things. Rāhula, who was renowned for his severe training, is present in the world even now, having sacrificed entrance into Nirvāṇa in order to lead sentient beings to salvation.

Many of the patriarchs in India who transmitted the true Law were of royal blood. The first patriarch in China, Bodhidharma, was the third son of the king of Kañcipura.[79] He transmitted the true Law to China, disregarding his future throne. You should now be able to realize just how exalted entrance into the monkhood really is. Why is it that people who are unequal to these royal personages, and should be quick to enter the monkhood, do not do so? What tomorrow are they waiting for? Our exhalation does not wait for our inhalation.[80] Thus, it is wise to enter the monkhood as quickly as possible. Furthermore, we should realize that the benevolence of the master who initiated us into the monkhood equals that of our own parents.

The first section of the *Ch'an-yüan Ch'ing-kuei* [Book of Regulations for Zen Monasteries][81] states: "All the Buddhas in the three stages of time have taught that one realizes enlightenment after having entered the monkhood. The twenty-eight Indian patriarchs and the six Chinese partiarchs who transmitted the Buddha-mind seal[82] were all monks. It may be said that it is because monks strictly observe the precepts that they are the paragons of the three worlds. Therefore if you wish to do zazen and pursue Buddhism, you should first observe the precepts. How can you expect to become a Buddha or patriarch if you do not guard against faults and prevent yourself from doing wrong?"

Even if a Zen monastery is under the influence of degenerate Buddhism,[83] it is like a fragrant flower garden. Monasteries of other sects can never be its equal. The situation is like having milk that has been diluted with water: if one wishes to drink milk, there is nothing to do but drink the mixture.[84] The correct transmission that all the Buddhas in the three stages of time have realized enlightenment after having entered the monkhood is the most exalted teaching of all. There has never been a Buddha in the three stages of time who failed to enter the monkhood. This is because entering the monkhood is the true Law, the excellent mind of enlightenment, and the supreme Bodhi-wisdom, which the Buddhas and patriarchs have correctly transmitted. *(Compiled by Dōgen's disciple in the summer of the seventh year of Kenchō [1255])*

TWO

Receiving the Precepts

(Jukai)

IT IS STATED in the *Ch'an-yüan Ch'ing-kuei:* "All the Buddhas in the three stages of time have taught that one realizes enlightenment after having entered the monkhood. The twenty-eight Indian patriarchs and the six Chinese patriarchs who transmitted the Buddha-mind seal were all monks. It may be said that it is because monks strictly observe the precepts that they are the paragons of the three worlds. Therefore if you wish to do zazen and pursue Buddhism, you should first observe the precepts. How can you expect to become a Buddha or patriarch if you do not guard against faults and prevent yourself from doing wrong?

"The manner in which the precepts are to be received is as follows: first, by way of preparation, the three types of *kaśāya,* eating bowls, and a ceremonial seating cloth, all new, should be obtained. If new *kaśāyas* are unavailable, old ones should be made pure by washing them thoroughly. When mounting the ordination platform to receive the precepts you should not borrow the sacred *kaśāyas* and eating bowls of others. Great care should be taken not to violate these regulations, for it is in this way that the dignity of the Buddha is maintained and his precepts are preserved. It is no small matter to come into possession of the same things that the Buddha used; it should not be treated lightly. If you mount the ordination platform and receive the precepts having borrowed the *kaśāyas* and eating bowls of others, you cannot truly be said to have received the precepts. Without having even once received the precepts, you will become a 'man of no precepts' for your entire life, willfully following scholastic Buddhism and vainly wasting the votive donations of others. Those who have only recently entered the monkhood have not yet had time to memorize the precepts and, without a master to guide them, are apt to become men of no precepts. It is for this reason that I dare to give you the following candid advice, which I hope will be taken to heart. If you have already received the precepts for a Śrāvaka,[1] you should further receive those for a Bodhisattva. This is the first step to becoming a Buddhist."

The Buddhas and patriarchs of India and China have all stated that receiving the precepts is the first step to entering the Way. Without having received them one cannot be considered to be a disciple of the various Buddhas or a follower of the patriarchs, for in practicing zazen and pursuing Buddhism it is necessary to guard against faults and prevent oneself from doing wrong. The words "receive the precepts first of all" already truly express the highest supreme Law. People who have become Buddhas and patriarchs have done so through having never failed to receive and observe this highest supreme Law. The Buddhas and patriarchs who correctly transmitted the highest supreme Law have unfailingly received and observed the precepts, for otherwise, it would have been impossible for them to become Buddhas or patriarchs. They received the precepts either directly from the Buddha himself or from one of his disciples. In either case they have all inherited the essence of the Way.

The precepts that the Buddhas and patriarchs correctly transmitted were passed down in China by Bodhidharma alone through the four patriarchs to Hui-nêng. His successors, Hsing-ssŭ of Mount Ch'ing-yüan[2] and Huai-jang of Mount Nan-yüeh,[3] further correctly transmitted them to the present day. What a pity it is that some careless senior monks are quite ignorant of this fact!

The admonition "receiving the precepts of a Bodhisattva is the first step to becoming a Buddhist" is something of which all trainees of the Way should be aware. The manner in which the precepts are to be received has been correctly transmitted to those who, by virtue of their long training, have realized the essence of the Buddhas and patriarchs, and not to those who have been negligent in their practice. The manner of receiving the precepts is as follows. The initiate should first burn incense and prostrate himself before the precept-bestowing master, asking his permission to receive the precepts for a Bodhisattva. Next, if permission is granted, he should purify his body by bathing, and then put on a new clean *kaśāya* if available, or a newly washed one if not, after having scattered flowers, burned incense, and respectfully prostrated himself to the *kaśāya*. By prostrating himself to various Buddhist images, the Three Treasures, and senior monks, it is possible to remove various hindrances and purify one's body and mind. These customs have long been correctly transmitted as the essence of the Buddhas and patriarchs.

Thereafter, in the ceremonial hall of the monastery the precept-bestowing master and his assistant instruct the initiate first to prostrate himself three times and then, kneeling before them with hands joined in *gasshō*, to repeat the following words: "I take refuge in the Buddha; I take refuge in the Law; I take refuge in the Buddhist community. I take refuge in the Buddha, the most venerable of human beings; I take refuge in the Law, venerable because it is free of desire; I take refuge in the Buddhist community, the most venerable community of all. I have taken refuge in the Buddha; I have taken refuge in the Law; I have taken refuge in the Buddhist community." [Repeated three times]

Next, the initiate is instructed to say, "The Tathāgata realized true supreme enlightenment and is my great teacher. I have now taken refuge in him. From now on I will not take refuge in evil spirits or non-Buddhist teachings. Please look with compassion on my humble vows. Please look with compassion on my humble vows." [Repeated three times]

Next, the master says, "Virtuous man! Since you have discarded wrong and taken refuge in good, the Buddhist precepts are already fulfilled. At this time you should receive the three pure precepts.

"The first precept is to do no evil. Can you observe the precept from now till you realize Buddhahood?" The initiate answers, "Yes, certainly." [Questions and answers are repeated three times.]

"The second is to do good. Can you observe this precept from now until you realize Buddhahood?" The initiate answers, "Yes, certainly."

"The third is to confer abundant benefits on all sentient beings. Can you observe this precept from now until you realize Buddhahood?" The initiate answers, "Yes, certainly."

"You must not break any of these three precepts. Can you observe this from now until you realize Buddhahood?" The initiate answers, "Yes, certainly."

The master then says, "Observe the precepts as you have promised. [The initiate prostrates himself three times and, kneeling, joins his hands in *gasshō*.]

"Virtuous man! You have already received the three pure precepts. Next, you must receive the ten grave prohibitions. They are the great precepts of the Buddhas and Bodhisattvas.

"Do not kill. Can you observe this from now until you realize Buddhahood?" The initiate answers, "Yes, certainly." [Questions and answers are repeated three times.]

"Do not steal. Can you observe this from now until you realize Buddhahood?" The initiate answers, "Yes, certainly."

"Do not engage in sexual relations. Can you observe this from now until you realize Buddhahood?" The initiate answers, "Yes, certainly."

"Do not lie. Can you observe this from now until you realize Buddhahood?" The initiate answers, "Yes, certainly."

"Do not deal in intoxicating beverages. Can you observe this from now until you realize Buddhahood?" The initiate answers, "Yes, certainly."

"Do not speak of the faults of Bodhisattvas, whether they be laymen or monks. Can you observe this from now until you realize Buddhahood?" The initiate answers, "Yes, certainly."

"Do not be too proud to praise others. Can you observe this from now until you become a Buddha?" The initiate answers, "Yes, certainly."

"Do not covet either the Law or property. Can you observe this from now until you become a Buddha?" The initiate answers, "Yes, certainly."

"Do not give way to anger. Can you observe this from now until you realize Buddhahood?" The initiate answers, "Yes, certainly."

"Do not disparage the Three Treasures. Can you observe this from now until you realize Buddhahood?" The initiate answers, "Yes, certainly."

"You must not break any of these ten precepts. Can you observe them from now until you realize Buddhahood?" The initiate answers, "Yes, certainly."

"Observe these precepts as you have promised. [The initiate prostrates himself three times.]

"The foregoing three refuges, the three pure precepts, and the ten grave prohibitions have all been received and observed by the various Buddhas. Can you observe these sixteen precepts from now until you realize Buddhahood?" The initiate answers, "Yes, certainly." [Repeated three times]

"Observe these precepts as you have promised." [The initiate prostrates himself three times.]

In conclusion the master chants the verse that begins: "The world around us is as vast as the sky,"[4] and says, "We take refuge in the Buddha; we take refuge in the Law; we take refuge in the Buddhist community." [The initiate then leaves the ceremonial hall.]

The Buddha and patriarchs have correctly transmitted the manner in which the precepts are to be received. Both T'ien-jan of Mount Tan-hsia[5] and initiate-monk Kao of Mount Yao[6] received and observed these sixteen precepts. Indeed, although some patriarchs never received the precepts for a Śrāvaka, all patriarchs have received and observed these sixteen precepts for a Bodhisattva, which the Buddhas and patriarchs have correctly transmitted. *[Date of writing omitted]*

THREE

The Merit of a *Kaśāya*

(Kesa Kudoku)

THE KAŚĀYA, WHICH HAS BEEN HANDED DOWN from Buddha to Buddha, patriarch to patriarch, as the material evidence of having realized enlightenment, was correctly transmitted to China only by the great master Bodhidharma of Mount Sung, the twenty-eighth patriarch in the line of the Buddha Śākyamuni.

In India a total of twenty-eight patriarchs correctly handed down the *kaśāya,* one to another. The twenty-eighth patriarch, Bodhidharma, personally went to China, where he became the first [Chinese] patriarch. In China five successive patriarchs transmitted it to Hui-nêng, the thirty-third patriarch after the Venerable Mahākāśyapa and the sixth after the great master Bodhidharma. Hui-nêng treasured throughout his life the *kaśāya* he had received in the middle of the night from his master Ta-man of Mount Huang-mei.[1] This *kaśāya* is still enshrined at Pao-lin temple on Mount Ts'ao-ch'i.[2] Successive emperors respectfully asked that it be brought to court, where, while bowing, they made venerative offerings to it. They protected it as the most consecrated treasure of the nation.

Three emperors of the T'ang dynasty, Chung-tsung,[3] Su-tsung, and Tai-tsung, each respectfully asked that this *kaśāya* be brought to his court in order that he might make venerative offerings to it. When requesting that it be sent and upon returning it, the emperors dispatched imperial messengers with their edicts. One such edict, issued by Emperor Tai-tsung at the time he returned the *kaśāya* to Mount Ts'ao-ch'i, stated, "We are now respectfully returning this *kaśāya* under the guard of General Liu Ch'ung-ching, who is in charge of pacifying the nation. We consider this to be a national treasure. Chief monk! You should see to it that it is enshrined in the temple in accordance with the Buddha's instructions, thereby enabling the monks to realize the essence of Buddhism. You should take stringent measures for its protection, ensuring against its loss."

The emperors of this small country[4] who see, hear of, and make venerative offerings to a *kaśāya* lead, I dare say, a much more excellent life than those who, in this transient life, rule over lands as innumerable as the sands of the Ganges river. *Kaśāyas* are present wherever the Buddha's teachings are found.

However, it was only Bodhidharma, the first patriarch in China, who personally received the *kaśāya* that had been handed down by the orthodox patriarchs and correctly transmitted it to his successors. No other patriarchs had *kaśāyas* conferred upon them in this way. For example, the teachings of the Venerable Buddhabhadra,[5] a collateral Zen master of the twenty-seventh patriarch, Paññatara,[6] were transmitted to a Chinese monk named Sêng-chao.[7] There was, however, no correct transmission of a *kaśāya* between them. In China even though the fourth patriarch[8] transmitted the Law to Fa-jung of Mount Niu-t'ou,[9] he did not present him with a *kaśāya*.[10]

The merit of the Buddha's Law is eternally boundless even to those who have not had a *kaśāya* bestowed upon them by the orthodox patriarchs. Still greater is the merit accruing to those to whom both the Buddha's Law and his *kaśāya* have been correctly transmitted. Therefore if any human or celestial being wishes to wear a *kaśāya* he should wear one that has been correctly transmitted by the Buddhas and patriarchs. In India and China, in the ages of true and formal Buddhism, even laymen wore a *kaśāya*. Now in Japan, which is far from the above countries and presently in the age of degenerate Buddhism, even those who, having shaved their head and beard, call themselves disciples of the Buddha wear no *kaśāya*. It is truly regrettable that they do not believe, know, or realize that they should wear one, still more that they do not know the materials, colors, or size of a *kaśāya* or even the way it should be worn.

A *kaśāya* has been called a "deliverance robe"[11] since ancient times. When one puts it on he is able to free himself from all the hindrances that are encountered during training—the effects of his wrong deeds in his present and past existences as well as of his delusive mind. If a dragon gets hold of even a piece of thread from a *kaśāya*, he can rid himself of the three sufferings.[12] If an ox touches it with even one of his horns, his wrongdoings will naturally disappear. The various Buddhas never failed to put on a *kaśāya* at the time of their enlightenment. It should be realized that the merit of a *kaśāya* is incomparable.

How regrettable it is that we were born in a corner of the world located far from India and China, and moreover, in the age of degenerate Buddhism! On the other hand, however, how joyful it is that we have been able to come into contact with this piece of the Buddha's clothing that the Buddhas and patriarchs have correctly handed down as the symbol of the Law! What other sect has ever correctly transmitted a *kaśāya* and the Law as ours has? Who, upon coming into contact with it, would not respectfully make venerative offerings? We should respectfully make venerative offerings to it even if each day we must sacrifice our lives, which are as numerous as the sands of the Ganges. We should pledge to make venerative offerings respectfully in whatever generation and world in which we come into contact with it.

We now live in Japan, which is more than one hundred thousand *ri* from India, where the Buddha was born. However, in spite of this vast distance we are able to come into contact with the true Way as a result of our good deeds in the past, obstructed neither by the mountains and oceans between Japan and India nor by the fact that we are a primitive people located in a remote area of the world. We are able to practice the Way night and day with single-hearted devotion, wearing a *kaśāya* that we have reverently accepted and will protect eternally. This is possible not merely because of the merit we have accrued as a result of our training under the guidance of one or two Buddhas, but rather is due to the merit accumulated through our various practices under the guidance of Buddhas as numerous as the sands of the Ganges River. We should be exceedingly glad that we have been able to come into contact with a *kaśāya* and respect it reverently, even though we came into contact with it as a result of our own efforts. Furthermore, we should show our respect to the patriarchs who transmitted the Law to us, realizing how deeply indebted to them we are. Since even animals show their appreciation for kindnesses done to them, how can human beings be unaware of the benefactions of others? If we are unaware, then we should be considered to be inferior to animals.

The only people who have realized the merit of the Way and of a *kaśāya* are those patriarchs who have transmitted the true teachings of the Buddha. If one wishes to follow in their footsteps, he should devote himself completely to the search for the transmission of the Law. The transmission of the Way in this manner should be considered as the transmission of the Truth, even tens of thousands of years from now. This is the Buddha's teaching. The evidence of its being the correct transmission is quite clear. This correct transmission should not be thought of as being like milk that has been diluted with water. Rather it is like a crown prince ascending the throne. If, desiring to drink milk, there is no milk available except that which has been diluted with water, it is permissible to drink it. However, no substance other than water, for example, oil, lacquer, or wine, should be mixed with the milk. The correct transmission of the Way is like this. Even though one may be training under an ordinary master, if that master has been the recipient of a correct transmission it is similar to having found an opportunity to drink milk, even though that milk may have been diluted with water. This is even truer when it is a question of the correct transmission of the Way by the Buddhas and patriarchs; truly it may be said to be just like the accession of the crown prince to the throne. Even in the lay world the successor to the throne says, "I will only wear that clothing which is in accordance with the regulations of the former king." How then could those engaged in the study of Buddhism wear anything other than the Buddha's *kaśāya?*

Since the tenth year of Yung-p'ing [A.D. 67] during the reign of Emperor Hsiao-ming of the Later Han dynasty, many monks and laymen have traveled one after another from China to India and back. None of them have said, however, that while in India they had encountered patriarchs to whom the Way had been correctly transmitted. Neither did they claim to have the genealogy of the direct transmission of the Way that had been initiated by the Tathāgata. Instead, they merely brought back with them various Sanskrit *sūtras* that they had studied under scriptural scholars while in India. It is for this reason that they neither mentioned having met with patriarchs to whom the Way had been correctly transmitted nor talked about the existence of patriarchs who transmitted the Buddha's *kaśāya*. It is clear that they had not plumbed the utmost depths of Buddhism. Consequently, they were unable to realize the true meaning of the Way that had been transmitted by the Buddha and patriarchs.

When the Buddha Śākyamuni bestowed the Venerable Mahākāśyapa with the supreme Bodhi-wisdom, he also presented him with a *kaśāya* that had been correctly transmitted from the Buddha Kāśyapa. This *kaśāya* was further directly transmitted down through the successive patriarchs to Hui-nêng of Mount Ts'ao-ch'i, the thirty-third patriarch. In addition, instructions concerning the kind of material, color, and size of the *kaśāya* were also handed down. Thereafter, the followers of Ch'ing-yüan and Nan-yüeh personally transmitted these instructions, making and wearing their *kaśāya* exactly as the Buddha had prescribed. Unless one has realized the essence of Buddhism that the successive patriarchs have directly transmitted, it is impossible to know how to wash and wear a *kaśāya*.

There are three kinds of *kaśāya,* made of five, seven, or nine strips of cloth. Mahāyāna trainees wear only these three kinds of *kaśāya* and do not attempt to obtain any other; for they are sufficient by themselves.

The first of these is worn when cleaning or doing other kinds of physical labor as well as when going to the lavatory, the second when participating in various ceremonies, and the third when engaged in giving instruction in the Way to human and celestial beings. Furthermore, the first is to be worn when one is alone, the second when in the company of other monks, and the third when entering a palace or other human habitation. During warm weather the first is sufficient; however, in cold weather the second may be added, and in bitterly cold weather the third may be worn as well.

In the past, on midwinter nights when the cold was so severe that it caused the bamboo to crack, the Tathāgata would wear a *kaśāya* of five strips during the evening, add a *kaśāya* of seven strips around midnight, and further put on a *kaśāya* of nine strips during the coldest part of the morning. At that time the Tathāgata thought to himself, "In the future, trainees of the Way can put on these three kinds of *kaśāya* to keep their bodies warm when they are unable to bear the bitter cold."

THE WAY OF WEARING A KAŚĀYA The normal method of wearing a *kaśāya* is to put it on so that one's left shoulder is covered, leaving the right exposed. There is also a method, followed by the Tathāgata and elderly senior monks, in which both shoulders are covered. In the latter case, however, even though the shoulders are covered, the upper part of the chest may or may not be exposed. A *kaśāya* made of sixty or more strips of cloth is used when covering both shoulders. When putting on a *kaśāya* its two ends should be placed one over the other on the left arm and shoulder. The overlapping part of the right end of the *kaśāya* should be placed on the left shoulder and hung over the outside of the left arm. In the case of a large *kaśāya* the overlapping part of the right end should be placed over the left shoulder and hung in back. Apart from these methods there are many other ways of wearing a *kaśāya*. In order to learn these methods it is necessary to undergo training for longer periods of time.

Over a period lasting hundreds of years in the Liang, Ch'ên, Sui, T'ang, and Sung dynasties many scholars of both the Mahāyāna and the Hīnayāna schools forsook lecturing on the *sūtras* because they realized that this practice was not the essence of Buddhism. Furthermore, as they trained in the Way that had been correctly transmitted by the Buddhas and patriarchs, they inevitably took off and threw away their former unorthodox robes and replaced them with a *kaśāya* that had been correctly transmitted by the Buddhas and patriarchs. They truly left the false and returned to the true.

The true Law of the Tathāgata originated in India. Most ancient and modern masters, however, gave instruction in the Way based on the narrow and delusive views of ordinary people. Originally, however, since the worlds of Buddhas and of ordinary people are beyond "bounded" and "boundless," it is impossible for the narrow minds of the latter in the present day to understand the teachings, practice, practitioners, or truth of the Mahāyāna and Hīnayāna schools. Furthermore, there are people in China who, failing to base their teaching on the true Law as found in India, substitute their own new and narrow views and take them for the Way. They are far from Buddhism.

Therefore, if someone with a Bodhi-mind puts on a *kaśāya,* it should be one that has been correctly transmitted, not a newly devised one. The former is a *kaśāya* that has been correctly transmitted from the Tathāgata down through the successive patriarchs to Bodhidharma, Hui-nêng, and their followers. During this period there was not even one patriarch who failed to wear such a *kaśāya*. The *kaśāya* that was newly devised in the T'ang dynasty in China, however, is far different from the correctly transmitted one. All the monks who have hitherto come from India have worn their *kaśāya* according to the correct transmission of the Buddhas and patriarchs. None of them has worn a *kaśāya* like that newly devised by monks belonging to the Vinaya school of Buddhism[13] in China. Only those unfamiliar with the correctly transmitted *kaśāya* believe in this new one, while those familiar with the former cast away the latter.

The merit of a *kaśāya* that has been correctly transmitted from Buddha to Buddha, patriarch to patriarch, is clear and easily believable. This orthodox *kaśāya* has been handed down as an inheritance by the patriarchs, its true appearance thus having been preserved to this day. All these patriarchs have been masters and disciples who realized enlightenment and to whom were transmitted the Law. We must therefore make a *kaśāya* according to the way that the Buddha and patriarchs have correctly transmitted. All beings, common or sacred, human or celestial, dragons or deities, have long realized that this is the only correct transmission.

As we have been born in an age when the correct method of making a *kaśāya* is known, if we wear it even once for only a short period of time, it will surely serve to protect us in our search for enlightenment. If we believe and immerse ourselves in even one word of the Buddha's teaching or one verse of the *kaśāya gāthā*,[14] this will become the seed of eternal light, which will finally lead us to the supreme Bodhi-wisdom. This is also the case when we devote ourselves to one teaching or one good action. Even though our body, mind, and thoughts are constantly in a state of rise and decay, the merit that results from the practice of Buddhism in this way will inevitably come to fruition. A *kaśāya* is not something that is "made" or "nonmade," "fixed" or "unfixed." Rather, it is the very essence of those who have realized enlightenment. The merit that trainees attain through wearing a *kaśāya* will inevitably be completely realized and comprehended. A person who has failed to do good in his previous lives will be unable to see, wear, believe, or comprehend the meaning of a *kaśāya* even in the course of one, two, or innumerable lives. In present-day China and Japan there are some who have been able to wear a *kaśāya* at least once and others who have been unable to. This has nothing to do with the questions of whether they are of noble or humble birth, foolish or wise. Rather it is a question of whether or not they have done good in their previous lives.

For this reason, those who are now able to wear a *kaśāya* should rejoice over the fact that they did good in their previous lives. One should not doubt the merit that has been accumulated in this way. A person who has not yet been able to obtain a *kaśāya* should, wishing to do so, quickly endeavor to sow the seeds in his present life that will enable him to obtain one in the future. If he encounters difficulties in doing so, he should make the following petition of repentance before the Buddhas and the Three Treasures: "How earnestly people in other countries wish to wear a *kaśāya!* How I wish that the Law and the *kaśāya* may be correctly transmitted to my country as they have been to China so that I may come into personal contact with them!" How ashamed and sorry we would be if the Law and the *kaśāya* had not been correctly transmitted to our country! Why is it that we have been so fortunate as to come into contact with the correctly transmitted Law and *kaśāya* of the Bhagavat? It is entirely due to the great merit we have accrued from having planted the seeds of Wisdom in our past lives.

Today in this age of degenerate Buddhism people are unashamed of having failed to receive the correct transmission and are jealous of others for having done so. Such as they are companions of the devil! What they own and the circumstances they find themselves in are the result not of Truth but of their past bad actions. They should simply take respectful refuge in the correctly transmitted Law. Realize that this is what those who truly study the Way should do.

We should understand that a *kaśāya* is something that all Buddhas have reverently respected and taken refuge in. It is known, therefore, as a Buddha-body and Buddha-mind. It is also called a robe of deliverance, good fortune, no form,[15] supremacy, endurance, the Tathāgata, great benevolence, victory, and the supreme Bodhi-wisdom. Truly, since it is all these things we should receive it respectfully without altering it in any way.

The materials for making a *kaśāya* may be either silk or cotton. Cotton is not necessarily pure, nor is silk necessarily impure. It is laughable to prefer silk over cotton! According to the traditional teachings of the Buddhas a *kaśāya* made of discarded cloth, that is, a *pāmsūla,*[16] is the best. There are either four or ten types of such cloth. The four types of cloth are those that have been burned by fire, munched by oxen, gnawed by mice, or worn by the dead. Indians throw this cloth away in the streets and in the fields just as they do their excreta. The name *pāmsūla* comes from this. Monks pick up such cloth and wear it after having washed and sewn the various pieces together. Although some of this cloth is cotton and some silk, no discrimination should be made between the two. We should deeply reflect on the meaning of a *pāmsūla.* In the past when the Śrāmaṇera[17] Jana washed his *pāmsūla* in Anavatapta Pond,[18] the Dragon King rained precious flowers on it in admiration and respect.

Masters of the Hīnayāna say that silk cloth is superior because it is mysteriously made from the thread of a silkworm. But students of the Mahāyāna laugh at this idea, knowing it to be sheer nonsense. The former do not realize that silk cloth is made of the thread of a cocoon produced by a silkworm. Adhering to their prejudiced views, they refuse to believe what is before their very eyes! We should realize that among the cloth we pick up there is some that is like silk and some like cotton. The types of cloth are as various as the customs of the districts in which they are made, so much so that it is impossible for an ordinary person to distinguish among them. Therefore, in picking up such cloth there should be no discussion of what it is made of. Simply call it a *pāmsūla.*

Even though human and celestial beings grow together with a *pāmsūla,* they are a *pāmsūla,* not sentient beings.[19] Even if pine trees or chrysanthemums grow together with a *pāmsūla,* they are a *pāmsūla,* not nonsentient beings. When we believe that a *pāmsūla* is made not of silk, cotton, gold, silver, pearls, or jewels, we can realize what a true *pāmsūla* is. Unless we stop discriminating silk from cotton, we do not stand even the slightest chance of understanding the true meaning of a *pāmsūla.*

A monk once asked a famous Zen master, "Was the *kaśāya* that was transmitted to Patriarch Hui-nêng at midnight on Mount Huang-mei made of cotton or silk?" The master answered, "Neither cotton nor silk." We should realize that this statement that a *kaśāya* is made of neither silk nor cotton is an excellent teaching of the Way.

The Venerable Śāṇavāsa[20] was the third [Indian] patriarch. He is said to have been born wrapped in a robe. As a layman this robe was that of an ordinary man, but after he entered the monkhood it became a *kaśāya.* Similarly, it is said, the Bhikṣuṇī Śuklā,[21] fulfilling a vow she had made, presented Śākyamuni with a carpet. Because of this good deed she was born with a *kaśāya* in every subsequent existence. Today, when we come into contact with the Buddha Śākyamuni and become monks, the ordinary dress that we received at our birth quickly changes into a *kaśāya,* just as in the case of the Venerable Śāṇavāsa.

It should now be clear that a *kaśāya* is not made of silk, cotton, or other materials. In similar fashion, the merit of the Law extends not only to self but to others as well. This is clearly the case with entering the monkhood and receiving the precepts too, though because of our ignorance we are unaware of this fact. Because of the universal nature of the teachings of the Buddhas, there is no reason to believe that this merit extends only to Śāṇavāsa and Śuklā and not to ourselves in accordance with our capacities.

The true meaning of the preceding should be made clear through your practice of the Way. It is said that a *kaśāya* made of neither cotton nor silk fell on the shoulders of the Venerable Mahākāśyapa when he appeared before the Buddha Śākyamuni and received the precepts from him. The way in which the Buddha teaches is beyond the understanding of ordinary people. The priceless jewel that the Buddha placed in the *kaśāya* is likewise beyond the understanding of those attached to scholastic Buddhism.

You should carefully study whether the kinds, colors, and sizes of the various Buddhas' *kaśāyas* are finite or infinite, with form or formless. This is something that all the patriarchs, both ancient and modern, in India and in China, have studied and correctly transmitted. There are those who, though they clearly know that the correct transmission of the *kaśāya* by the patriarchs is an incontrovertible fact, still do not wish to have it correctly transmitted to them. This attitude of theirs is unpardonable, due entirely to their extreme foolishness and unbelief. They have forsaken the Truth for falsehood, mistaken the branches for the roots. This shows their contempt for the Buddha.

Those who have awakened to the Bodhi-mind should definitely receive the *kaśāya* that has been correctly transmitted by the patriarchs. Not only have we been able to come into contact with the Law, but as grandchildren of the patriarchs, who have correctly transmitted the Buddha's *kaśāya,* we have been able to see, study, and receive one ourselves. This is equivalent to saying that we have seen the Tathāgata, listened to his sermons, bathed in his light, experienced his enlightenment, directly received his mind, and realized his essence. We stand covered with a *kaśāya* that has been directly given us by the Buddha Śākyamuni. In other words, submitting ourselves to the Buddha, we reverently receive his *kaśāya.*

THE METHOD OF WASHING A KAŚĀYA The unfolded *kaśāya* should be put in a clean wooden tub. Then, adding fragrant boiling hot water, let it soak for approximately two hours. Another method is to place the *kaśāya* in boiling hot water containing pure ash and wait for the hot water to cool. In our country this second method is commonly used and is known as *aku-no-yu.* After the hot water containing the ash has cooled and become clear, wash the *kaśāya* in it. When doing so, hold it with both hands, being careful not to crumple it up or trample on it. Continue washing the *kaśāya* until all the dirt and grease have been removed. When this has been done, rinse the *kaśāya* in cold water containing incense of aloes or beadwood, and so on. After having dried it thoroughly on a clean rod, fold it and put it in an elevated place. Then, burning incense and scattering flower petals, walk clockwise around it several times, prostrating yourself before it three, six, or nine times. Finally, kneeling before it in *gasshō,* pick it up and, after having recited the *kaśāya gāthā,* stand up and put it on in the prescribed manner.

The Bhagavat told his disciples: "In the past when I trained under the Buddha Dharmākara,[22] I was known as the Bodhisattva Avalokiteśvara.[23] At that time I made a vow to the Buddha Dharmākara: 'Buddha Dharmākara! Suppose that after I have realized Buddhahood someone becomes my disciple, enters the monkhood, and wears a *kaśāya.* Suppose further that although as a monk, nun, layman, or laywoman that person is guilty of having committed various grave crimes, such as breaking the ten grave prohibitions, becoming attached to false views, or ridiculing the Three Treasures because of his unbelief, yet he subsequently comes to reverently respect the *kaśāya,* as well as the Buddha, the Law, and the Buddhist community. At that time if his practice retrogresses because he is unable to receive a guarantee that he will realize Buddhahood in the future while in the three vehicles,[24] this is equivalent to deceiving the innumerable Buddhas of the whole world. Buddha Dharmākara! If there is even one person like this, I have no wish to realize the supreme Bodhi-wisdom!

" 'Suppose that after I have realized Buddhahood there is someone among celestial beings, dragons, demons, deities, and human and nonhuman beings who respectfully venerates, praises, and admires the wearer of a *kaśāya.* If he sees even one piece of a *kaśāya,* he will not retrogress in his practice while in the three vehicles.

" 'Buddha Dharmākara! Suppose that there are sufferers from hunger and thirst, poverty-stricken demons and deities, people of humble birth, and hungry ghosts. If any of them gets hold of even as much as a four-*ts'un*[25] piece of *kaśāya,* his hunger and thirst will be satisfied and his every wish quickly fulfilled.

" 'Suppose that there are those who, becoming antagonistic toward each other and feeling mutual resentment, continuously fight among themselves. Whether they be celestial beings, dragons, demons, deities, *gandharvas,*[26] *asuras, garuḍas,*[27] *kiṃnaras, mahoragas,*[28] *kumbhāṇḍas,*[29] *piśācas,*[30] or human or nonhuman beings, if any of them bears a *kaśāya* in mind, its virtue will cause him to have, successively, a compassionate, tender, nonresentful, enlightened, and controlled mind. Thus will he be purified.

" 'Suppose someone finds himself among those who intend to decide matters through various forms of armed and unarmed struggle. If he wears even the smallest part of a *kaśāya* that he has respectfully and reverently venerated, he will be protected so that they will be unable to injure, touch, or trifle with him. Thus he will always be able to overcome others, whatever difficulties may befall him.

" 'Buddha Dharmākara! If my *kaśāya* fails to have these five sacred merits, it means that I have deceived the innumerable Buddhas of the whole world. In this case, in the future I shall be able neither to realize the supreme

Bodhi-wisdom nor to save others. Thus the true Law will be lost and it will be impossible to destroy evil teachings.'

"Virtuous men! At that time the Buddha Dharmākara, stretching out his golden-hued right arm and patting me on the head, praised me, saying, 'Well said! Well said! Your words are like a great rare treasure, full of wisdom and virtue. You have already realized the highest supreme enlightenment. Your *kaśāya* is now endowed with the five sacred merits and able to bestow abundant benefits on all beings.'

"Virtuous men! When I heard the Buddha Dharmākara's words of praise I was filled with boundless joy. The hand of his golden-hued outstretched arm was as soft as a heavenly robe, his fingers slender and webbed. After I was patted on the head my body was transformed into that of a twenty-year-old youth.

"Virtuous men! All those present—celestial beings, dragons, deities, *gandharvas,* human and nonhuman beings—put their hands together in *shashu*[31] and, bowing respectfully, venerated me with various flowers and musical performances. After they had finished praising me in this way they became silent again."

It should be realized that these five preceding sacred merits form the core of the merits of a *kaśāya* as ennumerated in the *sūtras* and precepts for Bodhisattvas and Śrāvakas. This is as true now as it was when the Buddha was alive. Truly, a *kaśāya,* whose merits are immeasurable, is the clothing of all Buddhas in the three stages of time. To have received a *kaśāya* according to the teachings of the Buddha Śākyamuni, however, is superior to having received one according to the teachings of other Buddhas. This is because when the Buddha Śākyamuni made the five hundred great vows before the Buddha Dharmākara in his former existence as the Bodhisattva Avalokiteśvara, he made special vows about the merits of a *kaśāya.* How truly immeasurable and wondrous its merits are!

The essence of the Bhagavat has been transmitted through the *kaśāya* to the present time. Those patriarchs who have correctly transmitted the Eye Storehouse of the True Law have inevitably transmitted this *kaśāya.* Those who have received and respectfully preserved this *kaśāya* have never failed to realize enlightenment within two or three existences. Even if it is worn, in the beginning, simply as a joke or in order to make a profit, it inevitably becomes the basis for realizing enlightenment.

The Patriarch Nāgārjuna said, "Even if a monk fails to observe the precepts and commits a crime, he may still realize enlightenment after he redeems himself. In regard to this the *Utpalavarṇā-jātaka-sūtra* relates the story of a nun by the name of Utpalavarṇā who lived during the Buddha's lifetime. It was the custom of this nun, who had herself realized Arhathood and was endowed with the six powers for saving sentient beings, to visit the homes of noblewomen. At such times she would praise the act of entering the nunhood, saying, 'You should all become nuns.' They would answer, 'We are still young and healthy, and have attractive features. We are afraid it would be difficult for us to observe the precepts for nuns. Perhaps we might break the precepts.' 'Perhaps you will,' Utpalavarṇā answered, 'but even so it would be better for you to enter the nunhood.' 'But if we break the precepts,' they replied, 'we will inevitably fall into hell. How could we dare to break the precepts?' 'If that's what it takes, it's better to fall into hell,' she continued. Laughing at her, the noblewomen said, 'How can you say that it's all right for us to fall into hell when, if we were to do so, we would be punished?'

"Speaking from her own experience, the nun replied, 'In my previous existence I was a prostitute and often uttered licentious words while dressed improperly. Once, however, I put on nun's robes as a joke. Owing to this good deed, I was born a nun in the time of the Buddha Kāśyapa. My problems did not end here, however. Because of my noble birth and beauty I became proud and conceited, and consequently, I broke the precepts, falling into hell, where I was severely punished. After having redeemed myself and been born in the human world once more I was finally able to meet the Buddha Śākyamuni and reenter the nunhood. As a result I was able to realize Arhathood and become endowed with the six powers for saving sentient beings. Therefore, based on my own experience, I can tell you that even if you break the precepts after having entered the nunhood you will still be able to realize Arhathood. On the other hand, if you do wrong without having entered the nunhood, you will be unable to realize the Way. In the past I fell into hell for two consecutive generations because of my wrongdoings. Each time I left hell I became a bad woman and upon dying returned to hell without ever having realized enlightenment. This is why I know that even if you break the precepts after you have entered the nunhood, you will still be able to realize enlightenment.'"

It was the merit of the Bhikṣuṇī Utpalavarṇā's having worn a *kaśāya*, even though it was at first done as a joke, that laid the foundation for her eventual realization of Arhathood. In her following existence she was able to meet the Buddha Kāśyapa and become a nun. Finally, in her third existence she was able to meet the Buddha Śākyamuni and become a great Arhat, endowed with the three types of superior Wisdom and the six powers to save sentient beings. The three types of superior Wisdom are (1) eyes capable of seeing everything, (2) remembrance of one's former existences, and (3) perfect freedom. The six powers to save sentient beings are (1) free activity, (2) eyes capable of seeing everything, (3) ears capable of hearing everything, (4) insight into others' thinking, (5) remembrance of one's former existences, and (6) perfect freedom.

When Utpalavarṇā was simply a wrongdoer, she meaninglessly died and fell into hell, only to be reborn again later to repeat the same cycle. After having received the precepts, however, even though she later broke them and fell into hell, she was eventually able to realize enlightenment. Since she was able to realize enlightenment in three existences even though she initially wore a *kaśāya* as a joke, is it possible that a person wearing a *kaśāya* with a pure heart and searching for supreme Wisdom could fail to do otherwise?

How utterly immeasurable the merit of a person would be if he received and respectfully wore a *kaśāya* in this spirit for his entire life!

Those who have awakened to the Bodhi-mind should quickly receive and respectfully wear a *kaśāya*. Having had the good fortune to be born in this world, how regrettable it would be if we now failed to plant the seeds of our Buddhahood. Now that we have been born with human form, how foolish we would be if, having encountered the teachings of the Buddha Śākyamuni and received his *kaśāya* that the successive patriarchs have correctly transmitted, we wasted our lives meaninglessly!

The only true inheritors of the *kaśāya* are those who have had it correctly transmitted to them by the patriarchs. Those who have not received such a correct transmission can in no way be considered their equals. There is no little merit, however, in having received a *kaśāya* from even a member of this latter group, to say nothing of having received it from a true master. Such a person has truly become the Buddha's son and realized his essence. The *kaśāya* has been ceaselessly transmitted and protected by all the Buddhas, Bodhisattvas, Śrāvakas, and Pratyekabuddhas in the three stages of time and the whole world.

A *kaśāya* should be made of coarse cotton cloth. When this is not available, fine cotton cloth may be used. When neither of the preceding is available, plain silk cloth may be used. When neither silk nor cotton cloth is available, light figured silk cloth may be used.

These, then, are the materials [for making a *kaśāya*] of which the Tathāgata has approved. In countries that lack the preceding materials, however, he has also given permission for leather to be used.

A *kaśāya* should be dyed a dull blue, yellow, red, black, or purple. The Tathāgata always wore a dull red *kaśāya*. The *kaśāya* that the first patriarch [in China], Bodhidharma, transmitted was blue-black in color and made of large pieces of fine Indian cotton cloth. This *kaśāya*, which had been successively transmitted to the twenty-eight patriarchs in India and the five in China, is now enshrined on Mount Ts'ao-ch'i. All of Hui-nêng's disciples transmitted and preserved this *kaśāya* lineage. There is no comparison between this lineage and that of other monks.

The three types of *kaśāya* are: (1) that made of discarded cloth, (2) that made of furs, and (3) that made of worn-out cloth. The first type has been previously explained. The second type is made of the feathers of birds or the fur of animals. If trainees are unable to get hold of the first type of *kaśāya*, that is, a *pāmsūla*, they should make this second type. The third type of *kaśāya* is made of worn-out cloth that has been resewn. Monks should not wear *kaśāyas* made of fine materials prized by the ordinary world.

The Venerable Upāli[32] asked the Bhagavat, "Virtuous Bhagavat! How many kinds of *saṃghāṭī-kaśāya* are there?"

The Buddha answered, "Nine."

"What are they?"

"They are *kaśāyas* made of nine, eleven, thirteen, fifteen, seventeen, nineteen, twenty-one, twenty-three, and twenty-five strips of cloth. In making the first three types of *saṃghāṭī-kaśāya,* you should bear in mind that each strip consists of two long pieces and one short piece of cloth. In making the next three types, each strip should consist of three long pieces and one short piece of cloth. In the last three types, four long pieces and one short piece of cloth should be used. *Kaśāyas* using more than twenty-five strips of cloth are not allowed."

Upāli then asked the Buddha, "Virtuous Bhagavat! How many sizes of *saṃghāṭī-kaśāya* are there?"

The Buddha answered, "There are three sizes: large, medium, and small. The large size is three *hastas*[33] long and five *hastas* wide. The small size is two and a half *hastas* long and four and a half *hastas* wide. The medium size is that between these two."

Upāli continued: "Virtuous Bhagavat! How many kinds of *uttarāsaṃga-kaśāya* are there?"

The Buddha answered, "Only one, a *kaśāya* of seven strips of cloth. Each strip consists of two long pieces and one short piece of cloth."

Upāli then asked, "Virtuous Bhagavat! How many sizes of *kaśāya* of seven strips of cloth are there?"

The Buddha answered, "Three sizes: large, medium, and small. The large size is three *hastas* long and five *hastas* wide. The small size is half a *hasta* smaller in length and width. The medium size is that between these two."

And Upāli continued: "Virtuous Bhagavat! How many strips of cloth does the *antarvāsa-kaśāya* have?"

The Buddha answered, "It has five. Each strip consists of one long and one short piece of cloth."

Upāli continued: "How many sizes of *antarvāsa-kaśāya* are there?"

The Buddha answered, "Three sizes: large, medium, and small. The large size is three *hastas* long and five *hastas* wide. The medium and small sizes are the same as [for] the preceding [type of *kaśāya*]. Furthermore, there are another two sizes of *antarvāsa-kaśāya.* One of them is two *hastas* long and five *hastas* wide. The other is two *hastas* long and four *hastas* wide."

A *saṃghāṭī* is known as a double *kaśāya.* An *uttarāsaṃga* is known as an outer *kaśāya,* while an *antarvāsa* is known as an under or inner one. Furthermore, a *saṃghāṭī* is also called a great *kaśāya* and is worn when entering a king's palace or delivering discourses on Buddhism. An *uttarāsaṃga* is also called a *kaśāya* of seven strips or a medium *kaśāya,* and is worn when in the company of other monks. An *antarvāsa* is also known as a *kaśāya* of five strips or a small *kaśāya,* and is worn when training or doing work. These three kinds of *kaśāya* should be protected and preserved without fail. There is also a large *kaśāya* of sixty strips, which should be received and preserved in a similar manner.

It is said that in the past men lived to be approximately eighty thousand years old, just as they live to be approximately a hundred years old today. Some take the position that the size of a man's body has been affected by this change in life span, others that it has not. The latter is generally considered to be the correct transmission. There is an extreme difference in size between the body of a man and that of a Buddha. A man's body can be measured, while a Buddha's cannot. For this reason the Buddha [of the past] Kāśyapa's *kaśāya* was neither too long nor too large for the Buddha Śākyamuni to wear. Similarly, the Buddha Śākyamuni's *kaśāya* is neither too short nor too small for the Buddha [of the future] Maitreya[34] to wear. We should observe clearly, decide explicitly, realize completely, and discern carefully that a Buddha's body is beyond measure.

Even though King Brahma is in the heavenly world of form, he is unable to see the top of a Buddha's head. The Venerable Maudgalyāyana[35] went to the far distant world of Light Banner,[36] but he was still able to hear the Buddha Śākyamuni's voice as clearly as when he had been close to him. This is truly miraculous. You should bear in mind that all the merits of a Buddha are like this.

There are four correct ways of making a *kaśāya* depending on how the cloth is cut and sewn together. These are known as a *ko-chih-i,* a *hsieh-yeh-i,* a *shê-yeh-i,* and a *pata.*[37] We should wear whichever kind of *kaśāya* comes into our possession. The Buddha Śākyamuni has said, "The *kaśāya* of all the Buddhas in the three stages of time should definitely be made by backstitching."

Pure and clean cloth is considered to be the proper material for making a *kaśāya*. All the Buddhas in the three stages of time considered a *pāmsūla* to be the purest and cleanest *kaśāya* of all. In addition, *kaśāyas* given by faithful donors, or bought with their offerings, are also considered to be pure and clean. Although there are regulations governing the length of time in which a *kaśāya* is to be made,[38] since we are now living in the age of degenerate Buddhism in a country far from India, we should simply wear a *kaśāya* sewn out of deep faith [without regard to the length of time it takes us to make it].

It is the utmost secret of the Mahāyāna that both laymen and celestial beings have received and preserved the *kaśāya*. Both King Brahma and King Śakrendra wore a *kaśāya*. They are excellent examples of creatures in the worlds of desire and form. In the human world such instances are innumerable, for all lay Bodhisattvas have worn a *kaśāya*. In China, Emperor Wu[39] of the Liang dynasty and Emperor Yang[40] of the Sui also wore a *kaśāya*. So did Emperors Tai-tsung and Su-tsung, who trained under Buddhist masters and received the precepts for Bodhisattvas. In addition to these, there have been many laymen and laywomen, past and present, who have done the same.

In Japan, Prince Shōtoku wore a *kaśāya* as well as delivered discourses on the *Saddharma-puṇḍarīka-sūtra* and *Śrīmālā-sūtra.*[41] During the course of his delivery it is said that he felt as if celestial maids were raining precious flowers on him. It was subsequent to this that Buddhism spread throughout our country. Not only was Prince Shōtoku the regent of our country, he also became the teacher of all creatures in the human and celestial worlds, the messenger of the Buddha, and the spiritual father of all beings. In our country, although the size, color, and materials for making a *kaśāya* are mistaken, still, the fact that we can even hear the word *kaśāya* is due entirely to his efforts. What a regrettable position we would be in today if, at that time, he had not rejected falsehood and established the Truth! Subsequently, Emperor Shōmu[42] also wore a *kaśāya* and received the Bodhisattva precepts. Therefore, whether emperor or retainer, one should quickly put on a *kaśāya* and receive the Bodhisattva precepts. There is no greater human happiness than this!

Someone has said, "The *kaśāya* that laymen wear is called either a single-stitched or an ordinary robe. This former name stems from the fact that backstitching is not used in its making. Furthermore, when laymen go to a monastery to undergo training they should take the three kinds of *kaśāya,* a toothbrush, mouth rinse, eating utensils, and a sitting cloth with them, following the same pure practices as monks." Although many former masters have taught as has just been stated, the direct transmission of the Buddhas and patriarchs maintains that the *kaśāyas* that kings, ministers, lay monks, warriors, and ordinary people received all used backstitching. Hui-nêng is an excellent example of one who correctly transmitted the Buddha's *kaśāya.*

The *kaśāya* is the sign that we are the disciples of the Buddha. If we have received a *kaśāya* we should respectfully venerate it every day. Before putting it on we should place it on our head and, joining our hands in *gasshō,* chant the following verse:

> How wondrous this deliverance robe is,
> Like a field bestowing unlimited happiness!
> Now we unfold the Buddha's teachings,
> Making a vow to save all creatures.

After this *gāthā* is recited, the *kaśāya* is put on. A *kaśāya* should be regarded as if it were one's master or the Buddha's *stūpa.* The preceding *gāthā* should also be chanted when respectfully venerating a newly washed *kaśāya.*

The Buddha has said, "If one shaves his head and puts on a *kaśāya,* he will be protected by all the Buddhas and venerated by celestial beings." From this it can be clearly understood that when we shave our head and put on a *kaśāya* we will be protected by all the Buddhas. Through this protection we can completely realize the merit of the supreme Bodhi-wisdom, being venerated by both celestial and human beings.

The Bhagavat once told the Bhikṣu Jñānaprabha:[43] "A *kaśāya* has the following merits:

"1. It covers our body, prevents us from being ashamed, gives rise to feelings of repentance, and causes us to do good.

"2. It protects us from cold and heat, mosquitoes, dangerous animals, and poisonous insects so that we may undergo training in tranquillity.

"3. It gives us the appearance of monks, the sight of which delights others and detaches them from their delusive minds.

"4. It is the precious sign of human and celestial beings. Through respectfully venerating it we can be reborn as King Brahma.

"5. It eliminates the crimes of all beings and gives them unlimited happiness, for when wearing it we awake to the realization that it is a precious sign [of the Way].

"6. It keeps us from the five desires and avarice as a result of our dyeing it a dull color when we make it.

"7. It changes all delusions into eternal happiness because it is the pure robe of the Buddha.

"8. It extinguishes all our crimes and causes us to perform the ten good deeds[44] every moment we wear it.

"9. It advances the way of Bodhisattvas because it is like a fertile field.

"10. It protects us from being injured by the poisonous arrow of delusion because it is like armor.

"Jñānaprabha! You should realize, therefore, that when the Buddhas, Pratyekabuddhas, Śrāvakas, and pure monks in the three stages of time wear a *kaśāya* they all sit on the same deliverance seat, grasp the same Wisdom sword, and, defeating various devils, enter the same world of Nirvāṇa."

The Bhagavat further recited the following verse:

"Bhikṣu Jñānaprabha, listen carefully!
The *kaśāya* of good fortune has ten excellent merits.
Worldly clothing often increases our desires,
But the Tathāgata's robe does not.
Rather it prevents us from being ashamed,
Causing feelings of repentance and bringing good fortune.
Protecting us from cold, heat, and poisonous insects,
It strengthens our Bodhi-mind, leading us to enlightenment.
Giving us the appearance of monks and freeing us from avarice,
It cuts off the five mistaken views[45] and promotes true practice.
When we respectfully venerate the precious bannerlike *kaśāya,*
King Brahma bestows his blessings on us.
My disciple! Unfold a *kaśāya* as if it were a *stūpa,*
For it gives good fortune, extinguishes crimes, and saves both human and celestial beings.
A true monk is well ordered and respectful,
For his actions are not subject to worldly delusion.
All the Buddhas have praised it as being a fertile field,
The best of all things that give happiness to others.
The *kaśāya* is endowed with miraculous power,
For it is able to plant the seeds of Bodhi-practice.
It helps the sprout of Buddhist practice
To grow as if it were a spring plant,
The wondrous Bodhi-result [enlightenment] being like autumn's fruit.
Hard like adamantine armor, it protects us
From being injured by the poisonous arrow of delusion."

The Bhagavat continued in verse:

"I have now given a short explanation of the ten excellent benefits of a *kaśāya,*
Though I could continue talking about them forever.
If a dragon wears even a single thread of one,
He will be saved from being devoured by a *garuḍa.*
If one wears a *kaśāya* in crossing the sea,
There is no need to fear dragon-fish or demons.
When thunderbolts rain down from an angry heaven,
Wearers of a *kaśāya* need have no fear.
If laymen respectfully preserve a *kaśāya,*
No demons will be able to approach them.
When someone, awakening to the Bodhi-mind and becoming a monk,
Leaves the ordinary world and practices the Way,
All the demon palaces in the whole world shake,
And that person quickly realizes enlightenment."

The various merits of the Way are contained within these ten excellent benefits. We should carefully study these merits, which have been explained in the preceding *sūtra* and verses. We should not, however, read their contents once over lightly, thinking that sufficient. Rather, they should be studied word by word over a long period of time. These excellent benefits are the attributes of a *kaśāya* itself; they are not the result of the long hard training of monks. The Buddha said, "The miraculous power of a *kaśāya* is beyond comprehension." This is true whether one is an ordinary person or a Bodhisattva. In order to realize enlightenment quickly it is necessary to wear a *kaśāya.* No one, past or present, has ever realized enlightenment without wearing one.

Discarded cloth is, as has been previously mentioned, the purest and cleanest material for making a *kaśāya.* Its merit has been clearly expressed in the *sūtras,* rules of discipline, and treatises of the Mahāyāna and Hīnayāna. For more information about this, as well as other materials that may be used for making a *kaśāya,* you should consult with those well versed in Buddhism. All these things have been made clear and correctly transmitted by the Buddhas and patriarchs alone.

The *Mādhyam-āgama-sūtra*[46] states: "Virtuous men! Suppose that someone acts purely but speaks and thinks impurely. If a wise man sees this and becomes angry, it is necessary for him to eliminate his anger. Suppose again that someone acts impurely but speaks and thinks purely. If a wise man sees this and becomes angry, it is necessary for him to eliminate his anger. How can he do this? Virtuous men! He can do so by following in the footsteps of a solitary monk who picks up discarded cloth to make himself a *pāmsūla.* Like the monk, if he finds the cloth soiled with excreta, urine, nasal mucus, or anything else impure, he should pick it up with his left hand and, stretching it out with his right hand, tear off the unsoiled and holeless parts.

"Virtuous men! If someone acts impurely but speaks and thinks purely, do not think about his impure actions; rather simply think about his pure speech and thought. If a wise man sees such a person and becomes angry, he should eliminate his anger in the way I have described."

This is the way a solitary monk picks up discarded cloth to make a *pāmsūla*. Either four or ten types of cloth are used in making a *pāmsūla*. When picking up such cloth, first choose those parts that have no holes, then those that can be washed clean. Do not use those parts that have been stained irrevocably with urine or excreta.

The ten types of discarded cloth are (1) cloth munched by oxen, (2) cloth gnawed by mice, (3) cloth burned by fire, (4) cloth soiled by menstrual blood, (5) cloth soiled by the blood of childbirth, (6) cloth discarded at shrines, (7) cloth discarded in a cemetery, (8) cloth presented as an offering, (9) cloth discarded by government officials, and (10) cloth used to cover the dead.

People throw these ten types of cloth away when they have finished using them. After having been picked up, however, they become the cleanest materials for making a *kaśāya*. All the Buddhas in the three stages of time have praised and used such cloth. Therefore, the *pāmsūla* has been carefully protected and preserved by both human and celestial beings, as well as dragons and so on. We should definitely pick up such cloth to make a *kaśāya*.

How tragic it is that in present-day Japan, peripheral small country that it is, we are unable to find such unexcelled pure and clean materials for making a *kaśāya* no matter how hard we may try! Therefore, we should simply use the materials given to us by faithful donors or ordinary human and celestial beings. Money received from leading a pure life may also be used to buy the material for a *kaśāya*. Materials obtained in this way are not silk, cotton, gold, silver, pearls, jewels, twilled silk, light silk, brocade, or embroidery. They are simply discarded cloth. A *kaśāya* made of such cloth is not called a *pāmsūla* because of its appearance, whether ragged or beautiful. Rather it has been given this name simply because it is in accordance with the Law, having correctly transmitted the essence of all the Buddhas in the three stages of time, the Eye Storehouse of the True Law. When making a further study of its merits, you should seek the guidance of the Buddhas and patriarchs, not that of human and celestial beings.

POSTSCRIPT When I was in Sung China doing zazen on a long raised platform [at one side of the meditation hall], I noticed that every morning at the end of zazen the monk sitting next to me put a *kaśāya* on his head and, placing his hand in *gasshō*, quietly recited the following *gāthā*:

How wondrous this deliverance robe is,
Like a field bestowing unlimited happiness!
Now we unfold the Buddha's teachings,
Making a vow to save all creatures.

At that time I was filled with the deepest emotion and joy that I had ever experienced. Unknowingly I shed so many tears of gratitude that my collar became wet. Why? Although I had opened the *Āgama-sūtras* before and read the verse concerning the placing of the *kaśāya* on one's head, I did not know the details of the manner in which it was to be done. Seeing it at that time before my very eyes filled me with great joy. I said to myself, "Alas! When I was in Japan, no teacher told me about this, nor were there any fine friends to recommend this practice to me. How much time, sorry to say, I uselessly idled away! How fortunate it is that, owing to my good deeds in the past, I have now been able to see this! If I had remained in Japan, how could I have ever seen the monk next to me wearing the Buddha's *kaśāya?*" Filled with these mixed feelings of happiness and sorrow, I cried copiously. Then I vowed to myself, "With compassion for my fellow countrymen I will, unworthy though I am, become an heir to Buddhism, a right receiver of the true Way, and teach them the Law that was correctly transmitted by the Buddhas and patriarchs together with the *kaśāya.*

This vow was not in vain, for, I am happy to say, many laymen and monks are now wearing a *kaśāya*. Those who have received a *kaśāya* should respectfully venerate it constantly. By doing so they receive the highest supreme merit. It is not difficult to hear a word or verse of the Law, for even trees and rocks manifest it. No matter where one may travel, however, it is extremely difficult to encounter the merit of a *kaśāya* that has been correctly transmitted.

In October, the seventeenth year of Chia-shên [1224], two Korean monks, Chi Hyun and Kyung Oon,[47] came to Chingyüan-fu[48] in Sung China. Although they constantly gave lectures on the meaning of the *sūtras,* they were merely scholars of Buddhism. Their appearance was no different from that of ordinary men, for they possessed neither a *kaśāya* nor eating bowls. How tragic it is to be a monk in name but not in reality! This is probably because they also come from a small peripheral country. When Japanese monks go to other countries their appearance tends to resemble [that of] these two.

The Buddha Śākyamuni respectfully venerated his *kaśāya* for twelve years [before he realized enlightenment]. We, his followers, should study this fact. We should stop worshiping heaven, deities, kings, or ministers in pursuit of fame and profit, for nothing can give us greater happiness than respectfully venerating the Buddha's *kaśāya.* *(Shown to the assembly of monks at Kōshō-ji on October 1, the first year of Ninji [1240])*

FOUR

Awakening to the Bodhi-mind

(Hotsu Bodai-shin)

GENERALLY SPEAKING, there are three kinds of mind: *citta,* or the discriminating mind; *hṛdaya,* or the universal mind; and *īrita,* or the essence-embracing mind. It is through the discriminating mind that we are awakened to the Bodhi-mind. *Bodhi* is a Sanskrit word that is known [in China] as "the Way." *Citta* is also Sanskrit and is known [in China] as "the discriminating mind." Without the discriminating mind, we cannot awaken to the Bodhi-mind. This does not mean, however, that the discriminating mind is the same as the Bodhi-mind. Rather it is by using the discriminating mind that we awaken to the Bodhi-mind. To awaken to the Bodhi-mind means to vow and endeavor to help all sentient beings cross over to the other shore [of enlightenment] before doing so ourselves. Though of humble appearance, a person who has awakened to this mind is already the teacher of all mankind.

The Bodhi-mind is something that neither existed from the beginning nor arose recently. It is neither one nor many, neither free nor fixed. It neither exists within us nor extends throughout the universe. It is far from such differences as before and after, being and nonbeing. It is the essence neither of one's self nor of others' selves, nor of both. It does not rise spontaneously but accrues when there is a spiritual communion between sentient beings and the Buddha. We neither receive it from the Buddhas or Bodhisattvas nor produce it through our own ability, for as has been stated, it arises only when we have a spiritual communion with the Buddha.

The opportunity to awaken to the Bodhi-mind is, in general, limited to human beings. There are a few in the eight difficult realms,[1] however, who have done so. There are those who, after having awakened to the Bodhi-mind, practice the Way for innumerable *kalpas* of time. Some of them eventually decide to become Buddhas, while others choose first to help all sentient beings cross over to the other shore, thereby sacrificing their own Buddhahood.

Those who have awakened to the Bodhi-mind constantly endeavor in body, word, and mind to arouse this mind in all sentient beings and lead them to the Way. Simply fulfilling the worldly desires of human beings, however, is not what is meant by benefiting them. Awakening to the Bodhi-mind and practice-enlightenment[2] are superior to anything else, for these things are beyond delusion and enlightenment, the three worlds, and the attainment of Śrāvakas and Pratyekabuddhas.

The Bodhisattva Kāśyapa praised the Buddha Śākyamuni with the following verse:

> Awakening to the Bodhi-mind and enlightenment are two,
> But there is no difference between them,
> Though the former is more difficult to attain than the latter.
> We respect this awakening, for it means to help
> All sentient beings realize enlightenment before doing so ourselves.
> Those who have awakened to this mind
> Are already the masters of celestial and human beings,
> The superiors of Śrāvakas and Pratyekabuddhas.
> Awakening to the Bodhi-mind is beyond anything in the three worlds,
> The highest spirit of them all.

Awakening to the Bodhi-mind means, in the first instance, to vow to help all sentient beings realize enlightenment before doing so ourselves. Thereafter we should meet innumerable Buddhas and further arouse the Bodhi-mind through listening to their teachings, just as frost accumulates on snow.

To realize enlightenment is to attain the Buddha-result, the supreme Bodhi-wisdom. When comparing the supreme Bodhi-wisdom [ultimate enlightenment] with awakening to the Bodhi-mind, the former seems like a gigantic fire raging through the entire universe, the latter like a firefly. The difference between these two disappears, however, when we vow to help others realize enlightenment before doing so ourselves. [The Buddha Śākyamuni said,] "I have always given thought to how I could cause all creatures to enter the highest supreme Way and quickly become Buddhas." These words are the eternal life of the Tathāgata. A Buddha awakened to the Bodhi-mind practices the Way and realizes enlightenment in this manner.

To benefit others means to help them realize enlightenment, as has been previously stated, before doing so ourselves. After having aroused this mind, furthermore, we should not think of becoming a Buddha. Even though we have acquired sufficient merit to realize Buddhahood, we should place it at the disposal of all beings in order that they may realize the Way. This mind comes neither from self nor from other people or things. After awakening to this mind, everything we touch is changed, the earth becoming gold and the ocean nectar. When this happens even soil, sand, rocks, and pebbles manifest the Bodhi-mind, as do ocean spray, bubbles, and flames. Therefore, to offer others our castle, family, seven treasures, servants, head, brain, flesh, and limbs is a living manifestation of the Bodhi-mind. Even the discriminating mind, which is neither far away nor near at hand, neither in self nor in others, becomes the equivalent of awakening to the Bodhi-mind if we constantly keep in mind our vow to help others realize enlightenment before doing so ourselves. Hence, offering everything to which we are attached, be it grass, trees, tiles, pebbles, gold, silver, or rare treasures, for the sake of the Bodhi-mind is also equivalent to awakening to that mind.

Both the Bodhi-mind and all things exist within causal relationships. Therefore when we arouse this spirit for even a moment, all things aid in its growth. Awakening to the Bodhi-mind and realizing enlightenment are both subject to momentary birth and decay. If this were not true, neither momentary past wrong would disappear nor momentary present good appear. Only the Tathāgata has clarified the length of a "moment," for it is he alone who is able to produce and speak an entire word within as short a time as a *kṣaṇa*.

It is said that sixty-five *kṣaṇas* pass in the space of time it takes a young man in the prime of life to snap his fingers. Ordinary men, however, though they are aware of longer periods of time, are ignorant of this fact, just as they do not realize that their body and mind are in a constant state of birth and decay. Furthermore, they are unaware that there are 6,400,099,980 *kṣaṇas* in twenty-four hours, during which time their body and mind are also in a constant state of birth and decay. It is for these reasons that they are unable to awaken to the Bodhi-mind. Those who neither believe nor know the Law inevitably lack faith in the truth of momentary birth and decay, while those who have realized the supreme Mind of the Tathāgata, the Eye Storehouse of the True Law, inevitably believe it. Though we have been fortunate enough to have encountered the Tathāgata's teachings and seem to have understood them, in reality we have only understood that part which we [mistakenly] believe to be the whole, which is longer than 120 *kṣaṇas*. The fact that we cannot understand all of the Bhagavat's teachings is similar to our ignorance of the length of one *kṣaṇa*. We students of Buddhism should not be proud of our understanding, being, as we are, ignorant of both the minimum and maximum [periods of time].

It is the power of the Tathāgata's enlightenment that enables sentient beings throughout the universe to see. Life constantly changes, moment by moment, in each of its stages, whether we want it to or not. Without even a moment's pause our karma causes us to transmigrate continuously. Though subject to transmigration in this way, we should still quickly make the vow to help others realize enlightenment before doing so ourselves. Even if, deeply attached to body and mind, we refuse to awaken to the Bodhi-mind, there is no escape from birth, old age, sickness, and death, for in the long run, neither body nor mind belongs to us. Life, ever subject to birth and decay, passes by more quickly than we realize.

Once, during the Buddha Śākyamuni's lifetime, a monk came to him and, after having prostrated himself, asked, "Why does life pass by so quickly?" The Buddha answered, "Even if I explained it to you, you wouldn't understand." The monk then asked, "Isn't there a parable that explains it clearly?" The Buddha answered, "Yes, there is. I'll tell it to you. Suppose there were four skillful archers who, picking up their bows and arrows, stood back to back, ready to shoot their arrows in the four directions. If, at that time, a fast runner came by and said, 'Shoot your arrows at the same time, and I'll catch them all before they touch the ground,' do you think he would be a very fast runner?" The monk answered, "Indeed so, Bhagavat!" Continuing his explanation, the Buddha said, "Though such a man is a very fast runner, he is not the equal of a *yakṣa*[3] running on the ground, who himself is not the equal of a *yakṣa* flying through the air, while even the latter is not the equal of the Four-Quarter Kings.[4] Even these kings, however, cannot run faster than the chariots of the sun and moon, which themselves are not the equal of their celestial attendants. Although all of the preceding are very fast, they are no match for life, which, without a moment's pause, is in a constant state of birth and decay."

We monks should not forget for even a moment that our life is in a constant state of birth and decay. If, constantly keeping this in mind, we vow to help others cross over to the other shore before doing so ourselves, eternal life immediately appears before us. The Buddhas in the three stages of time and ten directions, together with the seven past Buddhas,[5] the twenty-eight patriarchs in India and the six in China, and the other patriarchs who have transmitted the supreme Mind of the Buddha—the Eye Storehouse of the True Law—have all preserved this Bodhi-mind. Those who have not awakened to the Bodhi-mind cannot be considered to be patriarchs.

Question 120 of the *Ch'an-yüan Ch'ing-kuei* asks, "Is enlightenment identical with the Bodhi-mind?" We should clearly understand that realizing the Bodhi-mind is the first step in the study of the Way of the Buddhas and patriarchs and, at the same time, is in accordance with their teachings. To realize the Bodhi-mind means to comprehend it thoroughly, to become enlightened. This enlightenment, however, is not equal to that of a Buddha. Even if one quickly realizes the ten stages[6] [in which the Wisdom of a Buddha is developed] he is still a Bodhisattva. The twenty-eight patriarchs in India, the six in China, as well as the various other great patriarchs were Bodhisattvas, not Buddhas, Śrāvakas, or Pratyekabuddhas.

Of those presently practicing the Way there is not one who clearly realizes that he is a Bodhisattva, not a Śrāvaka. How regrettable it is that the Way of the patriarchs has been lost in this age of degenerate Buddhism, because such as these, willfully calling themselves monks, are ignorant of this fact! Therefore, whether layman or monk, living in the world of celestial beings or humans, subject to pain or pleasure, we should quickly make the vow to help others cross over to the other shore before doing so ourselves. Even though the world of sentient beings is neither limited nor unlimited, we should arouse this mind, for it is none other than the Bodhi-mind.

It is said that when a Bodhisattva of the highest level of attainment[7] is about to descend to the human world he makes the following parting remarks to the celestial occupants of Tuṣita Heaven: "Because it preserves the Three Treasures, the Bodhi-mind is the way to enlightenment." We should clearly realize that the Three Treasures are preserved by the power of the Bodhi-mind. After this mind has once been aroused, it should be carefully and diligently protected.

The Buddha Śākyamuni said, "The Bodhi-mind is the one thing that a Bodhisattva should protect. A Bodhisattva always protects the Bodhi-mind in the same way that ordinary people protect their children, a one-eyed man protects his remaining eye, or people traveling in the wilderness protect their guide. This is the way in which a Bodhisattva protects the Bodhi-mind, for by doing so he is able to realize the supreme Bodhi-wisdom. Furthermore, having done this, he is now endowed with the four merits of enlightenment—eternity, bliss, absolute Self, and purity. It is because this is the highest supreme enlightenment that a Bodhisattva protects the Bodhi-mind."

This is the way in which the Buddha Śākyamuni clarified the meaning of protecting the Bodhi-mind. The reason that Bodhisattvas guard it so carefully and diligently may be explained by making the following comparison with phenomena in the ordinary world. There are three kinds of things that, though born, seldom reach maturity. One of them is a fish's eggs, another the fruit of the *āmra* tree,[8] and the third a Bodhisattva who has awakened to the Bodhi-mind. In addition there are many Bodhisattvas who become lax in their practice and lose this mind. We should be careful to protect this mind so that the same thing does not happen to us. Another reason a Bodhisattva tends to lose the Bodhi-mind in the early stages of his practice is that often he is unable to meet a true master and hear the true Law. The result is that he is likely to deny the existence of causality, enlightenment, the Three Treasures, the three worlds, and so on. Meaninglessly becoming attached to the five desires, he will be unable to realize enlightenment in the future.

Pāpīyas and his retainers sometimes disguise themselves as Buddhas, parents, Buddhist masters, relatives, and celestial beings in order to hinder trainees in their practice. Approaching a Bodhisattva, they deceitfully say to him, "Regrettably, the practice of the Way requires a long period of time during which you will have to undergo much suffering. It would be better if you first attained enlightenment for yourself before attempting to help others cross over to the other shore." Hearing these words, the Bodhisattva becomes lax in his practice and tends to lose the Bodhi-mind. We should clearly realize that statements like this are the work of demons and not to be followed. Without becoming lax in our vow and endeavors to help others cross over to the other shore before doing so ourselves, we should clearly realize that any statements that encourage us to do so should not be followed, for they are the teachings of demons, non-Buddhist religions, and bad friends.

"There are four kinds of demons: (1) the demon of desires, (2) the demon of the five aggregates, (3) the demon of death, and (4) Pāpīyas. The demon of desire is said to have either 108 or 84,000 desires. The demon of the five aggregates is composed of the source of desires. This source can be further divided into the four elements forming the body and its complements. These complements, the six sense organs, are called *rūpa-skandha*. The perception of the 108 desires and so on is called *vedanā-skandha*. The mental function that divides and unites various thoughts is called *samjñā-skandha*. The mental function, arising from likes and dislikes, that produces avarice, anger, and so on is called *samskāra-skandha.* The six consciousnesses, arising from the six sense organs that divide and unite all mental phenomena, are called *vijñāna-skandha.*[9]

"The demon of death, through transiency, destroys the continuity of the five aggregates and deprives the body of consciousness, temperature, and life. Pāpīyas is the king of the world of desire. Because of his deep attachment to and search for worldly pleasures, he falls victim to wrong views, hating and envying all who practice the Way. *Māra* [demon] is a Sanskrit word that is translated into Chinese as 'life-depriving person' [*nêng-to-ming-chê*]. Of the four kinds of demons, only the demon of death is able to physically deprive men of their life, hence he is also known as 'the destroyer.' The other demons, though able to deprive men of their wisdom, can only indirectly deprive them of their lives.

"Someone asked, 'Since the three other kinds of demons are included in the demon of the five aggregates, why are they divided into the four kinds?' He answered, 'There is really only one demon, but we describe him as four in order to explain his nature.' "

The preceding discourse was given by the Patriarch Nāgārjuna. We should study it diligently, taking care not to fall victim to demons or lose the Bodhi-mind. This is the meaning of protecting the Bodhi-mind. *(Shown to the assembly of monks at Yoshimine-dera, Yoshida-ken [county], Echizen, on February 14, the second year of Kangen [1244])*

FIVE

Veneration of the Buddhas

(Kuyō Shobutsu)

THE BUDDHA ŚĀKYAMUNI said in verse:

"Without past time
No past Buddhas would have been;
Without the Buddhas of the past
No one could become a monk."

We should clearly realize that there have been various Buddhas in the three stages of time. In regard to the Buddhas in the past, however, we should not assert that they either had or did not have a beginning, for the discussion of problems like this is not part of the study of Buddhism. If we respectfully venerate the various past Buddhas, enter the monkhood, and train under a master, we will, thanks to the merit we have realized, inevitably become Buddhas ourselves. There has never been anyone who has realized Buddhahood without having venerated at least one Buddha, for therein lies the origin of Buddhahood.

The *Fo-pên-hsing-chi sūtra*[1] states: "The Buddha Śākyamuni said to the Venerable Maudgalyāyana, 'In the past I sowed the seeds of goodness under innumerable Bhagavats and sought the supreme Bodhi-wisdom. Maudgalyāyana! In the past I once became King Cakravarti and encountered three billion Buddhas who were all named Śākyamuni. I revered and served all of them—from Tathāgatas to Śrāvakas—respectfully making venerative offerings to them of the four articles: clothing, food and drink, bedding, and medicine. At that time, however, none of these Buddhas prophesied that I would realize the supreme Bodhi-wisdom, become a Buddha, or be called a Lokavid,[2] Śāsta-deva-manusyānām,[3] Buddha, or Bhagavat in the future.

" 'Maudgalyāyana! In the past I once became King Cakravarti and encountered eight hundred million Buddhas who were all named the Buddha Dīpaṃkara.[4] I revered and respected all of them—from Tathāgatas to Śrāvakas—reverently making venerative offerings to them of clothing, food and drink, bedding, medicine, banners, canopies, flowers, and incense. At that time, however, none of these Buddhas prophesied that I would realize the supreme Bodhi-wisdom, become a Buddha, or be called a Lokavid, Śāsta-deva-manusyānām, Buddha, or Bhagavat in the future.

" 'Maudgalyāyana! In the past I once became King Cakravarti and encountered three hundred million Buddhas who were all named the Buddha Puṣya.[5] I made venerative offerings of the four articles to all of them, so that they were in want of nothing. At that time, however, none of these Buddhas prophesied that I would realize enlightenment.' "

Apart from the above offerings, the Buddha Śākyamuni, who had become King Cakravarti, also made venerative offerings to many other Buddhas. These venerative offerings of King Cakravarti, the ruler of the world and king of the universe, were so plentiful as to be beyond the comprehension of present-day ordinary men. Even had the Buddha himself attempted to explain how plentiful they were, it would still have been beyond their comprehension.

The eighth section, entitled "Pure Views," of the *Buddhagarbha-sūtra*[6] states: "The Buddha Śākyamuni told Śāriputra, 'In the past, when I was searching for the supreme Bodhi-wisdom, I encountered three billion Buddhas who were all named Śākyamuni. At that time I became King Cakravarti and made venerative offerings to them and their disciples of clothing, food and drink, bedding, and medicine for my entire life. Although I did this all for the sake of attaining the supreme Bodhi-wisdom, none of these Buddhas prophesied that I would become a Buddha in the future, for I had made the offerings with the expectation of gaining enlightenment.

" 'Śāriputra! In the past I encountered eight thousand Buddhas who were all named Dīpaṃkara. At that time I became King Cakravarti and made venerative offerings to them and their disciples of clothing, food and drink, bedding, and medicine for my entire life. Although I did this all for the sake of attaining the supreme Bodhi-wisdom, none of these Buddhas prophesied that I would become a Buddha in the future, for I had made the offerings with the expectation of gaining enlightenment.

" 'Śāriputra! In the past I encountered sixty thousand Buddhas who were all named Kuang-ming.[7] At that time I became King Cakravarti and made venerative offerings to them and their disciples of clothing, food and drink, bedding, and medicine for my entire life. Although I did this all for the sake of attaining the supreme Bodhi-wisdom, none of these Buddhas prophesied that I would become a Buddha in the future, for I had made the offerings with the expectation of gaining enlightenment.

" 'Śāriputra! In the past I encountered three hundred million Buddhas who were all named Puṣya. At that time I became King Cakravarti and made venerative offerings to them of the four articles. None of these Buddhas, however, prophesied that I would become a Buddha in the future, for I had made the offerings with the expectation of gaining enlightenment.

" 'Śāriputra! In the past I encountered eighteen thousand Buddhas who, living in the Shang-pa *kalpa* age,[8] were all named Shan-wang.[9] Shaving my head and putting on a monk's robe, I trained under them in search of the supreme Bodhi-wisdom. None of these Buddhas, however, prophesied that

I would become a Buddha in the future, for I had trained under them with the expectation of gaining enlightenment.

" 'Śāriputra! In the past I encountered five hundred Buddhas who were all named Hua-shang.[10] At that time I became King Cakravarti and made venerative offerings to them and their disciples so that they were in want of nothing. None of them, however, prophesied that I would become a Buddha, for I had made the offerings with the expectation of gaining enlightenment.

" 'Śāriputra! In the past I encountered five hundred Buddhas who were all named Wei-tê.[11] At that time I made venerative offerings to them so that they were in want of nothing. None of them, however, prophesied that I would become a Buddha, for I had made the offerings with the expectation of gaining enlightenment.

" 'Śāriputra! In the past I encountered two thousand Buddhas who were all named Kauṇḍinya.[12] At that time I became King Cakravarti and made venerative offerings to them so that they were in want of nothing. None of them, however, prophesied that I would become a Buddha, for I had made the offerings with the expectation of gaining enlightenment.

" 'Śāriputra! In the past I encountered nine thousand Buddhas who were all named Kāśyapa. At that time I made venerative offerings to them and their disciples of the four articles. None of them, however, prophesied that I would become a Buddha, for I had made the offerings with the expectation of gaining enlightenment.

" 'Sāriputra! In the past there was a period ten thousand *kalpas* long during which no [true] Buddha appeared. During the first five hundred *kalpas* of that period there were ninety thousand Pratyekabuddhas. Throughout my life I revered and respected them, making venerative offerings of clothing, food and drink, bedding, and medicine. During the next five hundred *kalpas* I did the same thing for eight thousand, four hundred billion Pratyekabuddhas.

" 'Śāriputra! After this period of one thousand *kalpas* no more Pratyekabuddhas appeared. At that time I died in the human world and was reborn in Brahma Heaven, where I became King Brahma. For the next five hundred *kalpas* I continued to be reborn in Brahma Heaven, where I became King Brahma, without at any time being reborn in the human world. After this period of five hundred *kalpas* I was born as the ruler of the human world before being reborn in the heaven of the Four-Quarter Kings. Upon my death there I was reborn in Trāyastriṃśa Heaven,[13] where I became King Śakrendra. For five hundred *kalpas* of time I went through continuous transmigration until I was born in the human world, whereafter, five hundred *kalpas* later, I was reborn in Brahma Heaven to become King Brahma.

" 'Śāriputra! During a period of nine thousand *kalpas,* with the exception of the one time I was born in the human world, I continued to be reborn in heaven. When this period was about to end I was born in Ābhāsvara Heaven[14] before being reborn in the newly formed Brahma Heaven. Śāriputra! During these nine thousand *kalpas* many beings fell into the three evil worlds because there were neither Buddhas nor Pratyekabuddhas.

" 'Śāriputra! Following this ten-thousand-*kalpa*-long period a single Buddha appeared. He was named the Buddha P'u-shou[15] and was also known as the one who (1) has come from the world of Truth, (2) is worthy of offerings, (3) knows everything perfectly, (4) sees the Truth and walks the Way satisfactorily, (5) has gone to the world of enlightenment, (6) understands the world, (7) is unsurpassed by anyone else, (8) controls men, (9) teaches celestial and human beings, and (10) is honored by the people of the world.[16] After my life in Brahma Heaven had ended, I was reborn in the human world, where I became King Cakravarti and was known as Kung-t'ien.[17] For a period of ninety thousand years I made venerative offerings of every conceivable kind to the Buddha P'u-shou and nine billion other monks for the sake of attaining the highest supreme enlightenment. Still, the Buddha P'u-shou did not prophesy that I would become a Buddha in the future, for I had not yet realized that all things are the manifestation of the Truth and was attached to my own selfish views.

" 'Śāriputra! Later, during this same *kalpa,* one hundred Buddhas appeared, each with a different name. At that time I became King Cakravarti and made venerative offerings of every conceivable kind to them and their disciples for my entire life, hoping to attain the supreme Bodhi-wisdom. None of these Buddhas, however, prophesied that I would become a Buddha in the future, for I had made the offerings with the expectation of gaining enlightenment.

" 'Śāriputra! During the seven hundredth *asaṃkhya-kalpa*[18] I encountered one thousand Buddhas who were all named Jambudvīpa.[19] At that time I made venerative offerings to them of the four articles for my entire life. None of these Buddhas, however, prophesied that I would become a Buddha, for I had made the offerings with the expectation of gaining enlightenment.

" 'Śāriputra! During the same *kalpa* I encountered six million, two hundred thousand Buddhas who were all named Chien-i-ch'ieh-i.[20] At that time I became King Cakravarti and made venerative offerings of every conceivable kind to them and their disciples for my entire life. None of these Buddhas however, prophesied that I would become a Buddha, for I had made the offerings with the expectation of gaining enlightenment.

" 'Śāriputra! During the same *kalpa* I encountered eighty-four Buddhas who were all named Ti-hsiang.[21] At that time I became King Cakravarti and made venerative offerings of every conceivable kind to them and their disciples for my entire life. None of these Buddhas, however, prophesied that I would become a Buddha, for I had made the offerings with the expectation of gaining enlightenment.

" 'Śāriputra! During the same *kalpa* I encountered fifteen Buddhas who were all named Canda.[22] At that time I became King Cakravarti and made venerative offerings of every conceivable kind to them and their disciples for my entire life. None of these Buddhas, however, prophesied that I would become a Buddha, for I had made the offerings with the expectation of gaining enlightenment.

" 'Śāriputra! During the same *kalpa* I encountered sixty-two Buddhas who were all named Shan-chi.[23] At that time I became King Cakravarti and made venerative offerings of every conceivable kind to them for my entire life. None of these Buddhas, however, prophesied that I would become a Buddha, for I had made the offerings with the expectation of gaining enlightenment.

" 'I went through continuous transmigration until I encountered the Buddha Dīpaṃkara and realized the stage of enlightenment in which the real nature of the phenomenal world is understood. At that time he prophesied that I would, after the passage of innumerable *kalpas,* become a Buddha in the future. I was to be named the Buddha Śākyamuni and also known as the one who (1) has come from the world of Truth, (2) is worthy of offerings, (3) knows everything perfectly, (4) sees the Truth and walks the Way satisfactorily, (5) has gone to the world of enlightenment, (6) understands the world, (7) is unsurpassed by anyone else, (8) controls men, (9) teaches celestial and human beings, and (10) is honored by the people of the world.' "

From the time the Buddha Śākyamuni first encountered three billion Buddhas named Śākyamuni up through the time he met the Buddha Dīpaṃkara, he, as King Cakravarti, respectfully made venerative offerings to them for his entire life. King Cakravarti lived to be more than eighty thousand years old, during which time he made venerative offerings of every conceivable kind. The Buddha Dīpaṃkara is also known as Ting-kuang.[24] Both the *Fo-pên-hsing-chi sūtra* and the *Buddhagarbha-sūtra* agree that the Buddha Śākyamuni encountered three billion Buddhas named Śākyamuni.

In the first *asaṃkhya-kalpa* the Bodhisattva Śākyamuni encountered, served, and made venerative offerings to seventy-five thousand Buddhas, the first of whom was named Śākyamuni and the last Ratnaśikhi.[25] In the second *asaṃkhya-kalpa* he encountered, served, and made venerative offerings to seventy-six thousand Buddhas, the first of whom was named Ratnaśikhi and the last Dīpaṃkara. Further, in the third *asaṃkhya-kalpa,* he encountered, served, and made venerative offerings to seventy-seven thousand Buddhas, the first of whom was named Dīpaṃkara and the last Vipassī.[26] Finally, during the following ninety-one *kalpas,* having realized the meaning of causation, he encountered, served, and made venerative offerings to six Buddhas, the first of whom was named Vipassī and the last Kāśyapa.

The way in which the Bodhisattva Śākyamuni gladly made venerative offerings to the various Buddhas of his life, castle, family, seven treasures, servants, and so on for innumerable *kalpas* is beyond the comprehension of ordinary men. Sometimes he offered silver bowls filled to the brim with golden unhulled rice, and sometimes gold and silver bowls filled to the brim with millet worthy of the seven treasures. In addition to these he also presented red beans, various kinds of flowers, incense made from the wood of the *candana* and *agara* trees, and so forth. Once he made a venerative offering to the Buddha Dīpaṃkara of five-stalked blue lotus flowers that he had bought for five hundred pieces of gold. On another occasion he presented him with deer leather.

We should quickly make venerative offerings to the Buddhas while there is still time, taking care not to spend our lives meaninglessly. Such offerings, however, are not made to the various Buddhas because they have need of them. For example, even though our offerings be gold, silver, incense, or flowers, they are of no use to the Buddhas. The reason that the Buddhas accept them is simply because, out of their great compassion, they wish to increase the merits of all beings.

The twenty-second section of the *Mahāparinirvāṇa-sūtra*[27] states: "The Buddha said, 'Virtuous men! One hundred billion *kalpas* ago the Buddha Śākyamuni lived in a world known as Sahā.[28] In this world he was also known as the one who (1) has come from the world of Truth, (2) is worthy of offerings, (3) knows everything perfectly, (4) sees the Truth and walks the Way satisfactorily, (5) has gone to the world of enlightenment, (6) understands the world, (7) is unsurpassed by anyone else (8), controls men, (9) teaches celestial and human beings, and (10) is honored by the people of the world. At that time he taught this *Mahāparinirvāṇa-sūtra* for the sake of all beings. Having been informed about this by a friend, I decided to listen to the Buddha Śākyamuni. I was so overjoyed upon hearing him speak that I decided to make venerative offerings to him. Coming from a poor family, however, I had nothing to give him. I thought about selling myself; but, being of little merit, I was unable to do so.

" 'As I was walking home I happened to meet a man along the way. In the course of our conversation I said to him, "I have been thinking about selling myself, and I am wondering if you might not be interested in buying me." He answered, "It is difficult to fulfill my needs, but if you are able to do so, I will buy you." I asked him, "What are your needs?" He answered, "I have a serious illness which, according to the doctor's prescription, requires that I eat three *liang*[29] of human flesh a day. If you are able to supply me with this amount of your flesh every day, I will give you five pieces of gold." Upon hearing this, I was delighted and said to him, "Give me the money and seven days to put my affairs in order." He answered, "Seven days is too long; I'll give you one day."

" 'Virtuous men! At that time I immediately took the money and, returning to where the Buddha was, prostrated myself before him, presenting the five pieces of gold. Thereafter I wholeheartedly listened to him as he continued to expound the *Mahāparinirvāṇa-sūtra*. Unfortunately, however, because of my stupidity, I was only able to understand the following verse:

> The Tathāgata who has realized the Truth
> Is eternally free from birth and death.
> If you listen to him with sincerity,
> Infinite happiness will be yours.

" 'Bearing this verse in mind, I returned to the sick man's house, where I gave him three *liang* of my flesh every day. Because I constantly recited the preceding verse, however, I felt no pain. A month passed in this way, by the end of which time the sick man had recovered from his illness. As for myself, I too returned to normal and was left without even a single scar. Upon seeing my body whole again, I awoke to the highest supreme Bodhi-mind. Considering the great merit of even this single verse of the *sūtra,* how much greater would that merit be which came from having read and recited it in its entirety!

" 'After having seen the benefits of this *sūtra* I redoubled my efforts to seek the supreme Bodhi-wisdom and, as the Buddha Śākyamuni, to realize the Way in the future. Virtuous men! I am now able to teach this *sūtra* to human and celestial beings because of the vast merit with which even one of its verses is endowed. The deepest secret storehouse of the teachings of all the Buddhas is contained in this profound *sūtra,* whose merits are immeasurable.' "

The Bodhisattva who sold himself at that time was the predecessor of the present Buddha Śākyamuni. According to other *sūtras,* this Bodhisattva, as a tilemaker named Ta-kuang-ming,[30] respectfully made venerative offerings to the Buddha Śākyamuni of the past at the beginning of the first *asaṃkhya-kalpa.* The venerative offerings that he made to this Buddha and his disciples consisted of three articles: meditation cushions, sweetened water, and tapers. He also made the following vow: "When I realize Buddhahood, may my name, life span, disciples, and country be like those of the Buddha Śākyamuni!"

The vow that he made at that time has now been realized. Therefore, when making venerative offerings to the Buddhas we should not be concerned about whether or not we personally or our families are poor. Selling oneself to make venerative offerings to the Buddhas is the true Law of our great teacher the Buddha Śākyamuni. Who could fail to be deeply moved and overjoyed by such an act? The daily giving of three *liang* of one's flesh to a sick man is not something that could be endured by an ordinary man, no matter how well intentioned he might be. The Bodhisattva Śākyamuni was able to do so because of his deep desire to make venerative offerings to the Buddha. We are now able to hear the Tathāgata's true Law because of his willingness to sacrifice his very flesh.

The value of the preceding verse is far beyond that of five pieces of gold. The merit of this verse is truly profound, for it has been transmitted from Buddha to Buddha, from life to life, over innumerable *kalpas* of time. We disciples of the Buddha should preserve and deeply revere this teaching. The Buddha has already taught the great merit of even this one verse. We should realize, then, how truly great the merit is that comes from preserving the entire *sūtra.*

The *Saddharma-puṇḍarīka-sūtra* states: "If someone respectfully makes venerative offerings of flowers, incense, banners, or canopies to the *stūpas,* statues, and portraits of the Buddha, he will eventually realize the Way. This is also true if his venerative offerings consist of having someone make music by striking drums and various kinds of gongs, blowing horns, reed organs, or flutes, or playing harplike instruments. Joyously singing of the virtues of the Buddha or praising him quietly are further acts of equivalent merit. Even though the person wishing to venerate a portrait of the Buddha does so in a disturbed state of mind, with an offering consisting of as little as a single flower, still he will be able to encounter innumerable Buddhas. Furthermore, if such a person venerates the Buddha by prostrating himself before a statue of the Buddha, or makes a *gasshō* with either one or both hands, or even merely lowers his head slightly, he will encounter innumerable Buddhas and, naturally realizing the supreme Way, be able to assist innumerable beings to cross over to the other shore."

Making venerative offerings in this way is the essence and life of the Buddhas in the three stages of time. Such actions on the part of these Buddhas should become the ideals toward which we strive, taking care, as Zen Master Shih-t'ou Wu-chi[31] has said, not to waste our time meaninglessly. Through the merit of having made venerative offerings we are able to realize Buddhahood. This has been true in the past, just as it is in the present and will be in the future, for the Truth is one, not two or three. Making venerative offerings to the Buddhas, then, is the cause of our realizing Buddhahood.

The Patriarch Nāgārjuna said, "Those who seek Buddhahood can realize their goal no matter how small an act they perform. Burning a pinch of incense, presenting a flower, or reciting the verse 'We take refuge in the Buddha' are all acts that fall into this category."

Even though these words originate with the Patriarch Nāgārjuna [not the Buddha Śākyamuni], we should still esteem them. Still more should we respect the teachings of our great teacher the Buddha Śākyamuni, which the Patriarch Nāgārjuna correctly transmitted. How fortunate we are to have been able to climb the treasure mountain and enter the treasure ocean of the Way! It is entirely due to the merit of having venerated the Buddhas for innumerable *kalpas* of time that we have been able to come into possession of this treasure. There is no doubt that we will be able to realize Buddhahood, for this is the teaching of the Buddha Śākyamuni.

Nāgārjuna continued: "Small causes produce great results. If someone, seeking the Way, burns a pinch of incense, or recites the verse 'We take refuge in the Buddha,' he will definitely realize Buddhahood. If, further, he realizes that all things are the manifestation of the Truth, that is to say, that all things are beyond birth and death, and acts according to the principles of causation, he cannot help realizing enlightenment."

The Patriarch Nāgārjuna has correctly transmitted these teachings of the Bhagavat himself. Even those of Nāgārjuna's teachings that originated with him are far more valuable than those of other masters. How fortunate we are to have been able to encounter the correctly transmitted teachings of the Buddha! These excellent teachings should not be compared with those mistaken theories of ordinary Chinese teachers.

The Patriarch Nāgārjuna continued: "The various Buddhas venerate the Law because of their respect for it. At the same time they take the Law as their master because they realize that all things are the manifestation of the Truth. Someone asked, 'Why do the Buddhas venerate the Law within others rather than within themselves?' The Buddha answered, 'Because it is customary to do so. If a monk wishes to venerate the Law-treasure he should not venerate the Law within himself; rather, he should venerate those who know, possess, and understand the Law. I also do the same, that is to say, even though the Law is within me I venerate the Law within other Buddhas.' Someone asked, 'Why do you venerate merit when you have no need of any further merit?' The Buddha answered, 'As a result of my training in innumerable past *kalpas* I have realized great merit and done various good acts. Still, because of my respect for merit I venerate it without seeking any reward.'

"Once, when the Buddha Śākyamuni was still alive, there was a blind monk who was sewing his robes though he could not see them. When his needle accidentally came unthreaded, he said, 'Is there no merit-loving person who will rethread my needle?' The Buddha came to him and said, 'Since I am a merit-loving person, I will rethread your needle.' Upon hearing the Buddha's voice, the blind monk realized who he was talking to. Quickly standing up and putting on his robes, he prostrated himself before the Buddha, saying, 'Why do you say you love merit when, as a Buddha, you have already realized perfect merit?' The Buddha answered, 'Although I have indeed realized perfect merit, I am deeply aware of the causes and rewards of merit, as well as its power. Because of this knowledge I have now realized the supreme Bodhi-wisdom. My love of merit is the result of this realization.' After having praised merit in this way, the Buddha continued to freely expound the Law. As a result the blind monk was able to see the Truth [realize enlightenment] more clearly than had his physical eyes been unimpaired."

I heard this story one night in my late master's [Ju-ching's] room. Later, while examining the tenth section of the *Mahāprajñāpāramitā* treatise,[32] I was able to verify its authenticity. The patriarchs have already transmitted the Law without omitting anything. In addition, they have clearly shown that the Buddha Śākyamuni and the various other Buddhas have all eternally taken the Law as their great master. Taking the Law as one's great master means to respectfully venerate the Three Treasures. Since innumerable *kalpas* in the past the various Buddhas have realized great merit and planted the seeds of goodness without seeking anything in return. They simply respected merit and venerated it. Even though the Buddha Sākyamuni had realized the supreme Bodhi-wisdom, he helped the blind monk thread his needle out of his love for even a little merit. This story truly tells us what the merit of Buddhahood is.

The merit of Buddhahood and the true nature of the Law are far beyond the comprehension of present-day ordinary men. They think that even wrong actions are manifestations of the Truth, and that it is correct to train with the expectation of achieving enlightenment. Even though they are able to comprehend eighty thousand *kalpas* of time, with mistaken views like these they inevitably hold that whatever existed in the past will disappear in the future. Why are such people unable to realize the true nature of the Law? Because they have failed to comprehend, as the Buddhas have, that all things are the manifestation of the Truth.

There are ten ways of venerating a Buddha: (1) making venerative offerings to the body [of a Buddha], (2) making venerative offerings to a *caitya,* (3) making venerative offerings to a *stūpa,* (4) making venerative offerings to a Buddha where there is no mausoleum, (5) personally making venerative offerings, (6) urging others to make venerative offerings, (7) making venerative offerings of goods and money, (8) making venerative offerings with a devout mind, (9) making venerative offerings with a nonseeking mind, and (10) making a venerative offering of one's practice of the Way.

The first way of veneration means to make offerings to the physical body of a Buddha. The second means to make offerings to a Buddhist mausoleum. According to the *Mahāsaṃghikā-vinaya,*[33] a *stūpa* receives its name from the fact that relics of the Buddha are enshrined therein. A *caitya,* on the other hand, is so named because it does not contain such relics. Sometimes, however, both of these are called by the latter name. *Stūpa* is a Sanskrit word that means [in Chinese] "four-cornered tomb" or "mausoleum." The word [pronounced as] *chih-chêng* [in Chinese], as found in the *Āgama-sūtras,* also refers to a *caitya.*

Although a *stūpa* and a *caitya* are similar, Abbot Hui-ssŭ of Nan-yüeh has written in his work *Fa-hua-ch'an-fa:*[34] "We respectfully prostrate ourselves before the relics and statues of the Buddha, as well as *caityas, stūpas,* the Buddha Prabhūtaratna,[35] and those *stūpas* dedicated to him." This clearly shows that *stūpas, caityas,* relics, and statues of the Buddha are all different.

The thirty-third section of the *Mahāsaṃghikā-vinaya* states: "There is the following story concerning the method of making a *stūpa.* When the Buddha Śākyamuni was living and expounding the Law in the country of Kośala,[36] he happened to meet a Brāhman who was tilling his field. When the latter saw the Bhagavat passing by, he laid his cattle prod on the ground and prostrated himself before the Buddha. Seeing this, the Buddha smiled. Some monks who noticed this asked the Buddha, 'Please tell us what prompted you to smile.' He answered, 'This Brāhman has just prostrated himself before two Buddhas.' 'Two Buddhas?' they asked. 'Yes, this Brāhman prostrated himself not only before me but also before the *stūpa* of the Buddha Kāśyapa, which is hidden in the ground beneath his cattle prod.' The monks continued: 'We would like to see this *stūpa.*' The Buddha replied, 'In that case, ask this Brāhman to give you the land [beneath his cattle prod].' The monks did so, and the Brāhman consented to give them his land.

"As soon as they had received this land the Buddha [miraculously] revealed a *stūpa* dedicated to the Buddha Kāśyapa, which was decorated with the seven treasures. This *stūpa* was thirty *li* high and fifteen *li* wide. When the Brāhman saw it, he said to the Buddha, 'Bhagavat! I am also named Kāśyapa; this *stūpa* has the same name that I do.' Hearing this, the

Buddha directed another *stūpa* dedicated to the Buddha Kāśyapa to be built near the Brāhman's house. In the process of building this new *stūpa,* some monks asked the Buddha, 'Bhagavat! Is it all right for us to present mud to be used for building this new *stūpa?*' The Buddha answered, 'Yes, it is,' and he continued with the following verse:

'Mud for making a *stūpa*
Given with a devout mind
Is far more valuable than
Vast quantities of gold.'

"The new *stūpa* that the Buddha directed to be built had a square foundation and was surrounded by a handrail. The tower itself consisted of two stories and was of circular construction, with four tusklike poles protruding from its sides. Banners and canopies were attached to these poles, while at the very top of the *stūpa* there was a tall ring-shaped crown. The Buddha said, 'This is the way in which a *stūpa* should be made.'

"After the *stūpa* had been completed the Bhagavat prostrated himself before it out of his respect for the Buddha Kāśyapa. Seeing this, the monks asked him, 'Bhagavat! May we do the same?' He answered, 'Yes, you may,' and continued with the following verse:

'Prostrating yourself before a *stūpa*
With a devout mind
Is far more valuable than
Vast quantities of gold.'

"Hearing that the Bhagavat had built a *stūpa,* many laymen came bringing incense and flowers, which they presented to him. The Buddha, out of his respect for the Buddha Kāśyapa, accepted these things in order to use them as venerative offerings to the *stūpa.* Seeing this, the monks asked him, 'May we do the same?' He answered, 'Yes, you may,' and continued with the following verse:

'Venerative offerings made to a *stūpa*
With a devout mind
Are far more valuable than
Vast quantities of gold.'

"Following this, a great number of monks gathered around the Buddha, and he instructed Śāriputra to deliver a discourse on the Law to them. The Buddha himself offered the following verse:

'Offering one word of the Law
That all beings practice
Is far more valuable than
Vast quantities of gold.'

"Hearing these words, one of those present realized enlightenment. The Buddha presented him with the following verse:

'Offering one word of the Law
That enlightens all beings
Is far more valuable than
Vast quantities of gold.'

"The Brāhman, deeply moved by what he had heard, made venerative offerings of food to the Buddha and other monks as an expression of his firm belief. King Prasenajit,[37] hearing that the Buddha had built a *stūpa* dedicated to the Buddha Kāśyapa, came to the Buddha with seven hundred cartloads of tile. Prostrating himself before [the Buddha], he said, 'Bhagavat! I want to build *stūpas* like this one throughout the country. May I do so?' The Buddha answered, 'Yes, you may,' and continued with the following story: 'Long ago, at the time of the Buddha Kāśyapa's death, there was a king named Kṛki[38] who wanted to build a *stūpa* decorated with the seven treasures. At that time one of the king's retainers said to him, "I am afraid that at some time in the future a wicked person may appear and commit the serious crime of destroying this *stūpa*. I would suggest, therefore, that you make the *stūpa* out of tiles and cover it with gold and silver. In this way even if such a person steals the gold and silver, the *stūpa* itself will remain intact." The king followed this advice and made the *stūpa* exactly as his retainer had suggested. It was thirty *li* high and fifteen *li* wide, with a copper handrail surrounding its base. Seven years, seven months, and seven days were needed for its construction. When completed, the king made venerative offerings to me and the other monks.' King Prasenajit then said to the Buddha, 'King Kṛki had great merit and much wealth. Although I also wish to build a *stūpa,* I am afraid it will be no match for his.' It took King Prasenajit seven months and seven days to complete his *stūpa*. Upon its completion he made venerative offerings to the Buddha and the other monks.

"The method of making a *stūpa* is as follows: first, build a square foundation and enclose it with a handrail. Next, construct a two-storied circular tower on top of this, with four tusklike poles protruding from its sides. Banners and canopies should be attached to these poles and a tall ring-shaped crown installed at the very top of the *stūpa*. If someone says, 'Although the Bhagavat is beyond avarice, anger, and ignorance, he still wants to have a *stūpa* built in his honor,' that person is guilty of having slandered the Buddha, and his karmic retribution will be great. This is the method of making a *stūpa*.

"The regulations to be followed when building a temple complex are as follows: first, select a suitable site for the construction of a *stūpa*. This site should be located in the eastern or northern part of the complex, not its southern or western part. When the monks' living quarters are built, care should be taken that they do not encroach on the area in which the *stūpa* is located, and vice versa. Furthermore, if the *stūpa* is situated near a cemetery, an outer fence should be constructed around it in order to prevent dogs from defiling the area by dragging the remnants of corpses onto it. Care should also be taken that water used in the monks' quarters, located in the western or southern part of the complex, does not run off onto the land where the *stūpa* is. It is permissible, however, for water from the *stūpa*'s site to run off onto the land where the monks' quarters are.

"The *stūpa* should be built on an elevated area commanding a fine view. *Kaśāyas* should not be washed, dyed, or dried within the area of the fence surrounding the *stūpa;* neither should shoes or sandals be worn nor cloth used to cover the head or shoulders, not to mention sniveling or spitting on the ground. If someone says, 'Although the Bhagavat is beyond avarice, anger, and ignorance, he still wants to have a *stūpa* built in his honor,' that person is guilty of having slandered the Buddha, and his karmic retribution will be great. These are the regulations to be followed when making a temple complex.

"There is the following story about the alcove [for enshrining images of the Buddha] in a *stūpa:* Once King Prasenajit came to the Buddha and, prostrating himself before him, said, 'Bhagavat! I have just built a *stūpa* dedicated to the Buddha Kāśyapa. May I build an alcove in it?' 'Yes, you may,' the Buddha answered, and continued: 'Long ago, at the time of the Buddha Kāśyapa's death, there was a king named Kṛki who built a *stūpa* dedicated to this Buddha. On its four sides he had alcoves built that were decorated at the top with carved images of lions and various multicolored paintings. Banners and canopies hung inside these alcoves, while flowers were placed outside, protected by a handrail. If someone says, "Although the Bhagavat is beyond avarice, anger, and ignorance, he still wants to have an alcove built for decorative purposes so that he may derive pleasure therefrom," that person is guilty of having slandered the Buddha, and his karmic retribution will be great. This is the meaning of the alcove of a *stūpa*.' "

It can now be clearly understood that the building of *stūpas* dedicated to past Buddhas, and the respectful veneration of them, is the traditional practice of all enlightened Buddhas. There are many other descriptions of *stūpas,* but I will limit myself to the preceding for the time being. The teachings of the Sarvāstivāda school[39] are among the best in Buddhism. The *Mahāsaṃghikā-vinaya,* which forms the core of this school, was first brought back to China [from India] by Fa-hsien[40] after he had climbed Vulture Peak[41] and encountered many difficulties. The Law that the patriarchs have correctly transmitted is in accordance with the teachings of the Sarvāstivāda school.

The third way of venerating a Buddha is to make venerative offerings to a *stūpa, caitya,* and other forms of a Buddha's body.

The fourth way is to make venerative offerings to a Buddha where there is no mausoleum. It is the same veneration of a Buddha, however, whether or not a mausoleum exists at the place where the venerative offerings are made. Although there is great merit in venerating a Buddha where such a mausoleum, *stūpa,* or *caitya* exists, there is even greater merit in doing so in their absence, for the object of veneration in the latter case is more encompassing. At any rate, the greatest merit can be had from venerating a Buddha in either of these ways.

The fifth way of veneration is to personally make venerative offerings to a Buddha or a *caitya*.

The sixth way is to urge those who have even a little money to readily make venerative offerings to a Buddha or a *caitya*. It is the same veneration of a Buddha, however, whether one does it himself or urges others to do so. Although the merit in the former case is great, the merit in the latter case is even greater. At any rate, the greatest merit can be had from venerating a Buddha in either of these ways.

The seventh way of veneration is to make venerative offerings of goods and money to a Buddha, his relics, a *caitya*, or a *stūpa*. There are three kinds of goods: (1) clothing, food, and so on, (2) incense, flowers, and so on, and (3) all types of precious decorative ornaments.

The eighth way is to make venerative offerings with a devout mind. There are three kinds of such veneration: (1) complete devotion to the making of venerative offerings, (2) the realization that belief in the great virtue of a Buddha with a pure and faithful mind is one form of veneration, and (3) the realization that the wish for Buddhahood is one form of veneration.

The ninth way is to make venerative offerings with a nonseeking mind. There are two forms of such veneration: (1) that done with a mind freed from attachment to nonmaterial things, and (2) that done with a mind freed from attachment to material things.

The tenth way is to make venerative offerings of one's practice of the Way. The result of such venerative offerings, that is, one's practice of the Way, is enlightenment. They are of either two or three forms. The two forms are (1) venerative offerings made through the Law and (2) venerative offerings made through one's training. The three forms are (1) venerative offerings of money and goods, (2) venerative offerings made joyfully, and (3) venerative offerings made through one's training.

This completes the explanation of the ten ways of venerating a Buddha. The ways of venerating the Law and the Buddhist community are the same as the above. The veneration of the Law means to venerate the teachings, principles, and practices of the Buddha as expressed in the *sūtras*. The veneration of the Buddhist community means to venerate all Śrāvakas, Pratyekabuddhas, and Bodhisattvas, as well as their statues, *caityas*, *stūpas*, and mausoleums. It also means to venerate ordinary monks.

There are six kinds of venerative mind: (1) the highest supreme mind of good fortune, which arises as a result of venerating the Three Treasures; (2) the highest supreme mind of benevolence, which arises as a result of venerating the Three Treasures; (3) the highest supreme mind of all sentient beings; (4) the mind as difficult to encounter as an *uḍumbara* flower; (5) the supreme mind in the whole world; and (6) the mind of Truth, which penetrates delusion and nondelusion. Because the Tathāgata is endowed with this mind, sentient beings are able to depend on him. There is infinite merit to be had from making even a small venerative offering, let alone a big one, to the Three Treasures with any of these six venerative minds.

We should definitely make venerative offerings with a sincere mind, as has been described, just as all the Buddhas have done. Descriptions of such venerative offerings are included in the *sūtras* and treatises on the rules of discipline; they have also been correctly transmitted by the Buddhas and patriarchs. Service rendered to the Buddhas and patriarchs is at the same time veneration of them. The methods of construction and the regulations governing the use of *stūpas, caityas,* and mausoleums form the essence of the Law, which the Buddhas, patriarchs, and their descendants alone have correctly transmitted. The same holds true for the rules governing the enshrinement of statues and relics of the Buddhas, as well as the making of venerative offerings. Had such methods and regulations not been correctly transmitted, they would be in discrepancy with the Law, in which case our veneration would be untrue and consequently of little merit. Therefore we should definitely offer our veneration in accordance with the Law and transmit it correctly.

Zen Master Ling-t'ao[42] spent many years attending the mausoleum of his master Hui-nêng. Hui-nêng as a young monk pounded rice day and night without rest in service to his fellow monks. Both of these are examples of offering veneration in accordance with the Law. There are many other such examples, but I do not have time to list them all. At any rate, we should venerate the Buddhas as has been described. *(Compiled by Dōgen's disciple in the summer of the seventh year of Kenchō [1255])*

SIX

Taking Refuge in the Three Treasures

(Kie Buppōsō-hō)

THE ONE HUNDRED TWENTIETH QUESTION of the *Ch'an-yüan Ch'ing-kuei* asks, "Do you venerate the Three Treasures or not?" This clearly shows that reverent veneration of the Buddha, the Law, and the Buddhist community is the essence of the correct transmission of the Buddhas and patriarchs in both India and China. Without taking refuge in the Three Treasures it is impossible to reverently venerate them. Without reverently venerating them it is impossible to take refuge in them. The merit of having taken refuge in the Three Treasures inevitably appears when there is spiritual communion between the trainee and the Buddha. Those who experience this communion inevitably take this refuge whether they find themselves existing as celestial or human beings, dwellers in hell, hungry ghosts, or animals. As a result, the merit that is accumulated thereby inevitably increases through the various stages of existence, leading ultimately to the highest supreme enlightenment. Even though we be led astray by bad friends or devils, with the result that we stop doing good and lose all hope of realizing enlightenment, still the merit of having previously taken refuge in the Three Treasures will continue to increase, and eventually we will resume doing good, ultimately realizing enlightenment.

Taking refuge in the Three Treasures means, first of all, to come with a pure faith. Whether it is during the Tathāgata's lifetime or after it, people should place their hands together in *gasshō* and, with lowered heads, recite the following: "From now until we realize Buddhahood we take refuge in the Buddha; we take refuge in the Law; we take refuge in the Buddhist community. We take refuge in the Buddha, the most venerable of human beings; we take refuge in the Law, venerable because it is free of desire; we take refuge in the Buddhist community, the most venerable community of all. We have taken refuge in the Buddha; we have taken refuge in the Law; we have taken refuge in the Buddhist community."

We are able to take refuge in the Three Treasures because of our desire for enlightenment. Having done so, we can be certain that even though our body and mind are in a constant state of birth and decay, our Law-body will continue to grow until we finally realize enlightenment. The *ki* of *kie* [to take refuge] means "to throw [oneself] into." *E* means "to depend on." This is the significance of the words "to take refuge in." Just as a child throws himself into his father's arms, we should throw ourselves into the Three Treasures. Just as the people depend on the king for their well-being, we should depend on the Three Treasures. We take refuge in the Buddha because he is our great teacher. We take refuge in the Law because it is good medicine. We take refuge in the Buddhist community because it is composed of excellent friends.

Someone asked, "Why do we take refuge in the Three Treasures alone?" He[1] answered, "Because in addition to being the ultimate foundation of the Way, they are able to free sentient beings from birth and death and lead them to enlightenment." The merit of the Three Treasures is truly wondrous!

In India, Śākyamuni is known as the Buddha. In China he is known as *Chüeh,* that is to say, "one who has realized the highest supreme enlightenment." In India the Law is called *Dharma* or *Dhamma,* in China *Fa.* In ordinary usage the word "law" is used to designate good, bad, or neutral phenomena. The Law as contained in the Three Treasures, however, signifies "a standard of judgment." In India the Buddhist community is called *Saṃgha,* and in China *Ho-ho-chung* [harmonious community]. Praise for the Three Treasures has been expressed by designating their components in this way.

[The Three Treasures may be classified into four categories.] The first of these is the Three Treasures of eternity. In this category, images of the Buddha and *stūpas* are the Buddha-treasure, *sūtras* are the Law-treasure, and those who shave their heads, dye their *kaśāyas,* and observe the precepts are the Buddhist-community–treasure. The second is the Three Treasures for enlightening deluded people. Here the Buddha Śākyamuni is the Buddha-treasure, his teachings are the Law-treasure, and his first five disciples, including Ajñātakauṇḍinya, are the Buddhist-community–treasure. The third is the Three Treasures of the Truth itself. The Law-body of five merits[2] is the Buddha-treasure, comprehension of the Four Noble Truths is the Law-treasure, and those who have realized or are about to realize Arhathood are the Buddhist-community–treasure. The fourth and final category is the Three Treasures of absolute unity. Full enlightenment is the Buddha-treasure, abiding pure and undefiled in this realm is the Law-treasure, and becoming thoroughly one with the Truth is the Buddhist-community–treasure.

We should reverently take refuge in the Three Treasures as has been described. Unfortunate and virtueless people are unable to hear even the name of the Three Treasures, let alone take refuge in them.

The *Saddharma-puṇḍarīka-sūtra* states, "Those who commit various wrong acts will, because of karmic retribution, be unable to hear even the name of the Three Treasures for countless *kalpas.*" The *Saddharma-puṇḍarīka-sūtra* explains the purpose of the various Buddhas having appeared in this world. It may be said to be the great king and the great master of all the various *sūtras* that the Buddha Śākyamuni taught. Compared with this *sūtra,* all the other *sūtras* are merely its servants, its relatives, for it alone expounds the

Truth. The other *sūtras,* on the other hand, include provisional teachings[3] of the Buddha, and therefore do not express his real intention.

It is a mistake to use the teachings of the other *sūtras* as the basis for determining the validity of those contained in the *Saddharma-puṇḍarīka-sūtra,* for without the merit-power of the latter, the former would be valueless. All the other *sūtras* find their origin in this *sūtra.* As the previously quoted sentence from this *sūtra* shows, the merit of the Three Treasures is truly of unsurpassed value.

The Bhagavat said, "There are many people who, out of fear, take refuge in the deities of mountains, forests, individual trees, gardens, non-Buddhist shrines, and so on. Taking refuge in such deities, however, is of no value whatsoever, for it is impossible to free oneself from pain and suffering in this way. All those who take refuge in the Buddha, the Law, and the Buddhist community are able to use their Wisdom-eye to view the Four Noble Truths. That is to say, they come to know that (1) all existence is suffering, (2) the cause of suffering is illusion and desire, (3) Nirvāṇa is the realm free from suffering, and (4) the practice of the Eightfold Noble Path[4] is the means of realizing Nirvāṇa. Therefore there is nothing more valuable than taking refuge in the Three Treasures, for release from suffering inevitably comes from doing so."

The Bhagavat has taught the preceding for the sake of all sentient beings. Therefore we should not act like those who, awe-struck, vainly take refuge in mountain deities and ghosts or worship at non-Buddhist shrines, for it is impossible to gain release from suffering in this way. There are also those who, following other non-Buddhist religions, think they can gain release from suffering and have their wishes fulfilled by doing such things as imitating the actions of a cow, deer, malicious devil, hungry ghost, deaf and dumb person, dog, chicken, or pheasant; smearing their body with ashes; growing long hair; sacrificing sheep to the deity of time after having cast a spell; worshiping the deity of fire for four months; fasting for seven days; or dedicating innumerable flowers to celestial beings. The truth is, however, that such actions are completely meaningless. No wise man would practice them, for he knows that those who do so suffer meaninglessly, without receiving anything in return.

On the basis of the preceding statements it is clear that we should not meaninglessly take refuge in the teachings and practices of such non-Buddhist religions. Even if a certain practice has not been specifically listed here, if it is similar in principle to worshiping the deities of trees and non-Buddhist shrines, we should not take refuge in it. Considering how difficult it is to be born as a human being, let alone come into contact with Buddhism, it would be a tragedy if, because of our mistaken views, we were to spend our whole life as the offspring of ghosts and goblins, subject to endless transmigration. Let us instead quickly take refuge in the Buddha, the Law, and the Buddhist community, seeking not only release from suffering but complete enlightenment as well.

The *Hsi-yu sūtra*[5] states, "Even if we were able to lead all sentient beings in the four continents and six lowest heavens to Arhathood, it would not equal the merit of our having led one person to take refuge in the Three Treasures." The four continents consist of Pūrvavideha, Aparagodānīya, Jambudvīpa, and Uttarakuru. Because the teachings of the Three Vehicles have not yet reached the fourth continent of Uttarakuru it is extremely difficult to lead its inhabitants to Arhathood. Even if we were able to do so, it would not equal the merit of our having led one person to take refuge in the Three Treasures. It is also extremely rare for anyone in the six lowest heavens to realize enlightenment. Even if we were able to lead someone there to Arhathood, it would not equal the profound merit of having led one person to take refuge in the Three Treasures.

The *Ekottara-āgama-sūtra*[6] states: "A celestial being living in Trāyastriṃśa Heaven saw the five marks of decay[7] appear on his body and realized he would soon die, probably to be reborn as a wild boar. Faced with this prospect he was grief-stricken, not knowing what to do. Hearing his lamentations, King Śakrendra said to him, 'You should take refuge in the Three Treasures.' The celestial being followed this suggestion, and as a result was able to avoid being reborn as a wild boar. In this regard the Buddha Śākyamuni recited the following verse:

'Those who take refuge in the Buddha
Do not fall into the three evil worlds.
Extinguishing delusion, they are reborn
In the human and celestial worlds,
Finally entering Nirvāṇa.'

"As a result of having taken refuge in the Three Treasures, the celestial being was born as a rich man's son and was eventually able to enter the monkhood, finally becoming an Arhat." The merit of taking refuge in the Three Treasures is immeasurable, beyond all conception.

Once, during the Buddha's lifetime, 2,600 million starving dragons came to him and, crying copiously, said, "Compassionate Bhagavat! We beseech you to save us. Once, in the past, we were able to become Buddhist monks. After that, however, we committed various bad acts, and as a result of karmic retribution we fell into the three evil worlds for innumerable *kalpas*. Eventually, because of additional karmic retribution, we became dragons, having to undergo much suffering." The Buddha said to them, "You should all immediately take refuge in the Three Treasures and do good with sincerity. By doing so, you will be able to meet the final Buddha, who is named Ruci,[8] during this present *kalpa*. After this Buddha has appeared in the world, your crimes will disappear." Upon hearing these words, the dragons all decided to take sincere refuge in the Three Treasures for their whole life.

The Buddha himself had no way or means to save the dragons but to have them take refuge in the Three Treasures. Although at one time in the past these dragons had taken refuge in the Three Treasures as monks, as a result of karmic retribution they had become starving dragons. There was no way to save them but to have them take refuge in the Three Treasures. We should realize that the Bhagavat himself has already borne witness to the fact that the merit of the Three Treasures is of unsurpassed value and unfathomable profundity. Therefore all living creatures should take this refuge.

There is no one who is able to grasp the depth of the Buddha's mind as expressed by his having had the dragons take refuge in the Three Treasures rather than recite the names of all the Buddhas in the ten directions. It is more important for people of today to take refuge in the Three Treasures than to meaninglessly recite the name of each and every Buddha. We should not be so foolish as to lose the great merit [of the Three Treasures].

The [*Ta-fang-têng-chi sūtra*][9] states: "There was once a blind female dragon whose mouth was covered with sores and filled to overflowing with various kinds of worms, giving it the appearance of excreta and the smell of a woman's private parts, this smell being almost unbearable. Worms had fed on her body, and mosquitoes, horseflies, and various kinds of venomous flies had bitten it, to the extent that pus was constantly oozing out. She presented a tragic sight indeed!

"The Bhagavat, looking at her pitiable condition with compassion, said to her, 'What was the cause of your having been born in such a condition? What did you do in the past to deserve this?' She answered, 'I am constantly subjected to various kinds of suffering, so much so that I am unable to talk freely. Looking back at the last three billion six hundred million years, I find that for a hundred thousand years I was a bad dragon incessantly subject to the same kinds of suffering I am undergoing now. The reason for this is that ninety-one *kalpas* ago, when I was a nun during the time of the Buddha Vipaśyin, I was overcome with sexual desires greater than those of a drunken man. Subsequently, I was no longer able to observe the Buddhist precepts for a nun and began to lead a licentious life, spreading bedding in the temple complex in pursuit of sexual pleasure, stealing others' possessions, and thirsting after venerative offerings. Because of these actions I was unable to be born in the human or celestial worlds for ninety-one *kalpas*, and instead fell into the three evil worlds, where I was engulfed in flames.'

"The Buddha asked her, 'If what you said is true, where do you think you will be reborn at the end of this present *kalpa*?' She answered, 'Due to my past bad actions I will be born in another [of the three evil] worlds. Even at the end of that *kalpa* my past bad karma will cause me to be reborn once again as a female dragon. Compassionate Bhagavat! I beseech you to save me [from this fate].'

"The Bhagavat, scooping some water in his hands, said to her, 'This water is known as the water of bliss. I tell you with all sincerity that in the past I willingly sacrificed my body and life, without the slightest doubt or hesitation, in order to save a dove. If what you have said is true, your afflictions will all be cured.' Saying this, the Bhagavat put some of the water in his mouth and sprayed it on her, completely healing all of her ill-smelling and affected parts. Upon being cured in this way the female dragon asked to be allowed to take refuge in the Three Treasures. The Bhagavat immediately gave her his permission, and she did so."

This female dragon had once been a nun during the time of the Buddha Vipaśyin. Although she ended by breaking the precepts, she had had the opportunity to come into contact with the Law. Thus, when she came directly into the Buddha Śākyamuni's presence, she asked to be allowed to take refuge in the Three Treasures. The Buddha, recognizing her essential goodness, granted her request. It was the merit of having taken refuge in the Three Treasures that enabled her to see the Buddha. Although neither female dragons nor animals, we are unable to encounter the Tathāgata, follow his teachings, or take refuge in the Three Treasures. We should be ashamed that we are so far from enlightenment and realize that the merit of taking refuge in the Three Treasures, which were given by the Bhagavat himself, is utterly profound and immeasurable. It was due to this profound merit that King Śakrendra prostrated himself before a wild fox and took refuge in the Three Treasures.

[The *Mahāparinirvāṇa-sūtra* states:] "Once, when the Buddha was residing in a grove of *nyagrodha* trees[10] near Kapilavastu Palace, Mahānāma came to him and asked, 'Who should be known as a devout layman?' The Buddha answered, 'He who, possessed of a sound body and mind, takes refuge in the Three Treasures is known as a devout layman.' Mahānāma asked once again, 'Who is known as a step-by-step devout layman?'[11] The Buddha answered, 'He who, after having taken refuge in the Three Treasures, further receives a single precept is known as a step-by-step devout layman.' " It is only by taking refuge in the Three Treasures that we can become disciples of the Buddha and be qualified to receive all the other precepts.

The *Dhammapada-sūtra*[12] states: "When King Śakrendra was about to die, he realized he would probably be reborn as a donkey. Grief-stricken at this prospect, he said to himself, 'Only the Bhagavat can save me from this fate!' Immediately going to the Buddha, he prostrated himself before him in veneration but died before he could stand up again, subsequently becoming a fetus in a donkey's womb. Some time later, the mother donkey grew restive, and she broke her bridle and damaged some china in a nearby china shop. The owner of the shop, seeing what had happened, became angry and struck her, rupturing her womb, with the result that the fetus was once again transformed into King Śakrendra. At that time the Buddha said to the newly reborn king, 'Because of the merit of your having taken refuge in the Three Treasures at death's door, the bad karma produced by your past actions was extinguished.' Upon hearing these words, King Śakrendra realized the first stage to Arhathood."[13]

No one is better able to save us from worldly suffering and misfortune than the Bhagavat. It is for this reason that King Śakrendra hurriedly prostrated himself before the Buddha, though he died in the process and subsequently became a donkey's fetus. It was due to the merit of his having taken refuge in the Three Treasures that the mother donkey broke her bridle, destroyed some china, and had her womb ruptured by the shop's owner. Thus the fetus was transformed once again into King Śakrendra, who realized the first stage to Arhathood upon hearing the Buddha's words. All of this is due to the merit-power of having taken refuge in the Three Treasures, which not only saves us from worldly suffering and misfortune but enables us to realize the supreme Bodhi-wisdom as well.

As has been seen, the power of having taken refuge in the Three Treasures not only saved King Śakrendra from falling into the three evil worlds but also enabled him to be reborn in his original form and realize the first stage to Arhathood. Truly the merit-ocean of the Three Treasures is unlimited and immeasurable! During the Buddha's lifetime there were many examples of such good fortune in the human and celestial worlds. Now that more than two thousand years have passed since the Buddha Śākyamuni's death, however, both human and celestial beings are at a loss what to do. We should remember, however, that the relics and images of the Tathāgata are still present in the world. If we reverently venerate them we can realize the same merit as in the past.

The *Wên-ts'êng-yu sūtra*[14] states: "The Buddha said, 'I recall a time, innumerable *kalpas* ago, when a wild fox lived on Mount Śītā in the great country of Vima.[15] Once when this fox was being chased by a lion who wanted to devour him, he fell into a deep well from which there was no escape. Three days later, faced with the prospect of death [from starvation], he recited the following verse:

> "How unfortunate I am to end my life in this well!
> Since all things are transient I do not regret dying,
> Though I would rather have been the lion's supper.
> May each and every Buddha see how unselfish and pure I am!"

" 'When King Śakrendra heard the fox invoking the names of the various Buddhas he was deeply moved and, lamenting to himself, said, "I live in isolation [from the Buddhas] without anyone to guide me and overcome with the five desires." Wanting to ask the fox why he invoked the names of the Buddhas, he quickly descended from heaven to the edge of the well, accompanied by eighty thousand celestial attendants. Looking into the well, he saw the fox vainly scratching its earthen walls with both front paws, trying to climb out. King Śakrendra once more thought to himself, "I am certain this is a Bodhisattva in disguise, not an ordinary fox. Yet could such a venerable personage be unable to save himself?"

" 'In order to resolve his doubt, King Śakrendra said to the fox, "Your previous poem was truly excellent. Might I ask you to expound the essence of the Law to us celestial beings assembled here?"

" 'The fox answered, "Even though you are a celestial king, you have nothing to teach. In spite of this, you dare to ask someone who is [physically] below you to expound the essence of the Law, without any regard for the proper etiquette involved. Why are you so proud? Don't you know the water of the Law is pure enough to save all people?" Hearing these remarks, the king became quite ashamed of himself. His attendants, on the other hand, burst out laughing in surprise. It was clear that the king had gained nothing by descending from heaven.

" 'King Śakrendra then told his attendants, "Restrain yourselves! You should not be surprised by what the fox said. It is all due to my stubbornness and lack of virtue. I certainly am in need of listening to the essence of the Law!" Saying this, the king lowered his heavenly robe into the well and helped the fox climb out. The celestial attendants prepared a meal of honeydew for him, which he gladly ate. Recovering his will to live, the fox thought to himself, "How fortunate I am to have been unexpectedly saved in this way!" Filled with boundless joy, he expounded the essence of the Law to King Śakrendra and his attendants.' "

The preceding is the story of how King Śakrendra came to prostrate himself before an animal whom he regarded as his master. It can now be clearly understood how difficult it is to hear the names of the Buddha, the Law, and the Buddhist community. This is clearly shown by the fact that King Śakrendra was willing to take even a fox as his master. Due to our past good deeds we have been able to come into contact with the Law left by the Tathāgata. Thus we can constantly hear the names of the Three Treasures for eternity. This is the essence of the Law. Since even Pāpīyas is able to free himself from suffering by taking refuge in the Three Treasures, it is certain that we will accumulate immeasurable merits if we do the same.

In order to practice the Way, we disciples of the Buddha should first respectfully venerate the universal Three Treasures and, requesting their presence, burn incense and scatter flowers before them. These excellent practices have been handed down by the Buddhas and patriarchs from long ago. It is the practice of taking refuge in the Three Treasures that distinguishes the teachings of Buddhism from those of Pāpīyas and other non-Buddhist religions. All the Buddhas and patriarchs have, without exception, taught that we should first take refuge in the Three Treasures. *(Compiled by Dōgen's disciple in the summer of the seventh year of Kenchō [1255])*

SEVEN

Deep Belief in Causality

(Jinshin Inga)

"WHENEVER ZEN MASTER HUAI-HAI of Mount Pai-chang[1] expounded the Law, an old man always came to listen to him together with the other monks; when the latter left the lecture hall, he left too. One day, however, he remained behind, and Huai-hai asked him who he was. The old man replied, 'To tell the truth, I am not a human being. Long ago, in the time of the Buddha Kāśyapa, I was the head monk here. One day, however, a monk asked me, "Is even an enlightened person subject to causality?" "No, he isn't," I answered. [As punishment] I have continued to be reborn as a fox for five hundred lives. I now beseech you to save me [from this fate] by teaching me the true nature of causality.' Continuing, he then asked, 'Is even an enlightened person subject to causality?' Huai-hai answered, 'No one can set aside [the law of] causality.' Upon hearing these words, the old man realized full enlightenment and, prostrating himself before Huai-hai, said, 'I am now saved from rebirth as a fox, and my corpse will be found on the other side of this mountain. I would humbly request that you bury me as a dead monk.'

"Huai-hai told the senior monk in charge of the meditation hall[2] to strike the wooden sounding block to inform the monks that there would be a funeral service for a dead monk following the midday meal. The monks were surprised by this announcement, for they were all healthy, and there was no one in the monastery sickroom. After they had eaten, Huai-hai led them to the foot of a massive rock on the far side of the mountain. There he used his staff to uncover the dead body of a fox and had it cremated in accordance with the proper [Buddhist] ritual.

"That evening, in the lecture hall, Huai-hai told the monks the whole story. Thereupon Huang-po[3] asked the following question: 'You have said the old man suffered rebirth as a fox five hundred times because he gave the wrong answer. Suppose, however, he had answered correctly; what would have happened then?' Huai-hai replied: 'Come up here, and I'll tell you!' After some hesitation, Huang-po went up to Huai-hai and slapped his face. Huai-hai, clapping his hands and laughing, exclaimed, 'I thought the barbarian had a red beard, but here is another red-bearded barbarian!' "[4]

The preceding story is to be found in the *T'ien-shêng Kuang-têng-lu.*[5] At present there are many Buddhist trainees who, blind to the law of causality, make the mistake of denying its existence. How regrettable it is that the Way, swept by the winds of degenerate Buddhism, is now on the decline! To believe that enlightened people are not subject to causality is to deny [the law of] causality. Those who believe this inevitably fall into the three evil worlds. To believe that [the law of] causality cannot be set aside is to have a deep belief in causality. By hearing [of the existence of causality] even those who are in the three evil worlds can be saved. You should harbor neither suspicions nor doubts [about this point]! At present, many of those who call themselves Zen trainees deny the existence of causality. This can be seen from the fact that they equate freedom from causality with subjection to it.

The nineteenth patriarch, the Venerable Kumāralabdha,[6] said, "The karmic retribution of good and evil occurs at three different periods in time. Ordinary people, however, seeing the merciful die young and the violent live long, the treacherous happy and the righteous unhappy, think that causality does not exist, and consequently that happiness and unhappiness are unrelated to it. They are unaware that a shadow follows its shape just as a sound does its voice. [The law of] causality will not disappear even in the course of one billion *kalpas* of time!"

It can now be clearly seen that the patriarchs have never denied causality. Because of their failure to study these ancient examples, however, latter-day trainees have not yet understood the great compassion of these patriarchs [in having taught the nature of causality]. Those who, in spite of this failure, dare to call themselves the spiritual leaders of human and celestial beings are actually the very opposite of what they claim to be, the detestable enemies of true students of the Way. You present-day trainees must not instruct initiates that there is no causality, for the denial of causality is a falsehood that is not to be found in the teachings of the Buddhas and patriarchs. It is because you are negligent in your practice that you cling to such false views.

Among present-day Chinese monks there are those who say, "Although we were born as human beings, and have come into contact with Buddhism, we are unable to understand our present life, let alone our future life. The former head monk of Mount Pai-chang, who became a fox, however, was acquainted with his past five hundred lives. Perhaps the reason he became a fox was not karmic retribution [for having denied causality] but the result of his desire, as an enlightened being, to save all deluded people, even if that meant temporarily becoming a fox." Such are the views of so-called great spiritual leaders! Actually, these views have nothing to do with the teachings of the Buddha and patriarchs, for the Bhagavat taught that although some men, foxes, and other creatures are born with the supernatural power to know of their former existences, this power is the result of their past bad karma, not enlightenment. Many Chinese monks are unaware of this, however, because they are negligent in their practice. How tragic! Even though they may know of their past one thousand or ten thousand lives, it has nothing to do with Buddhism. There are non-Buddhists who are said to be aware of periods of time as long as eighty thousand *kalpas;* but this, too, has nothing to do with Buddhism. The ability to know of one's past five hundred lives is of little importance.

The greatest weak point of present-day Chinese monks is their failure to recognize that freedom from causality is a false teaching. How regrettable it is that although the Tathāgata's teaching [about causality] is widely known and has been correctly transmitted from patriarch to patriarch, they choose to side with those mistaken people who would deny its existence! Their only hope is to awaken quickly to the law of causality. Huai-hai's statement that [the law of] causality cannot be set aside shows that he was well acquainted with its nature. When the law of causality is applied to the Way, it means that the "result" of enlightenment inevitably follows the "cause" of practice. Those who have not yet fully mastered the teachings of the Buddha should not willfully expound them to human and celestial beings.

The Patriarch Nāgārjuna said, "To deny, as non-Buddhists do, the existence of worldly causality is also to deny the existence of the present and future worlds. Further, to deny Buddhist causality is also to deny the Three Treasures, the Four Noble Truths, and the four stages to Arhathood."[7]

We should clearly understand that the denial of worldly and Buddhist causality is the teaching of non-Buddhist religions. What non-Buddhist religions mean when they deny the existence of the present world may be stated as follows: "Although the [human] body is present in this world, its inner nature is in [the world of] eternal enlightenment. The mind is the body's inner nature, for the body and mind exist independently of each other." Furthermore, what they mean by denying the existence of the future world is this: "When someone dies, he naturally returns to the great ocean of enlightenment [his original nature]. Therefore there is no need to practice the Way, and furthermore, there is no transmigration after death." This latter teaching is clearly a denial of causality.

Although their appearance may be that of monks, those who believe in the preceding mistaken teachings are without doubt the followers of non-Buddhist religions, not the disciples of the Buddha. They make the mistake of denying the existence of the present and future worlds because they deny [the law of] causality. Their denial comes from the fact that they have never trained under a truly excellent master, for those who have done so would never cling to such false teachings as that there is no causality. We should deeply believe and respectfully preserve the preceding compassionate teachings of the Patriarch Nāgārjuna.

Hsüan-chüeh was one of Zen Master Hui-nêng's foremost disciples. Originally he, like his fellow disciple Hsüan-lang,[8] had been a student of the *Saddharma-puṇḍarīka-sūtra* of the T'ien-t'ai sect. One day, however, a golden light filled his room as he read the *Nirvāṇa-sutra,* causing him to realize enlightenment. Thereafter he went to Hui-nêng and told him what had happened, whereupon the latter certified his enlightenment as being genuine.

Later, when Hsüan-chüeh wrote the *Chêng-tao-ko* [Song of Enlightenment] he included the following verse: 'Those [in the delusive world] who deny causality invite incalculable misfortune."

We should clearly understand that the denial of causality brings incalculable misfortune. Although all ancient monks of great virtue were well versed in [the law of] causality, present-day trainees are not. Filled with a pure Bodhi-mind in which Buddhism is studied for Buddhism's sake alone, we should, like the ancient monks, quickly become so. The denial of causality is clearly the teaching of non-Buddhist religions.

Zen Master Hung-chih[9] made the following versified comments on Huai-hai's story:

"Even a small cause may have a great result.
Thus, for five hundred lives a monk became a wild fox.
To talk about 'freedom from' or 'subjection to' causality
Is to remain captive to the discriminating mind.
Do you understand how laughable this is?
Transcend such conceptions and you will find a world
Where the words of enlightenment are freely spoken,
Where there is dancing and singing, as if before a shrine,
Where all clap their hands in unison, laughing merrily."

Hung-chih's statement that "to talk about 'freedom from' or 'subjection to' causality / Is to remain captive to the discriminating mind" shows that he [mistakenly] believed freedom from causality to be the same thing as subjection to it.

All the previous descriptions of causality have yet to explain it fully. [According to Huai-hai] the former head monk of Mount Pai-chang was finally able to escape rebirth as a fox. Strangely enough, however, he failed to state in which world that monk was subsequently reborn. It is clear that he must have been reborn somewhere, in the human or celestial world if not in the four evil worlds;[10] for the belief that sentient beings after death return either to the great ocean of enlightenment or to their true self is unmistakably the teaching of non-Buddhist religions.

Zen Master Huan-wu of Mount Chia[11] also made a versified comment on Huai-hai's story:

"When fish swim, the water becomes cloudy;
When birds fly, they lose their feathers;
For nothing can escape from the perfect mirror of causality,
Which is as vast and universal as the sky.
For five hundred lives the monk became a wild fox
Because he failed to understand Buddhist causality,
Which is as strong as a bolt of lightning or a raging typhoon,
As unchangeable as gold that has been purified many times over."

Even this verse has aspects that deny causality on the one hand and affirm the eternal nature of the [delusive] self and world on the other.

Zen Master Tsung-kao of Mount Ching[12] also made a versified comment on Huai-hai's story:

> "Freedom from causality and subjection to it
> Are as closely related as stone to earth.
> The monk's rebirth as a fox for five hundred lives
> Is like a silver mountain smashed to pieces.
> When Pu-tai of Mingchou[13] heard this story,
> He clapped his hands and laughed heartily."

Present-day Chinese monks regard the preceding masters as excellent patriarchs. Tsung-kao's comments, however, cannot even be called a provisional explanation of the Law, for they are close to denying causality. There have been more than thirty people who have made versified comments on and explanations of Huai-hai's story. None of them, however, has ever doubted that freedom from causality meant its denial.[14] How tragic it is that, wasting their whole life in meaningless discussion, they have failed to understand [the true nature of] causality! Buddhist trainees should first of all become well versed in causality, for those who deny causality are likely to fall victim to extremely mistaken views and, finally, to stop doing good. The law of causality, however, is both clear and impersonal: those who do evil inevitably fall [into hell]; those who do good inevitably ascend [into heaven]. If this were not so, the various Buddhas would not have appeared in this world, Bodhidharma would not have come to China, and we would not have come into contact with the Buddha or heard his teachings.

Causality was a mystery to both Confucius and Lao-tzŭ, for it has been understood and transmitted by the Buddhas and patriarchs alone. In this age of degenerate Buddhism, students of the Way are unable to understand causality because, as a result of their lack of virtue, they are unable to meet a true master or hear the true Law. Those who deny causality will be subject to incalculable misfortune as punishment for their mistaken view. Even though they do not create any additional bad karma, the harm [resulting from] this mistaken view is very great. Buddhist trainees therefore should, first awakening to the Bodhi-mind, repay the great benefaction of the Buddhas and patriarchs by quickly realizing [the true nature of] causality. *(Compiled by Ejō in the summer of the seventh year of Kenchō [1255])*

EIGHT

Karmic Retribution in the Three Stages of Time

(*San-ji Gō*)

When the Venerable Kumāralabdha, the nineteenth patriarch, was visiting central India, a virtuous monk named Gayata[1] said to him, "Although my parents have taken refuge in the Three Treasures for many years, they have often been subject to illness and economic misfortune. Our neighbor, on the other hand, who is a *caṇḍāla*,[2] is healthy and prosperous. Why is this?" The Venerable One answered, "Your doubt is easily dispelled. The karmic retribution of good and evil occurs at three different periods in time. Ordinary people, however, seeing the merciful die young and the violent live long, the treacherous happy and the righteous unhappy, think that causality does not exist, and consequently that happiness and unhappiness are unrelated to it. They are unaware that a shadow follows its shape just as a sound does its voice. [The law of] causality will not disappear even in the course of one billion *kalpas* of time!" Upon hearing these words, Gayata was immediately freed from his doubt [concerning karmic retribution].

The Venerable Kumāralabdha was the nineteenth successor to the Tathāgata. It is said that the Tathāgata himself prophesied that he would be his successor. Not only did the Venerable Kumāralabdha understand and correctly transmit the teachings of the Buddha Śākyamuni, but he also mastered the teachings of all the Buddhas in the three stages of time. After clearing Gayata of his doubt, he continued to give him guidance in the true teachings of the Tathāgata until finally the latter became the twentieth patriarch. It is said that the Buddha Śākyamuni also prophesied this succession.

As the previous example shows, whenever we are beset with doubts concerning the Law, we should study the teachings of such patriarchs as the Venerable Kumāralabdha. We should avoid associating with those deluded people in this present world who are ignorant of the law of causality and karmic retribution. They are unaware of the existence of the three stages of time and unable to distinguish good from evil.

The karmic retribution of good and evil occurs at three different periods in time: (1) retribution experienced in one's present life, (2) retribution experienced in the life following this one, and (3) retribution experienced in subsequent lives. This is the first thing we should study and understand when practicing the Way, for otherwise we are apt to make mistakes and come to hold wrong views, falling into evil worlds and undergoing a long period of suffering. Not only that, we will also stop doing good and thereby lose much merit, with the result that we will be unable to realize enlightenment for a long time. How regrettable!

As has been stated, the karmic retribution of good and evil occurs at three different periods in time. The first period, that is, retribution experienced in one's present life, means that we receive in our present life the matured results of the karmic seeds that we have sown in our present life. That is to say, we receive the karmic retribution of our acts, good or bad, in our present life. The following story is an example of a man who received his just reward for his bad actions in his present life.

[The *Abhidharma-mahāvibhāsā-śāstra* states:] "There once lived a woodcutter. One day when he was in the mountains a heavy snow fell and he lost his way. As twilight approached the snow lay even deeper, and it became colder and colder. Just as the woodcutter was about to freeze to death, he stumbled into a dense thicket and came upon a bear that was living there. The bear's fur was dark blue in color, and its eyes shone like two torches. The woodcutter was so frightened that he almost fainted.

"In reality, the bear was an incarnation of a Bodhisattva and, upon seeing how frightened the woodcutter was, consoled him, saying, 'Don't be afraid, for I, unlike some parents who harbor ill feelings toward their children, wish you no harm.' Having said this, the bear approached the woodcutter and, picking him up, carried him to a nearby cave. Once inside, it warmed him with its body and restored his spirits, bringing him various kinds of roots and nuts to eat. Furthermore, fearing that the woodcutter would be unable to digest this food, it continued day and night to warm him with its body and look after his other needs for the next six days.

"On the seventh day the weather cleared, and the woodcutter decided it was time to try to make his way back home. The bear, knowing of his feelings, once more prepared a dinner for him of numerous sweet nuts, then accompanied him to the edge of the thicket, where it bade him a polite farewell. The woodcutter, for his part, fell down on his knees in gratitude, saying, 'How can I ever repay you [for your kindness]?' The bear answered, 'I ask for nothing in return, other than that you protect my life as I have protected yours.' Respectfully agreeing to do so, the woodcutter picked up the firewood [he had previously cut] and left the mountains.

"As he neared home the woodcutter happened to meet two hunters, one of whom asked him if he had seen any wild animals in the mountains. He replied: 'Apart from one bear, I didn't see any wild animals.' Hearing this, the hunters asked him if he would show them where the bear was. The woodcutter agreed to do so on the condition that they give him two-thirds of the bear's body in return; and it was not long before the bear had been killed and its flesh divided into three parts. When the woodcutter reached out with both hands to pick up his promised flesh, however, his bad karma caused both his arms to fall off, just as if a string of pearls had suddenly broken or the root of a lotus flower had been cut.

"The hunters, seeing this, were both surprised and frightened, and they asked the woodcutter for an explanation. Deeply ashamed of what he had done, he gave them a detailed account of the whole story. The two said to him reproachfully, 'How is it possible that you were able to perpetrate such a treacherous crime against this bear when you were so deeply indebted to it? It's a wonder your whole body doesn't rot away!' Having said this, they took the flesh to a nearby temple and offered it to the community of monks.

"One of the senior monks in the temple, who was endowed with penetrating Wisdom, entered into *samādhi*[3] in order to see whose flesh it was. Seeing that it was actually the flesh of a great Bodhisattva who had bestowed abundant benefits and happiness on all beings, he immediately came out of *samādhi* and informed the other monks of its true nature. The other monks were quite surprised by this revelation, and they decided to cremate the flesh with incense wood. When this had been done, they further built a *stūpa* for the bear's bones and respectfully venerated them. As this story shows, bad karma never fails, sooner or later, to produce its result."

The preceding story is an example of a man who received the karmic retribution of his bad acts in his present life. As it shows, we should always aspire to reward those to whom we are indebted. At the same time, however, we should not seek any reward from those who are indebted to us. Should we commit treachery against or harm our benefactor, we will certainly receive our just punishment. We should definitely not act as the woodcutter did. On the one hand, he asked the bear at their time of parting at the edge of the thicket how he could ever repay its kindness. On the other hand, when he met two hunters at the foot of the mountain, he fell victim to his greed and demanded two-thirds of its flesh, thus bringing harm to his great benefactor. Whether laymen or monks, we should never forget those to whom we are indebted; for the woodcutter's bad karma caused his arms to fall off quicker than if they had been cut with a sword.

The following story concerns a man who was justly rewarded in his present life for his good actions.

[The *Abhidharma-mahāvibhāsā-śāstra* states:] "During the reign of King Kaniṣka[4] in the country of Gandhāra,[5] there was a eunuch who was employed to watch over the ladies-in-waiting of the court. One day when he was traveling outside the castle, he saw a herd of five hundred cattle being driven toward the castle. He asked the herdsman, 'What are you going to do with these cattle?' He answered, 'I'm taking them to be castrated.' At that time the eunuch thought to himself, 'Although I have a man's body, as a result of my past bad karma I am unable to function as a man. I should definitely use my wealth to save these cattle that are about to meet the same fate!' Thinking this, he bought all the cattle from the herdsman and set them free.

"As a result of his good karma the eunuch's male functions were restored.

Overjoyed at this occurrence, he decided to return to the castle and, approaching the castle gate, sent a messenger to the king, requesting an audience. The king called him in and asked him to explain himself. When the eunuch had finished, the king was both surprised and overjoyed, and presented him with numerous valuable gifts. Furthermore, he also assigned him new duties as the minister in charge of foreign affairs. As this story shows, good karma never fails, sooner or later, to produce its result."

It can now be clearly seen that although animals, such as cattle, are not necessarily to be pitied, we will still be rewarded if we help them, not to mention the even greater reward we will receive if we hold the virtuous and our benefactors in esteem and do good. This is what is known as receiving the retribution of our good acts in this life. There are many examples similar to the preceding, but I do not have time to list them all.

The second period, that is, retribution experienced in the life following this one, means that in our next life we receive the matured result of the karmic seeds that we have sown in our present life. That is to say, if we commit one of the five deadly wrongs in this life, we will inevitably fall into hell in our next life. Our next life refers to our next existence after this one. When we commit wrongs [other than the five deadly ones] it is also possible that we will fall into hell in our next life, though sometimes this does not occur until our subsequent lives. The committing of the five deadly wrongs, however, unquestionably results in our falling into hell in our next existence.

The five deadly wrongs are as follows: (1) killing one's father, (2) killing one's mother, (3) killing an Arhat, (4) injuring the body of a Buddha, and (5) causing disunity in the Buddhist community.

If we commit even one of the five deadly wrongs we will surely fall into hell in our next life. There have been those who have committed all five of these deadly wrongs. The Bhikṣu Hua-shang,[6] who lived at the time of the Buddha Kāśyapa, is an example of one of these. There have also been those who have committed only one of the five deadly wrongs. King Ajātaśatru,[7] who lived at the time of the Buddha Śākyamuni and is known to have killed his father, is an example of one of these. Further, there have also been those who committed three of the five deadly wrongs. Ajita,[8] who also lived at the time of Buddha Śākyamuni, is an example of one of these. He is said to have killed his father, his mother, and an Arhat. He committed these crimes when he was still a layman, however, and later was allowed to enter the monkhood.

Devadatta, who is also known as T'i-p'o-ta-tou, and whose name was translated [into Chinese] as T'ien-jê [heavenly heat], was a monk who committed three of the five deadly wrongs. That is to say, he caused disunity in the Buddhist community, injured the body of the Buddha, and killed an Arhat. The way in which he committed these crimes is as follows: "First of all, he deceived five hundred newly initiated and naive monks into following him to the top of Mount Gayā,[9] where he taught them the five false teachings,[10] thus causing disunity in the Buddhist community. When the Venerable Śāriputra learned of this, he caused Devadatta to go to sleep so that the Venerable Maudgalyāyana might lead the five hundred novices back [to the original community]. Just as the latter had started to do so, however, Devadatta awoke and, seeing what was happening, vowed to take revenge. This he did [sometime later] when, picking up a large rock fifteen *hastas* wide and thirty *hastas* high, he threw it at the Buddha. Although a mountain deity intercepted this rock with his hand, one small fragment struck the Buddha's foot, causing it to bleed."[11]

According to the preceding description, Devadatta caused disunity in the Buddhist community before injuring the body of the Buddha. According to other versions, however, the order is reversed. According to still other versions, he also killed the Bhikṣuṇī Utpalavarṇā, who was an Arhat, with his fists, thus committing the third deadly wrong.

The fifth deadly wrong of causing disunity in the Buddhist community is also committed when someone initiates false teachings or practices among the monks. The latter false practices are to be found throughout the whole world, with the exception of the northern continent [of Uttarakuru]. These false practices began when the Tathāgata was still alive and will continue until the demise of the Law. False teachings, on the other hand, existed throughout the world only when the Tathāgata was still alive. Following his death, they disappeared in all but the southern continent [of Jambudvīpa]. Expounding such false teachings is the most serious crime of all.

Devadatta fell into Avīci hell[12] as a result of having committed three deadly wrongs. As has been stated, there have been those who have committed all five deadly wrongs and others who have committed only one, or, as in Devadatta's case, those who have committed three. At any rate, all such people fell into Avīci hell, where those who had committed one deadly wrong suffered [one kind of] karmic retribution for a period of one *kalpa*,[13] while those who had committed all five underwent five kinds of retribution during the same period.

An ancient master said, "Both the *Āgama-sūtras* and the *Nirvāṇa-sūtra* state that in hell there are time periods as long as one *kalpa*, and that there are both strong and weak fires burning there. Furthermore, they also state that the suffering that the inhabitants of hell undergo varies according to [the seriousness of] their crimes."

Devadatta, who committed three deadly wrongs, had to undergo three times more suffering than those who had committed only one. Just as he was about to die, however, he started to repeat the invocation beginning "I take refuge in the Buddha." Although he died before he had completed this invocation, he was still able to free himself of his evil mind to some extent. How unfortunate [for him] that he could not complete the invocation! In Avīci hell he continued to take refuge in the Buddha Śākyamuni, even though the latter was far away, and eventually he was able to resume doing good.

In Avīci hell there are four other monks similar to Devadatta. One of them is the Bhikṣu Kokālika,[14] one of the Buddha Śākyamuni's one thousand disciples. One day when he and Devadatta were out riding, their horses stumbled and they fell off, losing their headpieces in the process. People nearby who saw this said to themselves, "Their study of Buddhism has been meaningless." Kokālika was a person who had slandered Śāriputra and Maudgalyāyana by spreading groundless rumors about them. The Bhagavat himself had warned him kindly about this, but he refused to stop. King Brahma had done the same with like result. In his next life he fell into hell for having slandered the two disciples, and to this day he has not acquired sufficient merit to resume doing good.

A monk who had attained the fourth stage of meditation is another of the inhabitants of Avīci hell. Just as he was about to die he slandered the Buddha, and as a result the intermediate world[15] disappeared and this hell immediately appeared before him, forecasting that this was his destination after death. The preceding are all examples of those who have experienced karmic retribution in the life following this one.

There are five reasons that the five deadly wrongs are known as deadly wrongs. The first reason is that those who commit these wrongs immediately fall into hell without going through the intermediate world. That is to say, they immediately receive the results of their actions in their next life. The second reason is that those who commit these wrongs experience continuous suffering. During the one *kalpa* of time that they are in Avīci hell, they are in a continuous state of suffering, unbroken by even a moment of pleasure. In this case the term "deadly wrong" receives its name from its result [rather than its cause].

The third reason is that the length of the karmic retribution that those who commit these wrongs undergo is unlimited. During the one *kalpa* they are in Avīci hell, they continue to suffer without interruption. The fourth reason is that the life span of those who commit these wrongs is unlimited. Once born in Avīci hell they continue to live there uninterruptedly for an entire *kalpa*. This is also a case of the term "deadly wrong" receiving its name from its result [rather than its cause]. The fifth reason is that the body of [each of] those who commit these wrongs fills Avīci hell completely. Avīci hell is eighty-four thousand *yojanas*[16] wide, and is so constructed that while even one person fills it completely, it is still possible for innumerable other people to be born there without disturbing each other. This is a further case of the term "deadly wrong" receiving its name from its result [rather than its cause].

The third period, that is, retribution experienced in subsequent lives, means that we receive the matured results of the karmic seeds that we have sown in our present life in our third, fourth, or following lives, even should these extend over a period of one hundred thousand *kalpas*. That is to say, we will receive the karmic retribution of our acts, good or bad, in our third, fourth, or subsequent lives up to and including our hundred thousandth life. The merit derived from the training of Bodhisattvas over innumerable *kalpas* of time usually appears in this third period. Those who are unaware of this fact, however, are likely to harbor doubts [about the appearance of a Bodhisattva's merit] even though they themselves undergo training. The Venerable Gayata, when he was still a layman, is a good example of this. Had he not met the Venerable Kumāralabdha, he would have been unable to free himself of his doubts. When we trainees determine to do good, evil disappears; but when we determine to do evil, the opposite is true.

[The *Abhidharma-mahāvibhāsā-śāstra* states:] "There once lived two men in the city of Śrāvastī.[17] One of them always did good, while the other always did bad. The one who did good had never once done any bad, while the one who did bad had never once done any good. At the time that the former was approaching death, the intermediate world leading to hell appeared before him as a result of his bad karma from his previous lives. At that time he thought to himself, 'I have done good my whole life, without having once done bad, and therefore should be reborn in heaven in my next life. Why, then, has the intermediate world leading to hell appeared before me?' [Thinking about this question,] he reached the following conclusion: 'The reason it has appeared is that the bad karma from my previous lives has now matured.' At the same time, he recalled all the good he had done in his life and was filled with great joy. As a result of this recollection, the intermediate world leading to hell disappeared, to be immediately replaced by the intermediate world leading to heaven. He then died and was reborn in heaven."

This man who always did good not only believed that he had to undergo the karmic retribution of his previous lives but further believed that he would certainly receive the effects of his good actions in his future lives. His great joy stemmed from this latter belief. It was because his beliefs were true that the intermediate world leading to hell disappeared, the intermediate world leading to heaven suddenly appeared, and he was reborn in heaven at his death. Had he been a bad person, and faced with the appearance of the intermediate world leading to hell as he approached death, he probably would have thought as follows: "Although I did good my whole life, I haven't gained any merit. If [the law of] causality is true, why is it that the intermediate world leading to hell has appeared before me?" Having thus doubted causality and slandered the Three Treasures, he would undoubtedly have fallen into hell at his death. Because he did not think this way, however, he was able to be reborn in heaven. We should be clearly aware of this fact.

[The *Abhidharma-mahāvibhāsā-śāstra* continues:] "When the person who did bad was about to die, the intermediate world leading to heaven suddenly appeared before him as a result of his good karma from his previous lives. He then thought to himself, 'I have done nothing but bad my whole life, without having once done any good, and therefore should be reborn in hell in my next life. Why, then, has the intermediate world leading to heaven appeared before me?' [Thinking about this question,] he came to the false conclusion that one does not receive the good, bad, or matured effects of one's previous actions. As a result of this false conclusion, the intermediate world leading to heaven disappeared, to be immediately replaced by the intermediate world leading to hell. He then died and was reborn in hell."

When this man who always did bad without ever doing any good was about to die, the intermediate world leading to heaven appeared before him; but he did not realize that it was the result of his good karma from his previous lives. Rather, believing that one does not receive the good and bad effects of one's previous actions, he thought he would be able to be reborn in heaven in spite of having done nothing but bad his whole life. It was because of this denial of causality that the intermediate world leading to heaven disappeared, the intermediate world leading to hell immediately appeared, and he fell into hell at his death. It was because of his false belief that the intermediate world leading to heaven disappeared.

Forsaking such false belief, we trainees should study what is true and what is false as long as we live. Denying causality, the three worlds, and enlightenment as well as slandering the Three Treasures are all false beliefs. We should understand that in this life we have only one life, not two or three. How regrettable it is if, fruitlessly holding false views, we vainly do wrong, thinking that we are not doing bad when, in fact, we are! The karmic retribution of our evil acts cannot be avoided even though we mistakenly assume that because we do not recognize its existence we are not subject to it. We should also be aware that bad intentions can change good karmic retribution into bad, for bad intentions, too, are a deadly wrong.

[The *Ching-tê-ch'uan-têng-lu* states:] "Hao-yüeh,[18] a monk who was engaged as counselor to the emperor, once said to Abbot Ching-ts'ên of Mount Chang-sha,[19] 'According to an ancient master [Hsüan-chüeh], the enlightened realize that karmic hindrance [past bad karma] is, in its essential nature, empty; the unenlightened, however, must repay their karmic debt. Why, then, did the Venerable Siṃha[20] and the Patriarch Hui-k'o have to repay their karmic debt?' Abbot Ching-ts'ên answered, 'You have not yet understood [what is meant by] "its essential nature is empty."' 'What, then, does "its essential nature is empty" mean?' '[It means] karmic hindrance,' Ching-ts'ên answered. 'Then what is karmic hindrance?' 'Its essential nature is empty!' At these words Hao-yüeh remained silent. Ching-t'sên then composed the following verse:

'Temporary existence does not really exist,
Nor does temporary nonexistence really not exist.
Nirvāṇa and the repayment of karmic debt
Have one nature, not two.' "

Ching-ts'ên had trained under Zen Master P'u-yüan of Nan-ch'üan[21] for many years and was one of his foremost disciples. Although he sometimes spoke the Truth [about the Law], as the preceding story shows, he had not yet even slightly understood the nature of karmic hindrance. It is clear that he had neither understood the words of a recent master like Hsüan-chüeh nor those of an ancient master like Kumāralabdha, let alone those of the Bhagavat. How can we respect someone who has not [correctly] transmitted the words of the Buddhas and patriarchs?

Karmic hindrance is one of the three hindrances, the other two being the hindrance of [worldly] desires and the hindrance of karmic retribution. Karmic hindrance denotes the five deadly wrongs. Even though Hao-yüeh may not have intended to ask about karmic hindrance as one aspect of the three hindrances, his question did in fact encompass all three. Basing his question on the belief that karma would never disappear, he asked about karmic retribution in subsequent lives. Ching-ts'ên's error was that when asked what "its essential nature is empty" meant, he answered, "[It means] karmic hindrance." This is truly a great mistake, for how could "karmic hindrance" mean "its essential nature is empty"? Since karmic hindrance is produced by our actions, how can something we have produced have emptiness as its essential nature? "Produced" and "nonproduced" exist only in relationship to one another. It is a non-Buddhist teaching to believe that karmic hindrance is, by nature, empty. Those who do evil, believing that the essential nature of karmic hindrance is empty, will never be able to realize enlightenment. If there were no enlightenment, the various Buddhas would not have appeared in this world, Bodhidharma would not have come to China, and P'u-yüan would not have existed. Had P'u-yüan not existed, who could have directed Ching-ts'ên toward the Way?

When Ching-ts'ên answered Hao-yüeh's question about karmic hindrance by telling him that its essential nature was empty, he missed the point. I think the reason for his failure lies in the fact that he dared to answer a thoroughly experienced trainee like Hao-yüeh on the basis of his own limited understanding. Later, he composed a verse in which he said, "Nirvāṇa and the repayment of karmic debt / Have one nature, not two."

I would ask Ching-ts'ên what "one nature" he is talking about. Which one of the three [moral] natures[22] does he mean? It is apparent that he does not know what "nature" is. What does he mean by "Nirvāṇa and the repayment of karmic debt"? Which Nirvāṇa is he talking about? That of Śrāvakas? Of Pratyekabuddhas? Of all the Buddhas? Whichever it is, it has nothing to do with repayment of karmic debt. His words are not those of the Buddhas and patriarchs. He should buy straw sandals and walk about [in search of a true teacher]!

There is no doubt that both the Venerable Siṃha and the Patriarch Hui-k'o were murdered by evil men. Since they had neither entered the *antima-deha* stage[23] nor lost the intermediate world [by committing the five deadly wrongs], it is impossible to think that they could have avoided karmic retribution in their subsequent lives. When the karmic seeds of retribution have matured, there is no question that we must receive their effects. It should now be clear that Ching-ts'ên had not yet understood karmic retribution in the three stages of time.

Buddhist trainees who wish to understand karmic retribution in the three stages of time should emulate the understanding of Kumāralabdha, for his understanding is the experience of the patriarchs. It should not be treated lightly. There is a total of eight kinds of karma[24] that should be thoroughly studied. Without having understood all of them we cannot receive the true Law of the Buddhas and patriarchs. Those who have not done so should not willfully call themselves the teachers of human and celestial beings.

The Bhagavat said, "Even though one hundred thousand *kalpas* of time elapse, karma will not disappear. You must inevitably receive the matured effects of your actions, good or bad. You should realize that if you do only good, you will receive only good matured effects. If you do only bad, the opposite is true. On the other hand, if you do both good and bad, you will receive a matured mixture of like results. Therefore you should stop doing bad, or a mixture of good and bad, and do good alone." The assembled monks, hearing the Bhagavat's words, were overjoyed and took them to heart.

The Bhagavat has shown that once good or bad karma has been produced, it will not disappear even in the course of one hundred thousand *kalpas* of time. We must inevitably receive the results of our actions, good or bad. Repentance, however, lessens the effects, bringing release and purity. When we rejoice at the good acts of others, our own good karma also increases. This is what is meant by the statement that karma does not disappear. There is no doubt that such rejoicing will produce its own [good] effect. *[Date of writing omitted]*

NINE

The Four Horses

(Shi-me)

ONE DAY A NON-BUDDHIST VISITED the Buddha Śākyamuni and asked him, "[What is] that which is neither spoken nor unspoken?" The Buddha remained sitting silently for some time, whereupon the non-Buddhist prostrated himself before him and said in praise, "Bhagavat, how wonderful! As a result of your great compassion the clouds of my delusive mind have vanished, and I have realized enlightenment." Saying this, he respectfully venerated the Buddha once more and departed. After his departure the Venerable Ānanda asked the Buddha, "What was it that caused that non-Buddhist to say he had realized enlightenment and praise you as he did?" The Bhagavat answered, "A good horse runs when it sees even the shadow of a whip."

From the time that Bodhidharma first came to China to the present day, numerous masters have used this story to give instruction to students of the Way, some of whom quickly understand it and come to believe in Buddhism, while others take many years. This story is known as "the non-Buddhist who questioned the Buddha." We should clearly realize that the Bhagavat has expounded the Law in two different ways—with speech and with silence. Those who have realized enlightenment on the basis of either of these two ways are all like a good horse that runs when it sees even the shadow of a whip. Those who realize enlightenment apart from these two ways are the same.

The Patriarch Nāgārjuna said, "[Realizing enlightenment] on the basis of having heard the Law expounded is like a fast horse that immediately enters the right path when it sees even the shadow of a whip." At various times and as a result of various causal relationships, we have the opportunity to learn of the nature of permanence and impermanence, the three vehicles, and the one vehicle.[1] Even though we sometimes fall into mistaken ways of thinking, we can return to the correct path through seeing the shadow of a whip, that is to say, through hearing the teachings of a true master. If we train under such a master or meet an enlightened person, we will find that the Law is being expounded everywhere and the shadow of the whip is always present. There are some who are able to see the latter immediately, others who must wait innumerable *kalpas,* and still others who must wait for an eternity. In the end, however, they are all able to enter into the right path [realize enlightenment].

The *Saṃyukt-āgama-sūtra*[2] states: "The Buddha said to the assembled monks, 'There are four kinds of horses. The first kind immediately follows its rider's will when, in surprise and fear, it sees the shadow of a whip. The second does likewise when the whip strikes its hair. The third, however, does not obey its master until after the whip has struck its flesh. The fourth, finally, does not do so until the whip has reached its very bones.

" 'The first horse is like someone who comes to dislike the transient world when he hears of the death of a neighboring villager. The second is like someone who feels this way when the deceased is a fellow villager. The third is like someone who does not feel this way until the deceased is one of his close relatives. The fourth is like someone who is not conscious of this feeling until he himself is faced with sickness [and death].' "

The preceding are the four kinds of horses as expounded in the *Saṃyukt-āgama-sūtra.* When undergoing training in the Way we should definitely study these examples, for they have been transmitted to us by those true masters—the patriarchs—who have appeared in the human and celestial worlds as messengers of the Buddha. Those who have not referred to these four horses cannot be considered to be the leaders of human and celestial beings. Trainees who, because of their good deeds, are close to the Way inevitably hear of these examples. Those who are far from the Way, however, are able neither to learn nor to hear of them. For this reason Zen masters should wish to explain, and disciples should wish to listen to, their meaning as quickly as possible. Even when the Buddha described the mind that dislikes the transient world with [only] a single word, various people understood him according to their own capabilities. Some rejoiced at this teaching, while others became fearful. Some disliked it, while others had their doubts resolved.

The *Mahāparinirvāṇa-sūtra* states: "The Buddha said, 'Virtuous men! There are four ways in which a rider controls his horse. The first is for the rider to strike the horse's hair, the second its skin, the third its flesh, and the fourth its bones. Just as a rider uses these four ways to control his horse, so the Tathāgata uses four methods to rid sentient beings of their delusion. When someone becomes a follower of Buddhism as a result of his having explained [the nature of] birth, it is similar to a rider who controls his horse by striking its hair. When he adds the question of old age to his explanation, it is similar to controlling it by striking its skin as well as its hair. The further addition of sickness is similar to controlling it by striking its hair, skin, and flesh. The fourth and final addition of death to the preceding three is similar to controlling it by striking its hair, skin, flesh, and bones. Virtuous men! Although a rider is not always successful in controlling his horse, the Tathāgata never fails to rid sentient beings of their delusion. It is for this reason that he is known as "the one who controls men." ' "

The preceding are the four horses of the *Mahāparinirvāṇa-sūtra.* There have never been any trainees who have failed to study these examples, nor any Buddhas who have failed to explain them. When we encounter, venerate, and become followers of the Buddha we should by all means listen to his explanation of these four horses. Whenever the Law is transmitted [from one Buddha to another] these examples are taught for the sake of all beings. This is something that will remain unchanged for innumerable *kalpas*. Whenever someone realizes enlightenment he teaches these examples for the sake of Bodhisattvas, Śrāvakas, and human and celestial beings, just as he did when he first awoke to the Bodhi-mind. It is for this reason that the essence of the Three Treasures is eternal.

It can now be clearly seen that the teachings of the various Buddhas are far different from those of Bodhisattvas. We should realize that there are four methods of controlling a horse, which consist of striking its hair, skin, flesh, and bones, respectively. Although it is not explicitly stated what is used to strike the horse, those masters who have transmitted the Law have understood it to be a whip. Controlling a horse, however, does not necessarily depend on the use of a whip, for there are methods of control in which it is not employed. That is to say, methods of horse control should not necessarily be limited to those using a whip. For example, take the case of a "dragon-horse," which is over eight *ch'ih*[3] in height. There are very few human beings who can control this horse. Or take the case of a "thousand-*ri* horse," which is able to run a thousand *ri* in a single day. Although this horse is said to sweat blood for the first five hundred *ri*, it later becomes refreshed and is able to run extremely fast. There are very few people who are able either to ride or to control this horse. It is to be found not in China but in other foreign countries.

I have never seen [it written] that either of these two kinds of horses was often struck with a whip. It is true, though, that one ancient master did say, "It is absolutely necessary to use a whip to control a horse, for it is impossible to control one without it. This is the way in which a horse is controlled." The four methods [of controlling a horse] consist of striking its hair, skin, flesh, and bones, respectively. Without [first] striking its hair, its skin cannot be struck; without striking both its hair and skin, its flesh and bones cannot be struck. For this reason we should realize that it is absolutely necessary to use a whip to control a horse. The fact that the use of a whip is not explicitly mentioned in the text [of the *sūtra*] is because of a deficiency in its content. Such deficiencies are to be found in many *sūtras*.

The Tathāgata—the one who controls men—also uses four methods to rid all sentient beings of their delusion, a task in which he is always successful. There are those who understand the Buddha's teachings when he explains [the nature of] birth, others who understand them when he adds old age, still others who understand them when he further adds sickness, and finally, still others who first understand them when he adds death to the preceding three. The last three categories of understanding, however, cannot exist apart from the first, just as a horse's skin, flesh, and bones cannot be struck without first striking its hair.

It was the Buddha Śākyamuni himself who [first] explained [the nature of] birth, old age, sickness, and death. He did so neither to separate sentient beings from these four categories nor to assert that the latter were in themselves the Way. Rather, he explained them in order that all sentient beings might realize the supreme Bodhi-wisdom. This is why the Tathāgata, who never fails to rid sentient beings of their delusion, is known as "the one who controls men." *(Compiled by Ejō in the summer of the seventh year of Kenchō [1255])*

TEN

A Monk at the Fourth Stage of Meditation

(Shi-zen Biku)

THE PATRIARCH NĀGĀRJUNA SAID, "One of the Buddha's disciples took pride in his attainment of the fourth stage of meditation and [mistakenly] believed he had reached Arhathood. [Previously] when he had attained the first stage of meditation, he thought he had also achieved the first stage to Arhathood. When he attained the second and the third stages, he continued to believe that he had achieved the corresponding stages to Arhathood. After he had achieved the fourth stage he became so proud that he stopped his practice altogether. When he was approaching death, the intermediate world associated with the fourth stage of meditation appeared before him. Seeing this, he thought to himself, 'The Buddha has deceived me; there is no Nirvāṇa!' As a result of his mistaken view, the intermediate world associated with the fourth stage of meditation disappeared and was immediately replaced by the intermediate world leading to Avīci hell. He then died and was immediately reborn in Avīci hell.

"The assembled monks asked the Buddha, 'Where was this monk who trained by himself reborn when he died?' 'In Avīci hell,' the Buddha answered. The monks were very surprised to hear this, and they further asked, 'How could this happen to him when he had always done zazen and preserved the precepts?' The Buddha answered, 'It is all because he took pride in his attainment of the fourth stage of meditation and [mistakenly] believed he had realized Arhathood. When he was approaching death, he saw the intermediate world associated with the fourth stage of meditation appear. Seeing this, he mistakenly thought to himself, "The Buddha has deceived me; there is no Nirvāṇa, for if there were, I, who am an Arhat, would not be reborn [in the human world]." At that time he immediately saw the intermediate world leading to Avīci hell appear, and when he died, he was immediately reborn there.' The Buddha then recited the following verse:

'Great learning, preservation of the precepts, and the practice of zazen
Are unable [in themselves] to extinguish our desires.
Though there is merit in these practices,
We find it difficult to believe in its existence.

He fell into hell because he slandered the Buddha.
It had nothing to do with his attainment of the fourth stage of meditation.' "

The [preceding] monk is known as a monk at the fourth stage of meditation, and also as a self-taught monk. This story is an admonishment against our thinking that because we have attained the fourth stage of meditation we have also realized Arhathood. It also teaches us to guard against false views that slander the Buddha. All human and celestial beings who have ever gathered together to listen to the Buddha's teachings are well acquainted with this story, for from the Tathāgata's lifetime to the present day, in both India and China, Buddhist masters have used it to admonish and ridicule those who cling to falsehood believing it to be the Truth.

This monk may be said to have made three mistakes. The first was his inability, as a self-taught monk, to distinguish the fourth stage of meditation from Arhathood. In spite of this weakness he meaninglessly trained in a secluded place without seeking the Buddha's guidance. Since he was fortunate enough to have lived during the Tathāgata's lifetime, he could have overcome this problem if he had been willing to pay frequent visits to the Buddha and listen to his teachings. In spite of this, however, he chose to train in a secluded place, neither visiting the Buddha nor listening to his teachings. Even if he did not visit the Buddha, he should [at least] have visited the various great Arhats [the Buddha's foremost disciples] and sought instruction from them. He chose, instead, to train alone and fell victim to his pride.

His second mistake was that just as he thought he had achieved Arhathood when he attained the fourth stage of meditation, he thought he had realized the corresponding stages to Arhathood when he achieved the first three stages of meditation. The various stages of meditation, however, are far below those to Arhathood, and they should not be compared with each other. This monk made the mistake of doing so because, as a self-taught monk, he refused to train under a master and consequently remained ignorant of the Law.

[The *Mo-ho-chih-kuan* states:] "One of the Venerable Upagupta's disciples, who had previously entered the monkhood because of his strong faith [in Buddhism], mistakenly believed he had also realized Arhathood when he attained the fourth stage of meditation. In order to correct his mistaken belief, Upagupta told him to travel to a certain area. Upagupta then used his supernatural power to create an incident that his disciple would encounter along the way.

"The incident involved a group of five hundred merchants who were attacked and killed by a band of robbers. When the disciple saw their bodies strewn here and there, he was overcome with fear and suddenly thought to himself, 'I guess I have not realized Arhathood after all; I must still be at the third stage.' Just then the daughter of a wealthy merchant, whose father was among the slain, approached him and said, 'Virtuous monk! Please take me with you.' He answered, 'The Buddha has forbidden us from traveling together with women.' She continued, 'Virtuous monk! In that case, you go first and I will follow you.' Taking pity on her, he allowed her to do so.

"When they came to a big river, which Upagupta had also miraculously created, the young woman said to him, 'Virtuous monk! Let us cross the river together.' [Agreeing to this,] the monk started to cross the river downstream, while she crossed upstream. Suddenly she slipped and, tumbling into the water, asked for the monk's aid. Offering her his hand, he pulled her out of the river. At that time, however, having felt her delicate soft skin, he fell victim to sexual desire and immediately realized, as a result, that he had not achieved the third stage to Arhathood either. This did not stop his affection for her from growing, though, and he decided to take her to a secluded place where they could have sexual intercourse.

"Actually, the woman was Upagupta in disguise. When the monk discovered this, he was filled with great shame and prostrated himself before his master. After he stood up, Upagupta said to him, 'Previously you thought you had realized Arhathood. How is it, then, that you decided to commit such a bad act?' Having said this, he took the monk back to the community of monks, where he instructed him to make repentance. He then further instructed him in the essence of the Law until finally the monk realized Arhathood."

Although this monk had at first a false view of the nature of birth and death, he still realized that he was not an Arhat when he became fearful at the sight of the [merchants'] bodies strewn all about. He committed a further mistake, however, when he then thought he had realized the third stage to Arhathood. Later, when he touched the delicate soft skin of a woman and fell victim to sexual desire, he realized that he had not achieved the third stage either. In spite of this, however, he neither slandered the Buddha or the Law nor forsook [the Buddha's] teachings. In this respect he is far superior to the monk at the fourth stage of meditation [who was previously introduced]. It was because of his study of the Buddha's teachings that he realized he had not achieved either the third or the fourth stage to Arhathood.

Present-day self-taught monks are quite unaware of the nature of Arhathood, let alone Buddhahood. It is because of this ignorance that, although they are neither Arhats nor Buddhas, they make the mistake of believing that they are. What a serious error! The first thing Buddhist trainees should do is learn the [true] nature of Buddhahood.

An ancient master said, "Those who study the Buddha's teachings are generally aware of their degree [of accomplishment]. Though they [sometimes] stray from the Way, they still find it easy to realize enlightenment." This ancient master has indeed spoken the truth! Even though we have a false view of the nature of birth and death, if we have studied the Law even slightly we will neither deceive ourselves nor be deceived by others.

[The *Mo-ho-chih-kuan* continues:] "It is said that a certain monk who thought he had realized Buddhahood once waited for the morning star to appear [just as Buddha Śākyamuni had done]. No matter how long he waited, however, it failed to appear, and he became convinced that a celestial demon was obstructing it. When at last it did appear, King Brahma failed to ask him to expound the Law [as he had done when the Buddha Śākyamuni realized enlightenment]. He then realized he had not really realized Buddhahood, though he thought he must at least have attained Arhathood. When someone subsequently criticized him, however, he became angry, and thus realized that he had not achieved Arhathood either, though he was still convinced that at the very least he had achieved the third stage [to Arhathood]. When he saw a young woman, however, he was filled with sexual desire, and finally he realized he had not even achieved the first stage. It was due to his knowledge of the Buddha's teachings that he recognized his shortcomings."

Those who, like this monk, know the Buddha's teachings are also aware of their own faults and are able to rid themselves of them quickly. On the other hand, those who do not know his teachings waste their lives in ignorance, transmigrating endlessly. Even though Upagupta's disciple originally believed that he had also realized Arhathood when he achieved the fourth stage of meditation, he later had the wisdom to realize that he was not an Arhat. If the [previously introduced] self-taught monk had only possessed the same wisdom to see that he too was not an Arhat, he would not have slandered the Buddha when he saw the intermediate world associated with the fourth stage of meditation appear as he approached death. In fact, however, in spite of the fact that this self-taught monk had realized the fourth stage of meditation long before [his death], he failed to understand the difference between his attainment and Arhathood, and consequently was unable to correct his error. Failing to revise his thinking, he at last fell victim to his false view.

The monk's third great mistake, which ensured that he would fall into Avīci hell, occurred as he approached death. Even had he mistaken the fourth stage of meditation for Arhathood throughout his entire life, he should have repented his mistake and realized that he was not an Arhat when he saw the intermediate world associated with the fourth stage of meditation appear as he approached death. Had he done so, he would never have doubted the Buddha's teachings concerning the existence of Nirvāṇa. In fact, however, because he had made the mistake of becoming a self-taught monk, he ended by slandering the Buddha. Thus the intermediate world leading to Avīci hell appeared before him, and he was reborn there at his death. Even had he actually realized Arhathood, how could he be compared with the Tathāgata?

Śāriputra was a virtuous monk who had realized Arhathood early in life. Setting aside the Tathāgata's Wisdom [for the moment], Śāriputra's wisdom was so great that even if the wisdom of all beings in the one billion worlds were added together, it would be less than one-sixteenth of Śāriputra's. In spite of his great wisdom, however, he never felt deceived by the Tathāgata, even when the latter taught something that contradicted his previous teachings. On the contrary, at such times he praised the Buddha by saying that even Pāpīyas was unable to contradict himself in this way. While Śāriputra had been unable to save Punyavadharna, the Tathāgata had done so.[1] This clearly shows the great difference between Arhathood and Buddhahood. Even if people as wise as Śāriputra and the Buddha's other disciples filled the whole world, they would still be unable to measure the Buddha's Wisdom.

In the teachings of both Confucius and Lao-tzŭ there is nothing that can be compared with the merit of the Buddha's Wisdom. Although those who study Buddhism have no difficulty in understanding [the teachings of] Confucius and Lao-tzŭ, none of those who have studied the latter two alone have ever realized the essence of the Law. In present-day China there are many who say that the teachings of Confucius and Lao-tzŭ are the same as those of the Buddha. Theirs, however, is a very distorted view about which I will have more to say later.

The [previously described] monk at the fourth stage of meditation took his distorted view for the Truth and, believing that the Tathāgata had deceived him, turned his back on Buddhism. The depth of his stupidity can only be compared with that of the six non-Buddhist religious philosophers.[2]

An ancient master said, "Even during the Great Master's lifetime there were monks who held distorted views, so it is no wonder that their number increased after his death; for they had no master [to guide them], and consequently were unable to achieve the fourth stage of meditation." The "Great Master" referred to here is the Bhagavat himself. Even during his lifetime it was impossible to prevent some of those who had entered the monkhood and received the precepts from falling victim to distorted views as a result of their having become self-taught monks. It is no wonder, then, that now that more than two thousand years have elapsed since his death, there are many more who have made this mistake, particularly in such a remote and ill-bred area as Japan. Even the [previously described] monks at the fourth stage of meditation made the same mistake, so it is not surprising that those who have not vowed even to achieve this fourth stage should do likewise, for they remain meaninglessly attached to fame and profit, hoping to become government officials and lead successful lives. As I have mentioned previously, in present-day China there are many ignorant and ill-informed monks who believe that the teachings of the Buddha are the same as those of Confucius and Lao-tzŭ.

In the Chia-t'ai era [1201–4] of the Sung dynasty, a monk named Chêng-shou[3] compiled the thirty-section *P'u-têng-lu*,[4] a copy of which he presented [to the emperor]. In it he says, "I once heard Chih-yüan of Mount Ku[5] say the following: 'The doctrine I teach is like a tripod, the legs of which are the teachings of the Buddha, Confucius, and Lao-tzŭ. If the tripod lacks one of its legs it will collapse.' Because of my high regard for Chih-yüan, I decided to study this question further, and came to the following conclusion: the essence of Confucianism is sincerity; the essence of Taoism is distinterestedness; and the essence of Buddhism is 'seeing into one's own nature' [the realization of one's Buddha-nature]. Although the essence of these three teachings is known by different names, in the final analysis they are one and the same."

This distorted view is not limited to Chih-yüan and Chêng-shou alone; there are many who subscribe to it. Their mistake is even worse than believing that one has realized Arhathood upon attaining the fourth stage of meditation. They slander not only the Buddha but the Law and the Buddhist community as well, denying as they do the existence of enlightenment, the three worlds, and causality. This [corruption of Buddhism] will undoubtedly engulf them in endless misfortune. They are no different from those who deny the existence of the Three Treasures, the Four Noble Truths, and the four stages to Arhathood.

The essence of Buddhism has never been to see into one's own nature. Which of the seven past Buddhas or twenty-eight Indian patriarchs ever said that the Law consisted merely of seeing into one's own nature? It is true that the sixth patriarch [Hui-nêng] spoke about this question in the *T'an sūtra*,[6] but as this is a forged writing it cannot be said to represent his true teachings or to have [correctly] transmitted the Law. We descendants of the Buddha should not rely on it at all. Chêng-shou and Chih-yüan were unaware of even one part of the Law. This is why they made the mistake of viewing Buddhism as one leg of a tripod.

An ancient master said, "Because both Lao-tzŭ and Chuang-tzŭ[7] were themselves attached to self and others, they were unable to understand the Hīnayāna teaching concerning the need to free oneself from attachment to these. It is no wonder, then, that they could not understand the Mahāyāna teaching that as both self and others are, in essence, empty, there is nothing to be attached to. Their teachings, therefore, are quite different from those of Buddhism. Foolish people, however, fall victim to their own superficial understanding of the teachings [of these two men] and, aided by their own attachment to the outer forms of zazen, imagine that their teachings concerning political morality and spiritual freedom are the same as those of the Buddha concerning enlightenment." From ancient times there have been those who, falling victim to their superficial understanding and ignorant of the Truth, have attempted to identify the Buddha's teachings with those of Chuang-tzŭ and Lao-tzŭ. No one who has understood Buddhism to even a slight extent, however, has ever held their teachings in high esteem.

The *Ch'ing-ching-pên-hsing sūtra*[8] states: "Yen-hui[9] is the Chinese reincarnation of the Bodhisattva Candraprabha,[10] Confucius is the Chinese reincarnation of the Bodhisattva Kuang-ching,[11] and Lao-tzŭ is the Chinese reincarnation of the Bodhisattva Kāśyapa." From ancient times there have been those who have used this *sūtra* to show that as Confucius, Lao-tzŭ, and others are reincarnations of [Indian] Bodhisattvas, and consequently the Buddhas's servants, their teachings are the same as those of the Buddha. They were quite mistaken in doing so, for an ancient master has said, "The various listings [of the *sūtras*] all note that this *sūtra* is a forgery." This ancient master's words clearly show that the Buddha's teachings are different from those of Confucius and Lao-tzŭ. Even if they really were Bodhisattvas, they would still be unequal to the Buddha.

It is only the various Buddhas and Bodhisattvas in the three stages of time who have the ability to take on the form of ordinary human beings in order to save them. Ordinary human beings are unable to do so, for they are born in this world as a result of their past [bad] karma, not from their desire to save human beings. Not only did Confucius and Lao-tzŭ fail to teach anything about this question, they were also quite ignorant of causality in the three stages of time. They merely taught loyal service to the emperor and filial piety, the latter seen as a method of regulating one's household. Their teachings concerned the present world only, ignoring the future, and therefore were one form of the denial of causality.

The reason that the [previously mentioned] ancient enlightened master had little use for Chuang-tzŭ and Lao-tzŭ was that the latter had failed to understand the teachings of Hīnayāna, let alone those of Mahāyāna. It has only been foolish men in later generations like Chih-yüan and Shêng-shou who have said the teachings of these two men were one with those of the Buddha. What qualified men like them to deny the teachings of this past master by asserting that these teachings were all the same? Their opinions concerning Buddhism are of no value whatsoever. They should put on their backpacks and set out in search of an enlightened master, for they know nothing about either Mahāyāna or Hīnayāna Buddhism. They have less knowledge of Buddhism than the monks who mistook their attainment of the fourth stage of meditation for Arhathood. How regrettable! In this present age, when the winds of degenerate Buddhism blow violently, there are many devils like them!

An ancient master[12] said, "The teachings of Confucius and Chou Kung-tan,[13] as well as those of the three founding emperors[14] and their five successors,[15] state that filial piety is used to regulate the home and loyalty the nation, thus aiding the nation and ensuring the welfare of the people. These teachings, however, are only concerned with the present world and have nothing to say about the past or the future. Thus, they are unequal to those of the Buddha, who speaks of benefiting sentient beings in all three stages of time. How could such teachings not be mistaken?"

How true this ancient master's words are! He had realized the ultimate meaning of Buddhism and at the same time was well acquainted with worldly truth. The teachings of the three founding emperors and their five successors are far inferior to, and should not be compared with, those of Kings Cakravarti, Brahma, and Śakrendra, for both the areas they deal with and the karmic benefits they produce are far fewer than those of these latter kings. Even these three kings, however, are inferior to someone who has entered the monkhood and received the precepts, let alone the Tathāgata. The writings of Confucius and Chou Kung-tan, too, are inferior to the eighteen Indian scriptures of Brahmanism, including the four Vedas.[16] The teachings of Brahmanism itself are unequal to those of Buddhism, not even reaching the level of those of Hīnayāna. How regrettable it is that in a small country like

China, far distant [from India], there is this mistaken teaching concerning the unity of Buddhism, Confucianism, and Taoism.

The Bodhisattva Nāgārjuna, the fourteenth patriarch, said, "Great Arhats and Pratyekabuddhas are aware of periods of time as long as eighty thousand *kalpas,* but Bodhisattvas and Buddhas are aware of eternity." Confucius, Lao-tzŭ, and so on, on the other hand, are unaware of the existence of either future or past life and consequently do not possess the supernatural power to know of events in their previous lives. It is not surprising, therefore, that they are unaware of even one *kalpa* of time, let alone a hundred, a thousand, or eighty thousand *kalpas* of time. How, then, can they be compared with the various Buddhas and Bodhisattvas, who are aware of eternity as clearly as they see the palms of their own hands? Such comparison is the height of stupidity! We should cover our ears whenever we hear talk about the unity of these three teachings, for it is the worst of all false views.

Chuang-tzŭ said, "High and low station in life, pleasure and pain, right and wrong, gain and loss all occur spontaneously." This view is similar to the non-Buddhist Indian view that all things occur spontaneously. Those who hold views like these are unaware that high and low station in life, pleasure and pain, and so on are all the result of past good and bad karma. Furthermore, they are unaware of those forms of karma that determine both the universal and the individual characteristics of existence. Since they are unaware of both the past and the future, they really do not know the present either. How, then, can their teachings be identified with those of the Buddha?

There are those who say, "Since the various Buddhas enlighten the whole world, all worldly phenomena express the enlightenment of the Buddhas. Therefore, since both self and others are encompassed in the enlightenment of the Buddhas, mountains, rivers, earth, sun, moon, stars, the four illusions,[17] and the three poisons[18] are all expressions of their enlightenment. Furthermore, since nothing is outside the Law, not even the three poisons and four illusions, the Tathāgata can be seen in mountains and rivers, just as the whole world can be seen in each of its individual phenomena. Thus, each individual act is an expression of the ultimate Truth." They designate all of this as [the meaning of] "great enlightenment" and assert that it is "the directly transmitted patriarchal Way."

In present-day China those who talk in this manner are as numerous as rice plants, hemp, bamboo, and reeds. Although it is uncertain whose [Law] descendants they are, it is clear that they have not understood the Way of the Buddhas and patriarchs. While it is true that mountains, rivers, and earth are encompassed in the enlightenment of the various Buddhas, the way in which ordinary men view them is far different from that of the Buddhas, for ordinary men have never learned or heard about the true nature of enlightenment. When they say it is possible to see the whole world in each of its individual phenomena, it is similar to saying that common people are the equals of their king. Why do they not also say that when the whole world is viewed, it is possible to see each and every one of its individual phenomena? If the Way of the Buddhas and patriarchs conformed to their views, neither the various Buddhas nor the patriarchs would have appeared in this world. Consequently, no one would be able to realize enlightenment. Attached to such views, they will never be able to realize that birth is [as it is] nonbirth.

The Venerable Paramārtha[19] said, "China is fortunate in two respects—it has no *rākṣasas* [man-eating devils] and no non-Buddhists." These words are truly those of a non-Buddhist Indian Brāhman. Although it may be true that there are no Chinese non-Buddhists who possess supernatural powers, this does not mean that there are no non-Buddhist views in that country. Although *rākṣasas* may not be found there either, it does not mean that there are no non-Buddhists like them. Since China is a small peripheral country, quite unlike central India, it is not surprising that while a few of its inhabitants practice the Way, none of them has realized the same enlightenment as those in India.

An ancient master[20] said, "At present there are many monks who are returning to secular life. Because they fear being forced to perform compulsory service for the king, however, they then become followers of non-Buddhist religions. Stealing the Buddhist doctrine, they secretly use it to develop the teachings of Chuang-tzŭ and Lao-tzŭ. The result is a mixture of these various teachings that confuses beginners, preventing them from deciding what is true and what is false. This is similar to the Vedas, which teach the unity of self and Brahman."

We should realize that it is indeed beginners who are confused as to which of the three teachings is true and which are false. Chih-yüan and Shêng-shou are both examples of such beginners. Merely to call them extremely foolish is insufficient, for it is quite clear that they also had no respect for [the teachings of] the past patriarchs. Among present-day Chinese monks there is not even one who is aware that the teachings of Confucius and Lao-tzŭ are inferior to those of the Buddha. Although it is true that, throughout China, those who call themselves descendants of the Buddhas and patriarchs are now as numerous as rice plants, hemp, bamboo, and reeds, not one of them, not even half of one of them, has understood that the Buddha's teachings are superior to [those of] the other two. It was only Ju-ching, my late master, who understood this fact and proclaimed it ceaselessly day and night. Even among those [Chinese] monks who thought themselves qualified to expound the meaning of the *sūtras* and *śāstras*,[21] there have been none who understood this fact. The so-called "*sūtra*-lecturers" of the past one hundred years, in particular, have attempted to make up for their own ignorance by studying the training methods of Zen monks, hoping to steal the latter's understanding. What a great mistake!

In the writings of Confucius we find reference to "a man of innate knowledge." In the Buddha's teachings, however, there is no such reference, though there is a teaching concerning the relics of the Buddha. About this latter subject Confucius and Lao-tzŭ have nothing to say. If we make a thorough comparison of these three teachings in this way, it will become impossible for us to mix them together even should we wish to do so.

The *Analects* of Confucius states: "Those who have innate knowledge of it [the Truth] rank highest, those who learn it through study are next, while those who learn it after much difficulty follow them. The lowest rank is assigned to those who are unable to learn it even after much difficulty." In Buddhism it is impossible for someone to be born with innate knowledge, for this would be a denial of causality. The reason the monk at the fourth stage of meditation fell into hell was that he committed the crime of slandering the Buddha as he approached death. Those who slander the Buddha by thinking that his teachings are the same as those of Confucius and Lao-tzŭ will not have to wait until their next life to reap the karmic retribution of their crime! Should we trainees fail to discard this false view quickly, we too will end by falling into hell.

We should clearly realize that Confucius and Lao-tzŭ were unaware of both the three stages of time and the law of causality. Furthermore, they were unaware of the existence of even one of the four continents, let alone all of them. It is not surprising, then, that they knew nothing about the six lowest heavens, the three worlds, the nine realms,[22] the one thousand worlds, the one million worlds, or the one billion worlds. Unlike the Tathāgata, who ruled over all these various worlds, Confucius and Lao-tzŭ were, because of their birth, unable to ascend the throne of even their own country.

The Tathāgata was respectfully venerated and guarded, day and night, by Kings Brahma, Śakrendra, and Cakravarti. They constantly requested that he expound the Law [for their benefit]. Confucius and Lao-tzŭ, however, lacked such virtue. Ordinary individuals that they were, they have continued to transmigrate endlessly and even now remain ignorant of the path to enlightenment. How can such as they be thought to have realized that all things are the manifestation of the Truth? If they have failed to realize this, how can they be said to be the Bhagavat's equals?

Confucius and Lao-tzŭ were unable to enlighten others, just as they had been unable to enlighten themselves. Being the Bhagavat's inferiors in this respect as well, how can their teachings be considered to be the same as his? Whereas the Bhagavat was able to see the smallest particle of matter and measure the shortest moment of time, Confucius and Lao-tzŭ, ignorant of both the finite and the infinite worlds, were unable to do either one. Confucius, Lao-tzŭ, Chuang-tzŭ, and Hui-tzŭ[23] were simply ordinary people, inferior even to those in the first stage to Arhathood, let alone the second, third, or fourth stages. How can their teachings be considered the same as those of the Buddha?

In spite of all this there are still Buddhist trainees who out of their ignorance continue to identify these people with the various Buddhas. This is the greatest delusion of all! Not only were Confucius and Lao-tzŭ unaware of the three stages of time and innumerable *kalpas*, they were completely ignorant of the three thousand worlds and the three viewpoints [concerning the nature of phenomena] encompassed in a single moment of thought.[24] For this reason they cannot be considered the equals of the deities of the sun and moon, let alone the Four-Quarter Kings and the various other celestial deities. Those who compare the Bhagavat with the likes of these do a disservice to both laymen and monks.

The *Lieh-ch'uan*[25] states: "Kuan-ling Yin-hsi was a government official in the Chou dynasty who was well versed in astrology. On one occasion he happened to see a strange sign in the eastern heavens. [Anticipating that this sign signified the coming of an important personage] he decided to go to meet this person, who, it turned out, was Lao-tzŭ. After greeting him, Yin-hsi requested that the other write a book containing more than five thousand words. Yin-hsi himself wrote a nine-section work, entitled the *Kuan-ling-tsu,* which was fashioned after the *Hua-hu-ching.*[26] When Lao-tzŭ subsequently decided to go to the Kuan-hsi district,[27] Yin-hsi asked if he could accompany him. Lao-tzŭ answered, 'If you really wish to go with me from the bottom of your heart, bring me the heads of seven people, including those of your father, mother, and others.' Yin-hsi immediately did as he was instructed and brought the seven required heads, which, however, had all turned into those of wild boars."

[In reference to this story] an ancient master said, "In secular books it is written that Confucianists practice filial piety by worshiping the wooden statues [of their ancestors]. Lao-tzŭ, however, taught Yin-hsi to kill his parents. The Tathāgata, for his part, based his teachings on [the need for] great compassion. Where, then, did Lao-tzŭ find the basis for his treacherous teachings?"

In the past there were misled people who thought that Lao-tzŭ was the Bhagavat's equal. At present there are foolish monks who think that both Lao-tzŭ and Confucius are his equals. They are truly to be pitied! Neither Lao-tzŭ nor Confucius is the equal of King Cakravarti, who practices the ten good deeds in order to guide ordinary people [in the Way]. They are not even the equals of the three founding emperors or their five successors. These latter personages themselves are far inferior to King Cakravarti, who as previously mentioned rules over the four continents and the one billion worlds, and possesses the seven treasures, the four kinds of wheels, and one thousand children.

All the Buddhas and patriarchs in the three stages of time have made respect for and veneration of one's parents, master, and the Three Treasures the basis of their teachings. They have further taught that venerative offerings should be made to sick people and others. None of them has ever made the killing of one's parents the basis of his teachings. How then can Lao-tzŭ's teachings be identified with those of the Buddha? Those who kill their parents become subject to karmic retribution in their next life and inevitably fall into hell. No matter how much Lao-tzŭ may talk about "disinterestedness," those who kill their parents cannot escape karmic retribution in their next life.

The *Ching-tê-ch'uan-têng-lu*[28] states: "The second [Chinese] patriarch [Hui-k'o] used to lament, 'The teachings of Confucius and Lao-tzŭ are concerned with public morality and decorum. No Taoist writings have ever expressed the supreme Truth.' [Later on he said,] 'I recently heard that Zen Master Bodhidharma is residing at Shao-lin temple.[29] Now that a Buddha [Bodhidharma] has come this close, I should go train under him [in my quest for enlightenment].' "

We present-day trainees should clearly realize that the Law was correctly transmitted to China by virtue of the second patriarch's training [under Bodhidharma]. Even though the latter had come all the way from India, if the second patriarch had not become his disciple he could not have transmitted the Law. If the second patriarch himself had not [further] transmitted the Law, it would not now exist in China. For this reason the second patriarch holds a very special position, incomparable to that of his successors.

The *Ching-tê-ch'uan-têng-lu* continues: "Hui-k'o, who lived for many years in the Loyang district, was a generous and learned man. He read widely and spoke of the ultimate Truth." There is a great difference between the wide reading of the second patriarch and that of present-day men. Even after the former realized enlightenment and received a *kaśāya* [as a sign thereof], he did not revise his opinion concerning the teachings of Confucius and Lao-tzŭ. This, we should realize, was because he was well aware that their teachings were quite different from those of the Buddha. What justification, then, do we, his present-day descendants, have for turning our backs on his teachings and asserting that all these teachings are the same? We should clearly realize that such assertions are quite false. Those who truly regard themselves as the descendants of the second patriarch should not believe in the teachings of Shêng-shou, Chih-yüan, and so on, any more than they should assert the unity of the three teachings.

[The *Mo-ho-chih-kuan sūtra*[30] states:] "During the Tathāgata's lifetime there was a non-Buddhist by the name of Lun-li.[31] He had given himself this name because he believed there was no one who could equal his great knowledge and debating ability. Responding to a request by five hundred noblemen [who wished to perplex the Buddha], he chose five hundred difficult questions to put to the Buddha. After coming into the Bhagavat's presence, he asked, 'Is the true Way one or many?' 'It is only one,' the Buddha answered. Lun-li continued: 'Each of the various teachers claims that his is the true Way. Because none of them believes in any teachings but his own, they continuously slander each other and debate which of them is right. Thus, [it would appear that] the Way is many.'

"It so happened that just at this time, Mṛgaśīrsa,[32] one of the Buddha's disciples who had realized Arhathood, came up and stood beside the Bhagavat. The Buddha then asked Lun-li, 'Which of these various teachings do you think is the best?' He answered, 'Those taught by Mṛgaśīrsa.' The Buddha then said, 'If his teachings are the best, why is it that he discarded them to train under me as my disciple?' Looking at Mṛgaśīrsa, Lun-li was overcome with shame and, prostrating himself in veneration before the

Buddha, asked his permission to enter the monkhood. At that time the Buddha recited the following verse:

'Each, attached to his own view,
Each, denying the views of others,
Talks of the true Way but knows it not.
They debate the ultimate Truth,
The victors proud, the defeated bitter.
A man of Wisdom, however, is beyond both feelings.
Lun-li! You should realize
That the Way of my disciples
Is beyond being and nonbeing.
What, then, are you searching for?
If you refute my teachings
It will come to naught.
It is difficult to clarify the whole Truth.
To do so is to destroy oneself.' "

The preceding are the golden words of the Bhagavat. Foolish people in China should not willfully turn their backs on his teachings by asserting that there are any other teachings similar to his. Those who do so slander both the Buddha and the Law. The Indian Brāhmans Mṛgaśirsa, Lun-li, Mahākauṣṭhila,[33] and Śrenika[34] were all men of great learning. No one in China, neither Confucius nor Lao-tzŭ, has ever equaled them [in this regard]. Yet in spite of this, they all gave up their own understanding [of the Truth] and entered the Way. Those who assert that the teachings of ordinary men like Confucius and Lao-tzŭ are similar to those of the Buddha commit a serious crime. Even those who merely listen to them must share [a part of] the guilt. Both Arhats and Pratyekabuddhas will eventually become Bodhisattvas, for no one has ever remained at the stage of Arhathood [for eternity]. How, then, can non-Buddhists like Confucius and Lao-tzŭ be identified with the various Buddhas? Those who do so commit a serious mistake indeed!

The various Buddhas and Bodhisattvas, Kings Brahma and Śakrendra, the twenty-eight patriarchs in India and the six in China, not to mention virtuous monks, have all praised the Tathāgata, for they realize that he is far beyond all things. We monks in this age of degenerate Buddhism should not believe those foolish Chinese monks who teach the unity of the three teachings. To do so is to show one's ignorance. *(Compiled by Ejō in the summer of the seventh year of Kenchō [1255])*

ELEVEN

One Hundred and Eight Ways to Enlightenment

(Ippyaku-hachi Hōmyō-mon)

[A CERTAIN SŪTRA[1] STATES:] "When the Bodhisattva Hu-ming[2] was about to descend [to the human world], he entered [*samādhi*] and surveyed the house in which he was to be born. Having done this, he instructed all the celestial beings in Tuṣita Heaven to assemble in the immense sixty-*yojana*-square Kao-ch'uang palace in order that he might expound the Law to them, as he had often done before. [After a number of them had entered the palace,] he said, 'Celestial beings! I am about to descend to the human world. Before I do so, however, I wish to expound [the meaning of] the various ways to enlightenment, the provisional methods of realizing the [real] state of all things. I have gathered you all together here in order to give you these, my last teachings. If you bear these teachings in mind, I am certain they will bring you happiness.'

"By the time the Bodhisattva Hu-ming had completed these introductory remarks, all the celestial beings in Tuṣita Heaven, including celestial maidens and their attendants, had assembled together [though many of them had to stand outside the palace because of insufficient room inside]. Although the Bodhisattva wished to begin [the main part of] his teaching, when he saw [this situation] he decided first to use his miraculous powers to build another celestial palace on top of the present one. The height and width of this new palace were so great that it covered the whole universe. With its indescribably well-proportioned lines and exquisite beauty, it was a joy to all those who beheld it. Decorated as it was with various jewels, its towering majesty was incomparable with that of any celestial palace in the world of desire. Were celestial beings in the world of form to see this miraculously created castle, they would realize that in comparison their own castles were nothing more than large sepulchers.

"Hu-ming was a Bodhisattva who was endowed with both fortune and merit as a result of his past good and honorable deeds. [Entering the newly built palace] he installed himself on the lion's seat,[3] which was decorated with innumerable jewels of various kinds. Furthermore, various celestial garments were spread on this seat, and various flowers of exquisite fragrance lay on the floor around it. The sweet smell of costly incense that had been burned in an extremely large and magnificent censer hung in the air, while the palace itself was filled with the reflected light of innumerable rare jewels that decorated its interior.

"The palace's exterior was covered with a magnificent net to which many golden bells were attached, all resounding in the sweetest tones. The palace itself emitted an infinite variety of light, with tens of thousands of exquisitely colored banners, canopies, and tassels attached to its sides. Guarded by the Four-Quarter Kings and the various Buddhas and Bodhisattvas, it was also respectfully venerated by both Kings Śakrendra and Brahma.

"The voices of innumerable celestial maidens could be heard inside the palace singing the praises of the Bodhisattva Hu-ming to the accompaniment of musical instruments. Each holding the seven treasures, they spoke of his indescribably vast merit: indescribably vast because it was the result of the good fortune with which he was endowed, that good fortune itself being the result of his long *kalpas* of past training.

"Seating himself on the lion's seat, the Bodhisattva Hu-ming at last commenced his address to the assembled celestial beings. He said, 'Celestial beings! A Bodhisattva of the highest level of attainment living in the Tuṣita palace is required, if he wishes to descend to the human world, not only to expound the one hundred and eight ways to enlightenment to all celestial beings but also to make sure that the latter bear them constantly in mind. Celestial beings! I therefore ask that you listen carefully to what I am about to say.

" 'What, then, are the one hundred and eight ways to enlightenment?

" 'Correct belief is the first way, for it preserves a steadfast mind.

" 'A pure mind is the second way, for it is without defilement.

" 'Joy is the third way, for it is the result of a peaceful mind.

" 'A desire [for the Truth] is the fourth way, for it promotes a pure mind.

" 'Correct conduct is the fifth way, for it is the result of pure physical actions, speech, and thought.

" 'Pure speech is the sixth way, for it dispels the mind leading to the four evil realms of hell, hungry ghosts, animals, and *asuras*.

" 'Pure thought is the seventh way, for it dispels greed, anger, and ignorance.

" 'Bearing the Buddhas in mind is the eighth way, for contemplation of the Buddhas is a pure act.

" 'Bearing the Law in mind is the ninth way, for contemplation of the Law is a pure act.

" 'Bearing the monkhood in mind is the tenth way, for it guarantees realization of the Way.

" 'Bearing offerings in mind is the eleventh way, for such offerings are given without any expectation of reward.

" 'Bearing the precepts in mind is the twelfth way, for the precepts embody all the vows [of a Bodhisattva].

" 'Bearing heaven in mind is the thirteenth way, for it gives rise to a cosmic mind.

" 'Benevolence is the fourteenth way, for it causes all beings to do good.

" 'Elimination of suffering is the fifteenth way, for it protects sentient beings from injury.

" 'Happiness is the sixteenth way, for it eliminates all unhappiness.

" 'Selflessness is the seventeenth way, for it extinguishes the five desires.

" 'Transiency is the eighteenth way, for it exposes worldly desire.

" 'Contemplation of suffering is the nineteenth way, for it extinguishes all [evil] desires.

" 'Contemplation of the nonself is the twentieth way, for it eliminates attachment to self.

" 'Contemplation of quiescence is the twenty-first way, for it preserves a tranquil mind.

" 'Shame is the twenty-second way, for it promotes a peaceful mind.

" 'Shyness is the twenty-third way, for it extinguishes external evils.

" 'Sincerity is the twenty-fourth way, for it deceives neither celestial nor human beings.

" 'Truthfulness is the twenty-fifth way, for it prevents self-deception.

" 'Acting in accordance with the Law is the twenty-sixth way, for such action is in accordance with the Truth.

" 'Taking refuge in the Three Treasures is the twenty-seventh way, for it purifies the three evil realms of hell, hungry ghosts, and animals.

" 'Gratefulness is the twenty-eighth way, for it promotes goodness.

" 'Repayment of kindness is the twenty-ninth way, for it does not deceive others.

" 'Nonself-deception is the thirtieth way, for it prevents self-praise.

" 'Benefaction on behalf of all beings is the thirty-first way, for it prevents the slandering of others.

" 'Practice of the Law is the thirty-second way, for it is in accordance with the Truth.

" 'Awareness of time is the thirty-third way, for it prevents frivolous speech.

" 'Control of pride is the thirty-fourth way, for it develops Wisdom.

" 'Absence of an evil mind is the thirty-fifth way, for it protects both self and others.

" 'Freedom from misunderstanding is the thirty-sixth way, for it prevents doubts from arising.

" 'Belief and comprehension [of the Buddha's teachings] are the thirty-seventh way, for they are the basis of realizing enlightenment.

" 'Contemplation of uncleanliness is the thirty-eighth way, for it extinguishes desire.

" 'Amity is the thirty-ninth way, for it prevents recourse to anger.

" 'Knowledge [of the Truth] is the fortieth way, for it prevents the taking of life.

" 'Pursuit of the Law is the forty-first way, for it means to search for the Truth.

" 'Love of the Law is the forty-second way, for it ensures realization of the Law.

" 'A wish to listen to the Law is the forty-third way, for the [real] state of all things is revealed thereby.

" 'Correct provisional [teachings] are the forty-fourth way, for they embody correct practice.

" 'Recognition that the self is a [temporary union] of the five aggregates is the forty-fifth way, for it removes doubts [concerning the Law].

" 'Removal of the cause of delusion is the forty-sixth way, for it ensures the realization of enlightenment.

" 'Detachment from feelings of both bitterness and affection [toward others] is the forty-seventh way, for the unity of these two feelings is promoted thereby.

" 'Recognition that suffering is the result of the temporary union of the five aggregates is the forty-eighth way, for it reveals the true nature of various afflictions.

" 'Recognition of the separate existence of the four elements is the forty-ninth way, for it eliminates the [false] view that all things have a unified independent nature.

" 'Recognition of the [real] state of all things is the fiftieth way, for it reveals the true nature of enlightenment.

" 'Recognition that neither birth nor decay exists is the fifty-first way, for enlightenment is realized thereby.

" 'Awareness of the body's uncleanliness is the fifty-second way, for all things manifest enlightenment.

" 'Awareness that all sensation is suffering is the fifty-third way, for it eliminates all [delusive] sensation.

" 'Awareness of the mind's transiency is the fifty-fourth way, for it recognizes the illusive nature of the mind.

" 'Awareness of the nonsubstantiality of all things is the fifty-fifth way, for it expresses perfect Wisdom.

" 'The four kinds of right effort[4] are the fifty-sixth way, for they eliminate all evil and promote every good.

" 'The four bases of supernatural power[5] are the fifty-seventh way, for they promote flexibility of body and mind.

" 'Belief [in the Three Treasures] is the fifty-eighth way, for it prevents belief in non-Buddhist teachings.

" 'Assiduous practice of the Way is the fifty-ninth way, for it promotes the realization of all Wisdom.

" 'Bearing the Buddha's teachings in mind is the sixtieth way, for it is the basis of all [good] conduct.

" '*Samādhi* is the sixty-first way, for it purifies the mind.

" 'Wisdom is the sixty-second way, for it enables all things to be seen as they are.

" 'The power of belief is the sixty-third way, for it is superior to the power of various devils.

" 'The power of assiduous practice is the sixty-fourth way, for it prevents laxness.

" 'The power of mindfulness is the sixty-fifth way, for it promotes an independent spirit.

" 'The power of *samādhi* is the sixty-sixth way, for it extinguishes all [delusive] thought.

" 'The power of Wisdom is the sixty-seventh way, for it eliminates the two extreme views.[6]

" 'The Wisdom of mindfulness is the sixty-eighth way, for it enables the nature of all things to be known.

" 'The Wisdom of the Law is the sixty-ninth way, for it illuminates all things.

" 'The Wisdom of assiduous practice is the seventieth way, for it enables the Truth to be known.

" 'The Wisdom of happiness is the seventy-first way, for it enables all forms of *samādhi* to be realized.

" 'The Wisdom of repose is the seventy-second way, for it allows freedom of action.

" 'The Wisdom of *samādhi* is the seventy-third way, for it recognizes the equality of all things.

" 'The Wisdom of nonattachment is the seventy-fourth way, for it eliminates attachment to all phenomena.

" 'Correct understanding [of the Law] is the seventy-fifth way, for it ensures the realization of enlightenment.

" 'Correct thinking is the seventy-sixth way, for it eliminates both discriminatory and nondiscriminatory thought.

" 'Correct speech is the seventy-seventh way, for it eliminates attachment to names, sounds, and words.

" 'Correct livelihood is the seventy-eighth way, for it eliminates all evil acts.

" 'Correct action is the seventy-ninth way, for it leads to the other shore [of enlightenment].

" 'Correct remembrance is the eightieth way, for it is beyond dualistic thinking.

" 'Correct *samādhi* is the eighty-first way, for it promotes a tranquil mind.

" 'The Bodhi-mind is the eighty-second way, for it preserves the Three Treasures.

" 'Dependence [on Mahāyāna teachings] is the eighty-third way, for it prevents dependence on Hīnayāna teachings.

" 'True belief is the eighty-fourth way, for it ensures the realization of the highest supreme Law.

" 'Promotion [of good] is the eighty-fifth way, for it hastens the realization of all good.

" 'The *pāramitā*[7] of offerings is the eighty-sixth way, for it promotes the appearance, moment by moment, of the thirty-two distinguishing marks of a Buddha, decorates the world of enlightenment, and saves sentient beings from greed.

" 'The *pāramitā* of preserving the precepts is the eighty-seventh way, for it eliminates the hardship that evil acts produce and prevents sentient beings from breaking the precepts.

" 'The *pāramitā* of perseverance is the eighty-eighth way, for it saves sentient beings from anger, pride, flattery, ridicule, and frivolity.

" 'The *pāramitā* of assiduous practice is the eighty-ninth way, for it ensures the realization of all good and prevents sentient beings from becoming lax [in their practice].

" 'The *pāramitā* of *samādhi* is the ninetieth way, for it hastens the realization of all forms of *samādhi* and supernatural powers and promotes tranquillity in human beings.

" 'The *pāramitā* of Wisdom is the ninety-first way, for it saves sentient beings from ignorance and attachment.

" 'Provisional [teachings] are the ninety-second way, for they enable sentient beings to understand the Truth according to their individual capacities.

" 'The four ways of leading sentient beings [to enlightenment][8] are the ninety-third way, for they ensure that all sentient beings will realize enlightenment for both self and others.

" 'Teaching sentient beings is the ninety-fourth way, for it prevents the pursuit of personal pleasure and promotes interest in teaching [others].

" 'Acceptance of the true Law is the ninety-fifth way, for it eliminates all the delusions of sentient beings.

" 'Gathering merit is the ninety-sixth way, for it benefits all sentient beings.

" 'Practice of *samādhi* is the ninety-seventh way, for it hastens the realization of the ten powers [of a Bodhisattva].[9]

" 'Quiescence is the ninety-eighth way, for it embodies the Tathāgata's enlightenment.

" 'Wisdom is the ninety-ninth way, for it enables the essence of all things to be realized.

" 'Freely teaching the Law is the hundredth way, for it clarifies the essence of the Law.

" 'Truth-embodying practice is the one hundred and first way, for it clarifies the essence of a Buddha.

" 'Attainment of the power that encompasses all in one is the one hundred and second way, for it preserves the teachings of all the Buddhas.

" 'Attainment of the power to teach [the Law] freely is the one hundred and third way, for it brings joy to all sentient beings.

" 'Acting in accordance with the Law alone is the one hundred and fourth way, for it is in accordance with the Truth.

" 'Realization that all things are beyond birth and decay is the one hundred and fifth way, for it ensures the future realization of Buddhahood.

" 'The stage at which the result [of the practice of the Way] is immutable is the one hundred and sixth way, for it embodies the teachings of all past Buddhas.

" 'Advancement in the various levels of Bodhisattvahood is the one hundred and seventh way, for it hastens the ceremony marking this advancement and the realization of all Wisdom.

" 'The highest level of Bodhisattvahood is the one hundred and eighth way, for it ensures entrance into the monkhood and realization of enlightenment.'

"Having finished this explanation, the Bodhisattva Hu-ming concluded his talk to all the assembled celestial beings by saying, 'Celestial beings! You should realize that I have now presented you with the one hundred and eight ways to enlightenment. Continuously bear them in mind, for they must not be forgotten.' "

These, then, are the one hundred and eight ways to enlightenment. When a Bodhisattva of the highest level of attainment is about to descend to the human world, he inevitably teaches these one hundred and eight ways to all the celestial occupants of Tuṣita Heaven.

The Bodhisattva Hu-ming was the name given to the Buddha Śākyamuni when he lived in Tuṣita Heaven as a Bodhisattva of the highest level of attainment. These one hundred and eight ways are enumerated in the *T'ien-shêng Kuang-têng-lu,* compiled by Li Fu-ma.[10] There are only a few Buddhist trainees, however, who are aware of their existence, while those who are unaware are as numerous as rice plants, hemp, bamboo, and reeds. It is for this reason that I have compiled this section. Those Buddhist initiates who one day hope to realize Buddhahood and become teachers of celestial and human beings should study them thoroughly. Those who have never lived in Tuṣita Heaven as Bodhisattvas of the highest level of attainment cannot be considered to be Buddhas. Buddhist trainees, therefore, should not be proud of their [minor] accomplishments. Bodhisattvas who have once lived in Tuṣita Heaven become Buddhas without passing through the intermediate world. *[Date of writing omitted]*

TWELVE

The Eight Aspects of Enlightenment

(Hachi Dainin-gaku)

THE VARIOUS BUDDHAS have all been enlightened persons. Their enlightenment is designated *hachi dainin-gaku* because it has eight important aspects, the comprehension of which lead to Nirvāṇa. It was the Buddha Śākyamuni himself who, in his last sermon on the eve of his death, clarified these eight aspects.

The first [important aspect] is freedom from greed. This means to forsake the five desires. The Buddha said, "Monks! You should know well that a person of many wants seeks both fame and profit, thus subjecting himself to great suffering. A person of few wants, however, seeks neither of these things and consequently does not suffer [at all]. Therefore you should quickly free yourselves from greed, both for this reason as well as because the merit of this freedom gives birth to various other merits. Furthermore, a person of few wants neither caters to the wishes of others nor becomes enslaved to his own sense organs. Satisfied with little, he has no worries and consequently is always calm. His freedom from greed will certainly ensure his entrance into Nirvāṇa. Such is the nature of freedom from greed."

The second is satisfaction. This means to be satisfied with whatever one has. The Buddha said, "Monks! If you wish to escape from suffering you should bear satisfaction in mind. To be satisfied is to have a happy and peaceful state of mind. A satisfied person is happy even though he must sleep on the ground. An unsatisfied person, however, even though he lives in a palatial mansion, is unhappy. Though the latter be rich, he is really poor; though the former be poor, he is really rich. A satisfied person takes pity on an unsatisfied person because the latter is continually enslaved to the five desires. Such is the nature of satisfaction."

The third is to enjoy quiet. This means to lead a solitary life, separated from all worldly disturbances. The Buddha said, "Monks! If you wish to enjoy the quiet of Nirvāṇa, you should lead a solitary life. A quiet person is respected by both King Śakrendra and celestial beings. For this reason you should give up attachment to self and others and lead a solitary life, thereby eliminating the root of suffering. Those who wish to be together with others will be disturbed by them, just as a large tree withers when many birds perch in it. Ordinary people cannot escape various kinds of suffering, just as an old elephant is unable to free himself once he becomes stuck in the mud. Such is the nature of a solitary life."

The fourth is diligence. This means to do good single-heartedly and continuously. The Buddha said, "Monks! If you are diligent [in your practice of the Way], it will not be difficult for you [to realize enlightenment]. For this reason you should be diligent, for running water, no matter how little, can eventually wear away a rock. If, however, you are often lax [in your practice], it is like someone who stops striking a flint before having ignited a fire. Can any [good] result be expected? Such is the nature of diligence."

The fifth is correct remembrance. This is also called the preservation of correct remembrance, the word "preservation" signifying the comprehension of the Law. The Buddha said, "Monks! If you wish to find a true master who can give you good advice, you should preserve correct remembrance, for those who do so remain free from various delusions. Therefore, always bear correct remembrance in mind, for if you fail to do so, you will lose its various merits. On the other hand, if you preserve it, you will remain unharmed even though surrounded by the five desires, like a soldier made invincible by a suit of armor. Such is the nature of correct remembrance."

The sixth is the practice of *samādhi*. *Samādhi* means to reside in the Truth, in an undisturbed state of mind. The Buddha said, "Monks! You enter into *samādhi* through controlling your mind, thus becoming aware of worldly birth and decay. For this reason you should always be diligent in your practice of the various forms of *samādhi*. If you do so your mind will remain undisturbed. Dikes are carefully maintained by those who fear floods. In like manner, you trainees should build the dike of *samādhi* to prevent the water of Wisdom from leaking out. Such is the nature of *samādhi*."

The seventh is the practice of Wisdom. Wisdom stems from enlightenment, which is the result of having practiced the Law that one has heard and thought about. The Buddha said, "Monks! When you possess Wisdom you are free from attachment to greed. Therefore, you should continually engage in self-reflection, taking care not to lose Wisdom, for this is the way to realize enlightenment. Those who fail to do this are neither Buddhist monks nor laymen.

"A person who possesses true Wisdom is like a stalwart ship sailing across the ocean of old age, sickness, and death; like a great bright lamp dispelling the darkness of delusion; like good medicine for all those who are sick; and like a sharp ax used to cut down the tree of illusion. The Wisdom resulting from having heard, thought about, and practiced the Law can thus be used to increase your merit [in the Way]. If a person has come into possession of the light of Wisdom, he has the power to see the Truth with his naked eyes. Such is the nature of Wisdom."

The eighth is to refrain from random discussion. This means to go beyond discriminatory thinking and realize the true nature of all things. The Buddha said, "Monks! Random discussion disturbs the mind, and even though monks, you will be unable to realize enlightenment. For this reason you should quickly give up such mind-disturbing random discussion. Only those who have done this can experience the bliss of enlightenment. Such is the nature of refraining from random discussion."

These, then, are the eight important aspects of enlightenment. Each of these aspects has eight different functions, for a total of sixty-four functions in all. In a broader sense, however, these eight actually have an infinite number of functions, the figure sixty-four being merely an abbreviated form of the latter. The Buddha Śākyamuni spoke the preceding, his last teaching and the essence of Mahāyāna, around midnight on February 15.[1] Thereafter, he said nothing more, remaining silent until his death.

The Buddha said [in conclusion], "Monks! Seek earnestly for the Way, for all worldly things, both transient and intransient, are subject to destruction and decay. Monks! Stop talking for a while, for time is slipping away, and I am about to die. These are my last words."

These final instructions are the reason that disciples of the Buddha never fail to study the teachings [that have been presented here]. Those who neither study nor practice them are not the Buddha's disciples, for these teachings are the Eye Storehouse of the True Law, the highest supreme Mind of the Tathāgata. In spite of this, however, there are at present many who are ignorant of these teachings and only a few who are aware of them. The former find themselves in this situation both because they have been led astray by devils and because of their own lack of past good deeds.

Formerly, during both the right and formal periods of the Law, all the Buddha's disciples studied and practiced the preceding eight aspects. Now, however, not even one monk in a thousand is aware of them. How regrettable! Truly this is the age of degenerate Buddhism! Still, [the eight aspects of] the Tathāgata's true Law continue to exist and are now to be found throughout the world. Therefore, taking care not to be negligent, we should quickly study them.

It is difficult even in the course of innumerable *kalpas* of time to come into contact with Buddhism. It is similarly difficult to be born as a human being. We, however, not only have been born as human beings but have had the good fortune to be born in the Jambudvīpa continent, the best of the three continents.[2] Here we are able to come into contact with the Buddha, hear his teachings, enter the monkhood, and realize enlightenment. Those who died before the Tathāgata did were unable either to hear of or to study the eight aspects. Due to the power of our past good deeds, however, we have been able to do both. In each successive rebirth we should study the eight aspects, for they increase our merit and inevitably lead to the supreme Bodhi-wisdom. If, further, we expound them to all sentient beings, then we ourselves are no different from the Buddha Śākyamuni. *(Written at Eihei-ji on January 6, the fifth year of Kenchō [1253])*

APPENDIX A

Zazen Postures

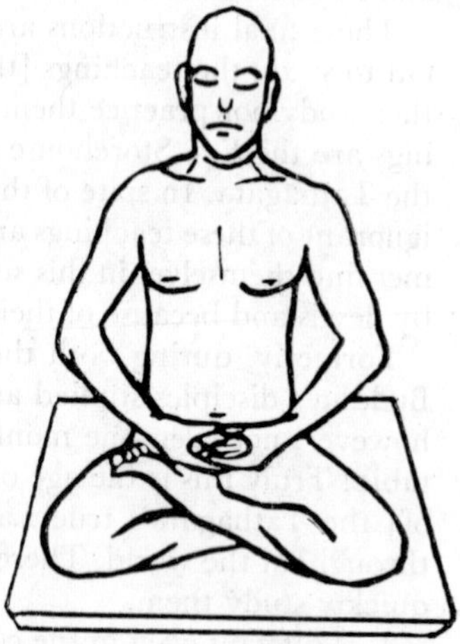

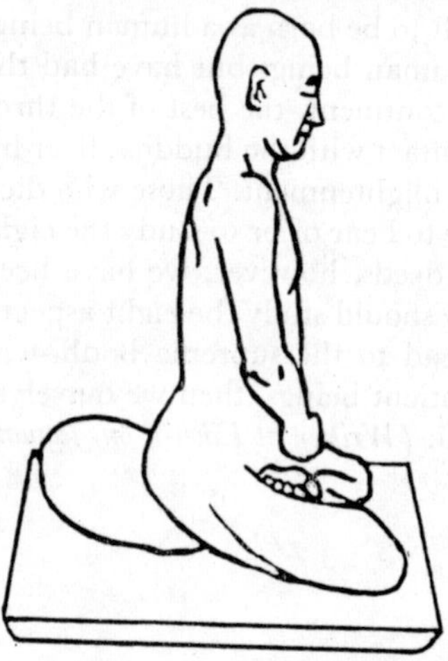

Upper left: the full lotus position, with the right foot over the left thigh and the left foot over the right thigh, both knees touching the mat. The eyes are half open, looking at a spot approximately three feet ahead. The hands are placed one on top of the other, the right hand beneath the left, and rest on the upward-turned soles of the feet. Upper right: the half lotus position, with the left foot over the right thigh and the right foot under the left thigh, both knees touching the mat. This position, while generally easier for beginners, is not as stable as the full lotus position. Lower left: a side view of the full lotus position, showing the ear aligned with the shoulder, back erect, and the tip of the nose aligned with the navel. Note that the buttocks rest on a round cushion. Such cushions measure anywhere from twelve to eighteen inches in diameter and from three to eight inches in thickness. Kapok makes the best filler because it fluffs out when placed in the sun.

APPENDIX B

Three Types of *Kaśāya*

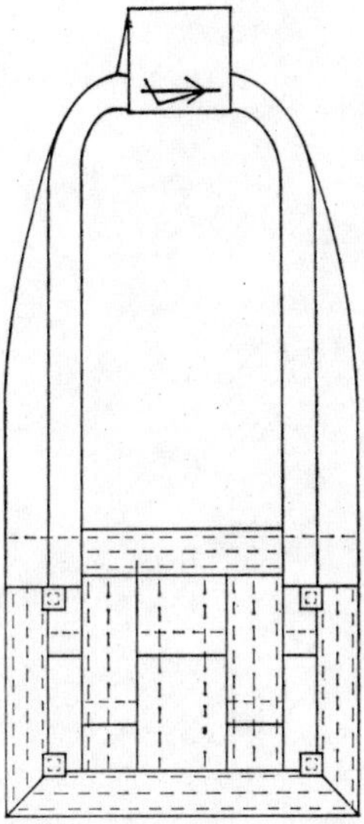

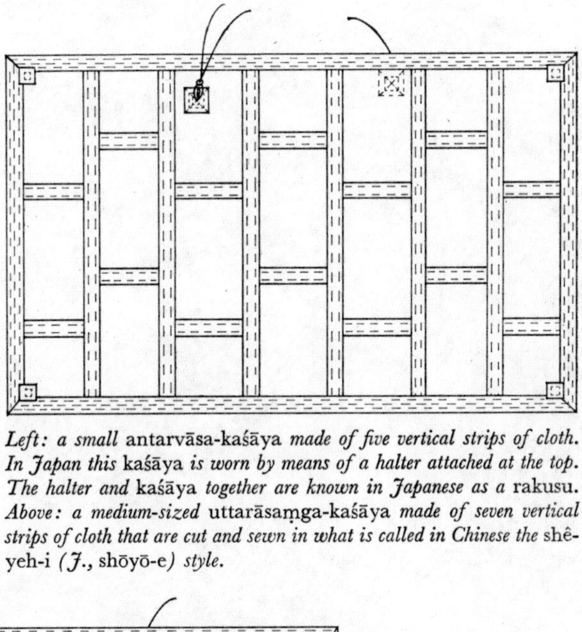

Left: a small antarvāsa-kaśāya *made of five vertical strips of cloth. In Japan this* kaśāya *is worn by means of a halter attached at the top. The halter and* kaśāya *together are known in Japanese as a* rakusu. *Above: a medium-sized* uttarāsaṃga-kaśāya *made of seven vertical strips of cloth that are cut and sewn in what is called in Chinese the* shê-yeh-i *(J.,* shōyō-e*) style.*

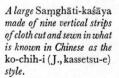

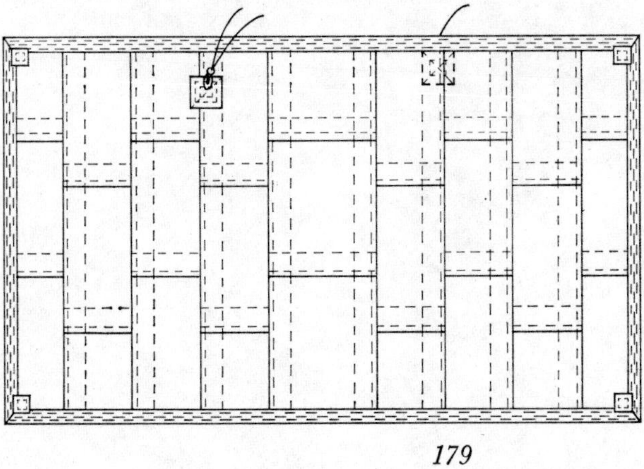

A large Saṃghāti-kaśāya *made of nine vertical strips of cloth cut and sewn in what is known in Chinese as the* ko-chih-i (J., kassetsu-e) *style.*

Notes

Part One

1. Introduction

1. Sitting in meditation (*dhyāna*) in either the full or half lotus position. *Dhyāna* is usually translated as "meditation," although it actually refers to a state in which discriminatory thinking has ceased and reality, the Truth, is experienced directly. See "A Universal Recommendation for Zazen" for a more detailed description.

2. Originally the Sanskrit word *buddha* meant anyone who is awakened or enlightened to the true nature of existence. In present usage, however, it often refers to the historical founder of Buddhism, Gautama Siddhārtha, the Buddha Śākyamuni, who was born around the year 565 B.C. as the first son of King Śuddhodana, whose capital city of Kapilavastu was located in what is now Nepal. At the age of twenty-nine he left his father's palace and his wife and child in search of the meaning of existence. One morning at the age of thirty-five he realized enlightenment while practicing zazen seated beneath the Bodhi tree. He spent the next forty-five years, until his death at the age of eighty, expounding his teachings of the Middle Path, the Four Noble Truths, and the Eightfold Noble Path in order that all sentient beings might realize the same enlightenment that he had. In this book, the term "a Buddha" denotes anyone who has realized enlightenment, while "the Buddha" refers to the historical Buddha, Śākyamuni. When reference is made to the Buddha principle, however, as in this passage, the definite article is also used. The plural, "Buddhas," naturally refers to all enlightened beings.

3. Founded by the Chinese Zen monk Lin-chi (J., Rinzai; d. 867), Buddhist heir of Huang-po.

4. The term *zenji* (Ch., *ch'an-shih*) is an honorific title used in Zen Buddhism and literally means "Zen master." In Japan, this honorific is always attached to the name of noted monks as a sign of respect. For the sake of brevity, however, the use of this title has generally been omitted in this book.

5. The literal meaning of *Dharma* is something that maintains a certain character constantly and becomes a standard of things. Signifying the universal norms or laws that govern human existence according to the Buddha's teachings, it is also translated in this book as "the Truth."

6. Sometimes translated as "Zen riddle," *kōan* (Ch., *kung-an*) originally meant a public notice issued by the Chinese government. However, it now refers to the statements, including answers to questions, made by famous ancient Zen masters. These statements are used as subjects for meditation by novices in Zen monasteries of the Rinzai sect as a means to transcend the realm of duality, such as the subject-object split.

7. A spiritual realm where the Buddhas and Bodhisattvas live in eternal bliss.

2. Japanese Buddhism before Dōgen

1. The Buddhist order or community consists of at least three monks or nuns.

2. Kegon, Hossō, Ritsu, Jōjitsu, Kusha,

and Sanron are commonly referred to as the six schools of the Nara period (710–94), although not all of them actually existed as independent entities.

3. Hōnen (1133–1212), the founder of the Jōdo (Pure Land) sect, taught that anyone, rich or poor, wise or foolish, could achieve rebirth in the Pure Land by sincerely invoking the name of the Buddha Amitābha (J., Amida) as expressed in the formula *Namu Amida-butsu* (Homage to the Buddha Amitābha). Nichiren (1222–82), the founder of the sect bearing his name, believed that the *Saddharma-puṇḍarīka-sūtra* (commonly known as the Lotus *Sūtra*) contained the ultimate teaching of the Buddha. He taught that to attain salvation one should invoke the title of this *sūtra* with the formula *Namu Myōhō-renge-kyō* (Homage to the *Sūtra* of the Lotus of the Supreme Law).

3. Dōgen's Life and Thought

1. One of the three sections of the Tripiṭaka (Buddhist canon). It consists of works, attributed to the Buddha's disciples or great Buddhist scholars, that attempt to state or interpret Buddhist doctrine systematically.

2. Deeds that are produced by the action of the mind, good deeds producing good results and bad deeds producing bad results at some time in the future. In common usage, "producing karma" means committing bad actions.

3. The two main branches of Buddhism. The southern branch (Theravāda, or Way of the Elders) arose in southern India, whence it spread to Ceylon, Burma, Thailand, and Cambodia. In Theravāda Buddhism one strives to become an Arhat, a person who has single-heartedly overcome his passions and ego, thereby gaining liberation for himself. Because of its emphasis on individual self-liberation, in northern Buddhist countries Theravāda is known, somewhat disparagingly, as the Hīnayāna (Lesser Vehicle). The northern branch (Mahāyāna, or Great Vehicle) spread from northern India to Tibet, Mongolia, China, Korea, and Japan. In contrast to Theravāda Buddhism, which tended to remain conservative and rigid, the Mahāyāna adapted itself to the needs of people of diverse racial and cultural backgrounds and varying levels of understanding. Its ideal became the Bodhisattva, one who is ever ready to sacrifice himself in the interest of those lost in ignorance and despair even at the cost of his own supreme enlightenment.

4. The Bodhi-mind refers to a person's aspiration to realize Bodhi-wisdom, that is, perfect enlightenment.

5. One *li* (J., *ri*) is a Chinese unit of distance equivalent to about 666 meters (0.4 mile).

6. The three kinds of square outer robes, which consist of the five-, seven-, and nine-strip *kaśāya*. See "The Merit of a *Kaśāya*" for a more complete explanation of these robes and their use.

7. The Bodhisattva of Supreme Wisdom. He is regarded as the idealization or personification of the Buddha's Wisdom, which is embodied in the practice of zazen.

8. Sōji-ji, the other head temple, was founded in 1321 by Keizan-*zenji* (1267–1325), the Zen master who was responsible for the growth of the Sōtō Zen sect among the common people. It has been regarded as one of the two head temples of this sect since it was made an Imperial Prayer Temple during the reign of Emperor Godaigo (1318–39). Originally located on the west coast of the main island of Honshū in present-day Ishikawa Prefecture, it is now located at Tsurumi in Yokohama.

9. The sixteen precepts that a Bodhisattva is expected to observe. See "Receiving the Precepts" for an enumeration of these precepts.

Part Two

1. A Universal Recommendation for Zazen

1. Wisdom (*prajñā*) is the function of the mind that makes decisions and eliminates doubts. It also enables the mind to gain a correct understanding of phenomena and is therefore closely associated with enlightenment itself. This Wisdom is not to be confused with Bodhi-wisdom (see "The Meaning of Practice-Enlightenment," note 6).

2. After Śākyamuni left his father's palace at the age of twenty-nine he is said to have undergone various kinds of religious training for six years.

3. Bodhidharma is supposed to have

journeyed from India to China, arriving on September 21, A.D. 519. After meeting Emperor Wu of the Liang dynasty (502–57), he crossed the Yangtze River and stayed at Shao-lin temple, where he did zazen for nine years facing a wall.

4. It is impossible to express in words the essence of zazen. This is something that can only be realized by one's own practice under the guidance of a true master.

5. Instruction in Zen is not something that is limited to words. The ninth-century monk Chü-chih, for example, seeing his master T'ien-lung raise his finger, became enlightened. Thereafter he is said to have merely raised his finger when asked about Buddhism. Nan-ch'üan (677–744), on the other hand, when asked by a monk, "How can we take another step on top of a hundred-foot pole?" is reported to have said, "Take another step." Nāgārjuna, seeing his disciple Kaṇādeva coming toward him, ordered someone to bring him a bowl of water. Seeing this, Kaṇādeva threw a needle away. Nāgārjuna, impressed by the depth of Kaṇādeva's enlightenment, was overjoyed. Finally, when the Buddha Śākyamuni was seated on a raised platform, the Bodhisattva Mañjuśrī struck a wooden block with a mallet, saying, "Realize the Buddha's teaching! This is it!"

6. Just as Zen instruction is not limited to words, the incidents that precipitate enlightenment are also varied. When Ch'ing-yüan (d. 740), for example, answered, "I have come from Mount Ts'ao-ch'i," Shih-t'ou (700–790) is said to have raised his *fu-tzŭ* (J., *hossu;* a short staff with horsehair at one end). In another incident Huang-po d. 850) raised his fist, saying, "Here are high priests from the whole country." Tê-shan (782–865), famous for his severe training, is said to have struck every newcomer with his staff. Lin-chi (d. 867), the founder of the Lin-chi (J., Rinzai) Zen sect, however, is said to have led others by shouting, "*Kwatz!*"

7. The legendary Yeh-kung was very fond of carving and painting dragons. But one day when a real dragon appeared in his room, he fainted from fright. Here "a real dragon" means zazen.

8. It is said that a group of blind men, each rubbing a different part of an elephant, argued among themselves as to what its shape was. In this context, "rubbing only one part of an elephant" serves as a warning against being too attached to letters to grasp the essence of Buddhism.

2. Points to Watch in Buddhist Training

1. Born into a Brāhman family (see "The Merit of Becoming a Monk," note 9) in South India in the second or third century A.D., he became one of the chief philosophers of Mahāyāna Buddhism and is considered to be the fourteenth patriarch in the lineage of the transmission of the Law. He advocated the theory that all phenomena are relative, having no independent existence.

2. In Mahāyāna Buddhism it is believed that the historical founder of Buddhism, the Buddha Śākyamuni, went through numerous transmigrations before finally realizing enlightenment. It is also believed that prior to the historical Buddha there had been a thousand people who had already realized Buddhahood, one of them being the Buddha Puṣya. When the Buddha Śākyamuni in one of his previous lives met this Buddha, Śākyamuni is said to have kept one foot raised for seven days and nights and to have chanted a *sūtra* to show his respect for Puṣya.

3. Kiṃnara is an Indian god of music. The *kalavinka* is a mythical Indian bird with a beautiful voice.

4. These two women are said to have been among the most beautiful courtesans in ancient China.

5. "True teachings" refer primarily to those of the *Saddharma-puṇḍarīka, Avataṃsaka,* and *Mahāparinirvāṇa sūtras;* "expedient teachings" include all other teachings.

6. The esoteric teachings are found in the Japanese Shingon and Tendai sects and refer to those doctrines and rituals, deeply influenced by Hinduism, that developed in India during the seventh and eighth centuries. These teachings, having magical properties, can only be revealed to those who have been properly initiated. The exoteric teachings refer to all other teachings.

7. The universe in its entirety is thought to consist of one billion worlds.

8. The other three insights are (1) that the body is impure, (2) that perception leads to suffering, and (3) that the mind is impermanent. Meditating on these four insights is said to eliminate delusion.

9. The red droplet represents the ovum of

the mother, the white one the father's sperm.

10. The position that enlightenment comes gradually, as a result of reading the *sūtras* and accumulated practice, was held by the Northern Zen school in China. Eventually this school died out, and only the Southern Zen school, advocating the sudden realization of enlightenment, survived.

11. Another name of the Buddha Śākyamuni. It signifies a person who has arrived from and gone to *tathatā*, that is, the absolute reality that transcends the multitude of forms in the phenomenal world.

12. The cutting off of an arm refers to Hui-k'o (481–593), the second Zen patriarch in China, who is said to have cut off an arm in the presence of Bodhidharma at Shao-lin temple to show how sincere was his desire to train under that master. The cutting off of a finger refers to one of the disciples of Chü-chih, who is said to have demonstrated the meaning of Buddhism to others by simply mimicking his master's habit of raising his finger. One day Chü-chih, discovering what his disciple was doing, cut off his disciple's finger to make him realize the true nature of Buddhism.

13. Teachings of Śrāvakas and Pratyekabuddhas. Śrāvakas are people who exert themselves to become Arhats, that is, those who have realized enlightenment for themselves but do not attempt to save others. Pratyekabuddhas are people who have realized enlightenment through independent study, without the guidance of a master. They also do not attempt to save others.

14. Lived 606–706. The founder of the Northern Zen sect in China, he was a leading disciple of Hung-jên, the fifth Zen patriarch. His understanding of the Way was highly intellectual, preventing him from realizing full enlightenment.

15. Lived 637–712. The Buddhist heir of Hung-jên, he is said to have realized enlightenment when pounding rice while training on Mount Huang-mei.

16. Lived 778–897. The Buddhist heir of Nan-ch'üan, he is famous for the *kōan* known as "Chao-chou's *wu*" (related on page 56).

17. Nothing more about her is known.

18. Lived 514 or 515 to 577. He is considered to be the second patriarch of the Chinese T'ien-t'ai sect. After having trained under Hui-wêng's guidance, in 570 he moved to Mount Nan-yüeh, where later he died. He is famous for having written a number of important books on Buddhism.

19. Lived 665–713. He is famous for having written the "Song of Enlightenment" (*Chêng-tao-ko*).

20. On the surface, the immediately preceding admonition to avoid "thought, discrimination, and so forth" seems to be contradicted here. However, these two statements are not actually in conflict; for the "thought and so on" that are to be used in the latter instance, rooted as they must be in actual practice, are not the conceptual thought and so forth of the former. This is one of the key points of Sōtō Zen.

21. The twenty-eight generations in India begin with the Buddha's chief disciple, Mahākāśyapa, and extend to Bodhidharma; the six generations in China are, in chronological order, Bodhidharma, Hui-k'o, Sêng-ts'an, Tao-hsin, Hung-jên, and Hui-nêng. The patriarchs of the five Zen schools are Yün-mên, Wei-yang, Ts'ao-tung, Lin-chi, and Fa-yen.

22. See "A Universal Recommendation for Zazen," note 7.

23. The potentiality to realize enlightenment, which all things possess by nature.

24. Absolute being, which is beyond the relative concepts of being and nonbeing.

3. The Meaning of Practice-Enlightenment

1. The three lower realms of the six realms of existence in which the souls of living beings are traditionally thought to transmigrate until they finally realize Nirvāṇa. The three lower realms, in ascending order, are those of hell, hungry ghosts, and animals. The three upper realms, in ascending order, are those of *asuras* (pugnacious devils), human beings, and celestial beings.

2. Sanskrit, *añjali*. A symbolic gesture of reverence, representing the unity of body and mind, in which the hands are joined at the palms, fingers extended, and placed near the breast.

3. An honorific title of the historical Buddha, literally meaning "world-honored one," that is, one worthy of being honored because he has destroyed all illusions and rid himself of all defilements.

4. This precept applies only to laymen and is essentially a prohibition against

adultery. The comparable precept for monks or nuns prohibits sexual relations altogether. See "Receiving the Precepts."

5. The wisdom of the Buddha's enlightenment acquired as the result of cutting off the two hindrances, passions and illusory conceptions. The Sanskrit term *bodhi* (J., *bodai*) itself is frequently translated as "wisdom," but in this book the two words are used together in order to distinguish Bodhi-wisdom from both secular wisdom and *prajñā* (Wisdom).

6. Monks, nuns, laymen, and laywomen.

7. Womb-born, egg-born, moisture-born, and metamorphically born.

8. Ching-k'ang is said to have taken pity on an imprisoned tortoise and freed it. Some time later, when Ching-k'ang was in the process of carving a seal, the tortoise caused its image to appear on the seal as a sign of its gratitude.

9. Yang-pao is said to have helped a sparrow that had been injured by a bird of prey. To express its gratitude the sparrow later presented him with four silver rings.

PART THREE

Introduction to the *Shōbō-genzō*

1. Some versions list ninety-five rather than ninety-two sections.

2. It was the noted modern Zen scholar Dōshū Ōkubo who first designated these twelve sections as Dōgen's "later writings," contrasting them with the first eighty sections, or "earlier writings," which make up the main body of the *Shōbō-genzō*. The present translation is based on the edition of the *Shōbō-genzō* edited by Ōkubo and published by Chikuma Shobō (Tokyo, 1969).

1. The Merit of Becoming a Monk

1. Traditionally, laymen should observe five precepts: (1) not to take life, (2) not to take what is not given to one, (3) not to engage in improper sexual conduct, (4) not to lie, and (5) not to drink intoxicants.

2. The Mahāyāna precepts for monks consist of ten major and forty-eight minor items of morality. The ten precepts are (1) not to kill, (2) not to steal, (3) not to engage in sexual relations, (4) not to lie, (5) not to deal in intoxicants, (6) not to speak of the faults of others, whether they be laymen or monks, (7) not to be too proud to praise others, (8) not to covet either the Law or property, (9) not to give way to anger, and (10) not to disparage the Three Treasures (the Buddha, the Law, and the Buddhist community).

3. A Hindu belonging to the highest of the four castes of ancient India. Male members of this caste were responsible for conducting religious ceremonies.

4. One of the ten great disciples of the Buddha. Śāriputra is said to have been the disciple most excellent in wisdom.

5. An evil spirit who, it is popularly believed, is the lord of the highest of the six heavens in the world of desire. Together with his followers, Pāpīyas hinders people from adhering to Buddhism.

6. Utpala was born into a noble family in the city of Rājagṛha in ancient India. When she discovered that her husband had committed adultery with her mother, she left him. Later, after she had remarried, she was shocked to find that the mistress of her second husband was her own daughter by her first marriage. This discovery drove her to such despair that she left her second husband and became a prostitute. Still later, she became a nun under the guidance of Maudgalyāyana, one of the ten great disciples of the Buddha.

7. A stage before Buddhahood in which one is free from all craving, rebirth, and other defilements. In Arhathood perfect knowledge has been attained, so that there is nothing left to be learned, and one is worthy of receiving respect and offerings.

8. The six powers of (1) free activity, (2) eyes capable of seeing everything, (3) ears capable of hearing everything, (4) insight into others' thinking, (5) remembrance of one's former existences, and (6) perfect freedom.

9. The sixth of the seven Buddhas who are said to have lived prior to the Buddha Śākyamuni.

10. Donated to the Buddha Śākyamuni and his disciples as a place to pursue religious training by Sudatta, a rich merchant, in the city of Śrāvasti.

11. A cousin of the Buddha and one of his ten great disciples. He accompanied the Buddha for more than twenty years and was famed for his excellent memory.

12. The Wheel-Rolling King. King Cakravarti is said to have thirty-two distinguishing marks and to rule the world by rolling the wheels bestowed on him by heaven at his enthronement. He manifests himself in four ways: (1) as the Gold-Wheel-Rolling King he rules the four continents (see note 13); (2) as the Silver-Wheel-Rolling King, the eastern, western, and southern continents; (3) as the Copper-Wheel-Rolling King, the eastern and southern continents; and (4) as the Iron-Wheel-Rolling King, the southern continent.

13. According to ancient Indian geography, the world consists of four continents lying in the ocean surrounding Mount Sumeru: Jambudvīpa to the south, Pūrvavideha to the east, Aparagodānīya to the west, and Uttarakuru to the north.

14. The seven treasures here are (1) fine rings, (2) elephants, (3) horses, (4) jewels, (5) beautiful court attendants, (6) retainers gifted in financial affairs, and (7) retainers gifted in military affairs. Another set of seven treasures, sometimes called the seven precious things, is listed in note 24.

15. The ten wrong acts are (1) to kill living things, (2) to steal others' belongings, (3) to engage in improper sexual conduct, (4) to lie, (5) to deceive others, (6) to be two-faced, (7) to speak ill of others, (8) to be greedy, (9) to become angry, and (10) to hold false views.

16. The first and lowest of the four meditation-heavens in the world of form. The beings there are said to be without sexual desire.

17. The thirty-two distinguishing marks on the body of the Buddha: (1) flat soles, (2) the *Dharmacakra* (wheel of the Law) on the soles, (3) slender fingers, (4) supple limbs, (5) webbed fingers and toes, (6) rounded heels, (7) long legs, (8) slender legs like those of a deer, (9) arms extending below the knees, (10) a concealed penis, (11) an armspan equal to the height of the body, (12) light radiating from the pores, (13) curly body hair, (14) a golden-hued body, (15) light radiating from the body ten feet in each direction, (16) supple skin, (17) legs, palms, shoulders, and neck harmoniously proportioned, (18) swollen armpits, (19) a dignified body like that of a lion, (20) an erect body, (21) full shoulders, (22) forty teeth, (23) firm white teeth, (24) four white canine teeth, (25) full cheeks like those of a lion, (26) flavored saliva, (27) a long slender tongue, (28) a beautiful voice, (29) blue eyes, (30) eyes shaped like those of a bull, (31) a bump between the eyes, and (32) a bump on the top of the head.

18. One of the guardian deities of Buddhism.

19. Utpala (see note 5).

20. The celestial world of unenlightened people, which is divided into three: (1) the world of desire, whose inhabitants have appetite and sexual desire; (2) the world of form, whose inhabitants have neither appetite nor sexual desire; and (3) the formless world, whose inhabitants have no physical form.

21. The second, fifth, and sixth of the six powers for saving sentient beings (see note 7).

22. Located to the north of Mount Sumeru. The inhabitants of Uttarakuru are said to live for a thousand years and to enjoy constant happiness. They have never heard the teaching of the Buddha.

23. A pagoda, generally of a domelike form, that is erected over sacred relics of the Buddha or at places consecrated because he performed significant deeds there. *Stūpas* are made of various materials, such as clay, elaborately worked brick, carved stone, and wood.

24. The seven precious things (also called the seven treasures) are gold, silver, mother-of-pearl, agate, coral, amber, and emerald.

25. In the Buddhist community, seats for taking meals or doing zazen are assigned according to the length of time elapsed since a person has entered the monkhood. The seats for novice monks are said to be the lowest, while those for senior monks are the highest.

26. The four elements are (1) earth, which has hardness as its nature and can support things; (2) water, which has moisture as its nature and can contain things; (3) fire, which has heat as its nature and can bring things to perfection; and (4) wind, which has motion as its nature and can cause things to mature.

27. In Buddhist philosophy, all physical, mental, and other elements in this phenomenal world are classified into five kinds of aggregates: (1) *rūpa-skandha*, a generic term for all forms of matter; (2) *vedanā-skandha*, perception; (3) *samjñā-skandha*, mental conceptions and ideas; (4) *samskāra-skandha*,

volition; and (5) *vijñāna-skandha,* consciousness of mind. In the case of man, the *rūpa-skandha* is his body, the *vijñāna-skandha* is the totality of his mind, and the other three *skandhas* are mental functions. Thus the five *skandhas* compose the body and mind of all sentient beings in the world of desire and the world of form, while those sentient beings in the formless world of pure spirit have no material element.

28. The eight kinds of suffering are (1) the suffering of birth, (2) the suffering of old age, (3) the suffering of sickness, (4) the suffering of death, (5) the suffering that comes from being apart from those whom one loves, (6) the suffering that comes from being together with those whom one hates, (7) the suffering that comes from the fact that one cannot have what one wants, and (8) the suffering that comes from the fact that one is attached to the five elemental aggregates (*skandhas*) of which one's body, mind, and environment are composed.

29. A measure of time said to be equal to one sixty-fifth of a second.

30. A Buddha mentioned in the *Saddharma-puṇḍarīka-sūtra.* According to this work, Candrasūryapradīpa expounded the same *sūtra* innumerable *kalpas* ago. He is said to be as brilliant as the sun and the moon, for which he is named.

31. A Buddha mentioned in the *Saddharma-puṇḍarīka-sūtra.* He is said to have attained enlightenment three thousand dust-atom *kalpas* ago.

32. The *Sūtra* of the Lotus of the Supreme Law, or Lotus *Sūtra.* This work, composed of eight sections divided into twenty-seven or twenty-eight chapters, is one of the most important documents of Mahāyāna Buddhism. It teaches that perfect enlightenment was achieved by the Buddha many *kalpas* ago, and that even followers of the Theravāda school are able to attain perfect enlightenment.

33. Nothing more about this king is known.

34. The son of the Buddha, born before his father's renunciation of the world. One of the ten great disciples of the Buddha.

35. When Śākyamuni forsook the world and entered the monkhood, his father ordered five men to accompany him. They practiced asceticism with Śākyamuni but left him when he abandoned it. Later, when he realized Buddhahood, they joined him in the Deer Park near Benares and became his disciples. The five monks were Ajñāta-kauṇḍinya, Aśvajit, Bhadrika, Mahānāman, and Daśabala-kāśyapa.

36. He became the Buddha's disciple shortly before the latter's death and is therefore known as the Buddha's last disciple. Subhadra was able to realize Arhathood immediately after hearing the Buddha's last sermon.

37. The king of the world of the dead. Yama judges the dead to determine whether they have committed any wrongdoing during their lifetime. He reigns over the realm of the dead because he was the first human being to die.

38. Also known as Śakra *devānām* Indra. He is one of the guardian gods of Buddhims. He lives in Sudarśana Palace on top of Mount Sumeru, ruling Trāyastriṃśa Heaven (the Heaven of the Thirty-three Gods; see note 60).

39. The rank at which monks progressively realize the Four Noble Truths within themselves.

40. Nuns must observe 348 precepts.

41. The highest aspect of the threefold body of the Buddha; the absolute nature of the Buddha-mind. It is ineffable, unmanifested, and nonsubstantial (*śūnyatā*).

42. The body of a Buddha that is produced upon entering Buddhahood. It is a result of the vows taken and the religious practices undergone while the Buddha was still a Bodhisattva.

43. The five deadly wrongs are (1) killing one's father, (2) killing one's mother, (3) killing an Arhat, (4) injuring the body of a Buddha, and (5) causing disunity in the Buddhist community.

44. The preaching of a Buddha. The Law is likened to a wheel because it crushes all illusions.

45. A *kalpa* is the period of time required for a celestial maiden to wear away a ten-mile-cubic stone if she touches it with her garments once every three years, that is, an infinitely long period of time.

46. Prince Siddhārtha was the name of the Buddha before his renunciation of the world. Siddhārtha is variously translated as "he who has accomplished his aim," "he whose desire has been fulfilled," "he who has been successful in his endeavors," and so on.

47. A servant of Prince Siddhārtha. He

led the white horse Kanthaka, on whose back the prince was riding on the night of his renunciation of the world. Later Chandaka became a disciple of the Buddha.

48. Fabulous gems capable of responding to every wish and dispelling evil. The *mani* jewels are obtained from the Dragon King in the ocean.

49. The highest of the four heavens in the world of form. Beings in this heaven have only the faculty of mind and the sensation of freedom from pain and pleasure.

50. Taken at face value, Dōgen here seems to be denying the possibility of women achieving Buddhahood, a fundamental contradiction of the basic Buddhist tenet that all beings have the Buddha-nature. In other sections of the *Shōbō-genzō,* however, Dōgen states that all people, regardless of sex, are able to practice the Way, and that even a girl of seven can become a teacher of the Way if she awakens to the Bodhi-mind. What Dōgen is stressing here is the importance of entering the monkhood in order to realize one's Buddha-nature. In this Buddha-nature, that is, the ultimate expression of one's true Self, there are no relative distinctions, such as man and woman or child and adult.

51. He was born in the ancient Indian kingdom of Magadha. After he realized enlightenment, Dhītaka spread Buddhism throughout central India.

52. He was born in the Indian kingdom of Mātaṅgā. Upagupta was the Buddhist heir of Śāṇavāsa, the third Indian patriarch. He is famous for having encouraged the construction of more than 84,000 *stūpas* in India.

53. It is traditional practice in Buddhism for a novice monk or nun to undergo training in the Way as part of the Buddhist community. Hence, "staying at home" signifies the life of a layman, while "leaving home" denotes a person who has left his home and family in order to join the Buddhist community, that is, enter the monkhood.

54. The desires for property, sexual love, eating and drinking, fame, and sleep.

55. Lived 726–79. The eighth emperor of the T'ang dynasty (618–907).

56. Lived 711–62. The seventh emperor of the T'ang dynasty.

57. Lived 638–713. The sixth patriarch in the lineage of the Chinese Zen sect. He originally made his living by selling firewood. While on his rounds one day, Hui-nêng heard the *Vajra-sūtra* (Diamond Wisdom *Sūtra*) being chanted. At that he awakened to the Bodhi-mind. He became a disciple of Hung-jên and realized enlightenment after only eight months' training.

58. P'ang Yün (740–803) is said to have thrown all his property into a river and to have practiced the Way under the guidance of Shih-t'ou and Ma-tsu before finally realizing enlightenment.

59. Died 740. One of the prominent disciples of Hui-nêng, the sixth Chinese Zen patriarch.

60. The six lowest heavens are (1) the Heaven of the Four-Quarter Kings, (2) the Heaven of the Thirty-three Gods (Trāyastriṃśa Heaven), (3) the Heaven of King Yama, (4) Tuṣita Heaven, (5) Nirmāṇarati Heaven, and (6) Paranirmita-veśavartin Heaven.

61. The first, second, and third meditation-heavens in the world of form are said to consist of three heavens each—nine in all; the fourth meditation-heaven consists of nine heavens, making a total of eighteen.

62. These are the heavens of (1) boundless knowledge, (2) infinite emptiness, (3) nonattachment to knowledge or emptiness, and (4) nonthought and non-nonthought.

63. See note 53.

64. One of the ten great disciples of the Buddha. He became a disciple about three years after the Buddha attained enlightenment and is said to have become an Arhat after being with the Buddha for only eight days. He is regarded as the first patriarch of Zen Buddhism.

65. The five moral powers: faith, exertion, mindfulness, meditation, and wisdom.

66. According to one tradition, he was a son of the Buddha and fell into hell because of false views.

67. Son of Mahāprajāpati, Śākyamuni's aunt and foster mother.

68. At first Devadatta was a follower of the Buddha, but later left him and attempted to kill him. He sent a maddened elephant against the Buddha; but, it is said, the Buddha "overcame it with love," and it became calm.

69. A Sanskrit title denoting a monk who is a full-fledged member of the Buddhist community. *Bhikṣuṇī* indicates a female member.

70. The four stages of meditation that enable one to be favored by bliss in the world of form. At this level, the delusions that one cherishes in the sensory world are removed. In the first stage, the five states of mind—investigation, reflection, joyfulness, and a concentrated state of mind—are realized. They are accompanied by the eight kinds of feelings and the ten virtues. In the second stage there are four states of mind: serenity of mind, joyfulness, bliss, and a concentrated state of mind. The third stage is characterized by five states of mind: equanimity, remembrance, wisdom, bliss, and a concentrated state of mind. In the fourth stage there are four states of mind: neither suffering nor joy, equanimity, remembrance, and a concentrated state of mind.

71. These are the powers of (1) distinguishing right from wrong, (2) knowing the relation of karma and its result, (3) comprehending various kinds of meditation, (4) judging the inferiority or superiority of the people's capacities, (5) seeing into what people understand, (6) knowing people's lineage, (7) understanding the law of rebirth, (8) remembering the past, (9) knowing the birth and death of people throughout the three periods of time, and (10) rightly knowing how to extinguish every affliction in oneself and others.

72. The five delusions are avarice, anger, pride, jealousy, and stinginess.

73. This flower is said to bloom only once every three thousand years. For this reason it is often used as an illustration of how difficult it is to come in contact with the true Law.

74. The fifth of these regulations is unknown.

75. King of the ancient Indian kingdom of Kapilavastu and father of King Śuddhodana, the Buddha's father.

76. The Buddha's cousin and one of his ten great disciples. Having once fallen asleep in the presence of the Buddha, he vowed that he would never sleep again. He eventually lost his eyesight but acquired the "miraculous eye" that enabled him to see intuitively.

77. Another of the Buddha's cousins. When still a layman he made venerative offerings to the Buddhist community as an expression of his deep faith.

78. One of the five monks (see note 35).

79. An ancient country in South India.

80. This passage refers to the transient nature of life.

81. Written by the famous Chinese Zen master Tsu-chiao in 1101. The oldest extant book of regulations for a Zen monastery, it consists of ten sections.

82. A sign of the correct transmission of the Law from a Zen master to his disciple.

83. According to traditional Buddhist belief, after the Buddha's death Buddhism will pass through three stages or periods. During the first period, that of the true Law, the Buddha's teachings, practice, and enlightenment exist. In the second period, that of the formal Law, only the Buddha's teachings and practice exist, while in the third period, that of the degenerate Law, only the Buddha's teachings remain. Although it is generally agreed that the third period will last for ten thousand years, there are various views on the duration of the first two periods, some believing that each period is only five hundred years long and others that each is one thousand years long.

84. In this analogy "milk" refers to the true Law, while "water" refers to degenerate Buddhism.

2. Receiving the Precepts

1. *Śrāvaka* literally means "disciple." In Mahāyāna Buddhism it refers to a person in the Hīnayāna school who exerts himself to attain the stage of Arhat by observing 250 precepts in the case of monks and 348 precepts in the case of nuns. From the Mahāyāna point of view this is a lower stage than that of Bodhisattva.

2. See note 59, "The Merit of Becoming a Monk."

3. Lived 677–744. One of the prominent disciples of Hui-nêng. He is considered to be the seventh Chinese Zen patriarch.

4. The entire verse is as follows: "The world around us is as vast as the sky, / As pure as lotus flowers rising from muddy water. / My mind is pure and beyond the ordinary world. / I pay homage to the most excellent Buddha."

5. Lived 739–834. He first studied Confucianism but later entered the Buddhist monkhood and became a Buddhist heir of Shih-t'ou.

6. A novice monk who pursued the Way under Wei-yen of Mount Yao (751–834).

His dates are unknown. It is said that T'ien-jan and he never received the precepts for a Śrāvaka.

3. The Merit of a *Kaśāya*

1. Lived 602–75. He was the Buddhist heir of Ta-i Tao-hsin.

2. A temple where Hui-nêng lived, located in present-day Hsinchou, Kwangtung Province.

3. Lived 656–710. The fourth emperor of the T'ang dynasty.

4. Sung China. Compared with India, the home of the Buddha, China was a spiritually small country.

5. Born in northern India, he was well versed in the Zen rules of discipline. He went to Ch'ang-an in 406.

6. Born in eastern India, he was the Buddhist heir of the twenty-sixth patriarch, Punyamitra. Paññatara is said to have commissioned Bodhidharma to introduce the Law to China.

7. Died 414. Born in Ch'ang-an, he was well versed in the *sūtras,* the rules of discipline (*vinaya*), and Buddhist philosophical treatises (*śāstras*).

8. Ta-i Tao-hsin (580–651). He was the Buddhist heir of Sêng-ts'an.

9. Lived 594–657. Said to have been well versed in the *sūtras* and Buddhist history by the age of nineteen, he was the collateral Buddhist heir of Ta-i Tao-hsin.

10. The fourth Chinese Zen patriarch, Ta-i Tao-hsin, conferred Hung-jên with a *kaśāya,* signifying that he, not Fa-jung, was to be considered his spiritual successor.

11. Wearing a *kaśāya* is thought to enable one to be delivered from delusion and realize enlightenment.

12. The three sufferings unique to a dragon: (1) having its body scorched by a hot wind, (2) having its precious robe carried off by an evil wind, and (3) being attacked by a *garuḍa* (see note 27).

13. *Vinaya* is the Sanskrit term denoting the rules of discipline that monks are required to follow. The Vinaya school was so named because it placed particular emphasis on these rules.

14. A *gāthā* is a verse praising the Buddha or restating succinctly major points of Buddhist doctrine.

15. As a physical entity a *kaśāya* has, of course, a form. For Dōgen, however, a *kaśāya* is also the concrete expression of absolute Truth, and in this sense it is beyond form.

16. Literally, "excreta-sweeping robe."

17. A *śrāmaṇera* is a Buddhist male novice who has vowed to observe the ten precepts for monks.

18. A pond, said to be located north of Mount Sumeru, where one of the eight Dragon Kings lives.

19. Here the *pāmsūla* represents the concrete manifestation of enlightenment.

20. Born in central India, he was the Buddhist heir of the second patriarch, Ānanda.

21. Nothing more about her is known.

22. The name of the Buddha Amitābha before his enlightenment, when he was a Bodhisattva. He made forty-eight vows to bring all sentient beings to the Pure Land.

23. The Bodhisattva who personifies great compassion, mercy, and love. He has vowed to save all beings through great compassion.

24. The three divisions of the teachings of the Buddha. In Mahāyāna Buddhism these are (1) the Śrāvakayāna or Hīnayāna, in which one rightly understands the Four Noble Truths and becomes an Arhat; (2) the Pratyekabuddhayāna or Mādhyamyāna, in which one rightly understands the twelve links of causation and becomes a Pratyekabuddha; and (3) the Bodhisattvayāna or Mahāyāna, in which one becomes a Bodhisattva as a result of religious practice over innumerable years.

25. A *ts'un* is a Chinese unit of measure equivalent to approximately 3 centimenters (1.2 inches).

26. A deity of celestial music.

27. A mythical gigantic golden-winged bird that is said to eat dragons.

28. A deity with a snakelike head.

29. An earthly demon who sucks human blood and eats human flesh.

30. A heavenly demon who sucks human blood and eats human flesh.

31. An expression of respect similar to the *gasshō.* The hands are joined, fingers curled, and placed on the breast.

32. One of the ten great disciples of the Buddha. He became a monk together with Ānanda and was known for his strict observance of the precepts.

33. A *hasta* is an Indian unit of measure equivalent to 45.7 centimeters (18 inches).

34. This Bodhisattva is believed to be

living in Tuṣita Heaven (the fourth of the six heavens in the world of desire), waiting for the time when he will come down to this world and succeed the Buddha Śākyamuni. It is held that he will appear in this world 5,670 million years after the death of Śākyamuni.

35. One of the ten great disciples of the Buddha. He is said to have possessed supernatural powers.

36. Nothing more about this world is known.

37. A *ko-chih-i* is made by sewing small precut pieces of cloth together, while a *hsieh-yeh-i* is made of larger uncut pieces of cloth. The method in which a *shê-yeh-i* and *pata* are made is difficult to explain simply, both of them having to do with the way in which the cloth is handled during making. The Chinese terms for the first three of these four types of *kaśāya* are used because the Sanskrit has been lost.

38. The *vinaya* state that a *kaśāya* of nine strips of cloth is to be made in five days, one of seven strips in four days, and one of five strips in two days.

39. Lived 464–549. It is said that in his later life he was more devoted to Buddhism than to administration of the government.

40. Lived 569–618. He is known for his study of literature and the arts, as well as for having excavated a great canal.

41. This *sūtra* transmits the teachings of the one vehicle (that of the Buddha) and ultimate Truth. It has fifteen chapters and is addressed to a devout queen, Śrimālā.

42. Lived 701–56. The forty-fifth emperor of Japan, he reigned 724–49. Embracing Buddhism wholeheartedly, he built numerous temples throughout the country, including the famous Central Cathedral, Tōdai-ji, in Nara. Seven years before his death he abdicated and entered the monkhood.

43. Nothing more about him is known.

44. The opposite of the ten wrong acts. (See "The Merit of Becoming a Monk," note 15, for the ten wrong acts.)

45. The five mistaken views are (1) to be attached to self and to other people and things, (2) to believe either that the self is eternal or that it is noneternal, (3) to deny causality, (4) to hold mistaken views like the above to be the Truth, and (5) to regard adherence to the precepts as the way to enlightenment.

46. One of the four *Āgamas* (early collections of the teachings of the Buddha), it consists of 60 sections, 5 *adhyāyās,* 18 *vargas,* and 222 *sūtras.* It sets forth such teachings as the Four Noble Truths and the twelve links in the chain of causation. It also contains much material dealing with subjects like the origin of Buddhism, parables, and the lives of the Buddha and his disciples.

47. Nothing more about them is known.

48. Present-day Ningpo-fu in Chekiang Province.

4. Awakening to the Bodhi-mind

1. The eight difficult realms are (1) hell, (2) animals, (3) hungry spirits, (4) the heaven of long life, (5) remote places, (6) the state of being blind, deaf, or otherwise handicapped, (7) secular prejudice, and (8) the period of absence of the Buddha.

2. As previously stated, Dōgen taught that practice and enlightenment, as expressed by the Japanese Zen term *shushō,* are one and the same thing.

3. One of the eight kinds of demons. *Yakṣas* are sometimes regarded as protectors of Buddhism.

4. Four mythical kings said to live halfway down Mount Sumeru. They protect the eastern, southern, western, and northern continents.

5. The seven past Buddhas are Vipaśyin, Śikhin, Viśvabhū, Krakucchanda, Kanakamuni, Kāśyapa, and Śākyamuni.

6. The ten stages are (1) joy at benefiting oneself and others, (2) freedom from all possible defilement, (3) emission of the light of Wisdom, (4) glowing Wisdom, (5) overcoming extreme difficulties, (6) the realization of Wisdom, (7) proceeding far, (8) the attainment of immobility, (9) the attainment of expedient Wisdom, and (10) the ability to spread the teachings over the *Dharmadhātu* (the phenomenal world) as clouds overspread the sky.

7. It is said that a Bodhisattva attaining this level will be born as a Buddha in his next existence.

8. A variety of mango tree.

9. See "The Merit of Becoming a Monk," note 27.

5. Veneration of the Buddhas

1. A sixty-section biography of the Bud-

dha and his chief disciples that was compiled in India and translated into Chinese by Jñānagupta. The Sanskrit original has been lost.

2. One of the ten epithets of the Buddha, denoting "one who understands the world."

3. One of the ten epithets of the Buddha, denoting "one who teaches gods and men."

4. A Buddha of the past who eventually assured the Buddha Śākyamuni, in one of the latter's previous lives, that he would someday realize enlightenment.

5. Nothing more about this Buddha is known.

6. Composed of either three or four sections, this *sūtra* was translated into Chinese by Kumārajīva. It emphasizes the need for Bodhisattvas to train apart from Śrāvakas.

7. Nothing more about this Buddha is known; the Chinese pronunciation of his name is used here because the original Sanskrit has been lost.

8. Nothing more about this *kalpa* age is known; the Chinese pronunciation is used here because the original Sanskrit has been lost.

9. Nothing more about this Buddha is known; the Chinese pronunciation of his name is used here because the original Sanskrit has been lost.

10. Nothing more about this Buddha is known; the Chinese pronunciation of his name is used here because the original Sanskrit has been lost.

11. Nothing more about this Buddha is known; the Chinese pronunciation of his name is used here because the original Sanskrit has been lost.

12. Nothing more about this Buddha is known.

13. The Heaven of the Thirty-three Gods. (See "The Merit of Becoming a Monk," notes 38 and 60.)

14. The third of the three heavens comprising the second group of meditation-heavens in the world of form. (See "The Merit of Becoming a Monk," note 61.)

15. Nothing more about this Buddha is known; the Chinese pronunciation of his name is used here because the original Sanskrit has been lost.

16. These are the ten epithets of the Buddha, presented here in their translated rather than original Sanskrit form.

17. Nothing more about this Buddha is known; the Chinese pronunciation of his name is used here because the original Sanskrit has been lost.

18. An infinitely long *kalpa*. *Asaṃkhya* is a Sanskrit word denoting an astronomical number.

19. Nothing more about this Buddha is known.

20. Nothing more about this Buddha is known; the Chinese pronunciation of his name is used here because the original Sanskrit has been lost.

21. Nothing more about this Buddha is known; the Chinese pronunciation of his name is used here because the original Sanskrit has been lost.

22. Nothing more about this Buddha is known.

23. Nothing more about this Buddha is known; the Chinese pronunciation of his name is used here because the original Sanskrit has been lost.

24. The Chinese pronunciation is used here because the original Sanskrit has been lost.

25. Nothing more about this Buddha is known.

26. Nothing more about this Buddha is known.

27. A Mahāyāna *sūtra* that claims to be the last sermon of the Buddha. It has been preserved in Chinese versions alone, the Sanskrit original having been lost.

28. The world of ordinary people.

29. A Chinese weight equivalent to approximately 15 grams (0.5 ounce).

30. Nothing more about this Bodhisattva is known; the Chinese pronunciation of his name is used here because the original Sanskrit has been lost.

31. Lived 700–790. The Buddhist heir of Ch'ing-yüan, under whose guidance he is said to have realized enlightenment.

32. A hundred-section philosophical commentary on the *Mahāprajñāpāramitā-sūtra* attributed to Nāgārjuna and translated into Chinese by Kumārajīva. It stresses the doctrine of "emptiness" (Skt., *śūnyatā*; J., *kū*).

33. A forty-section treatise on the rules of discipline (*vinaya*). It was translated into Chinese during the Ch'in dynasty (c. 221–206 B.C.) by Buddhabhadra and Fa-hsien.

34. A one-section work compiled by Chih-i, third patriarch of the Chinese T'ien-t'ai sect (not Hui-ssŭ, to whom Dōgen mistakenly attributes it). It contains in-

structions for trainees in their practice of the Way.

35. A Buddha appearing in the *Saddharma-puṇḍarika-sūtra*. When the Buddha Śākyamuni had expounded the first ten chapters of this *sūtra*, he appeared to witness to its truth.

36. One of the sixteen major countries in India during the Buddha's lifetime; present-day Oude in the Gogra Valley.

37. The king of Kośala, and later also of Kāśi, in central India. He was the same age as the Buddha, and ascended the throne the year that the latter attained enlightenment. Together with his wife and son, he became a devout follower of the Buddha.

38. Nothing more about him is known.

39. One of the twenty Theravāda (Hīnayāna) schools of Buddhism. Its chief teaching is that time and existence are eternal.

40. A Chinese monk of the Eastern Chin dynasty (317–420). In 399 he left China for India, finally arriving after six years of hard travel. After studying Sanskrit and obtaining many Sanskrit texts of the Tripiṭaka, he returned to China in 414 by sea. After his return he not only translated these texts but also wrote a record of his travels. He died when he was either eighty-two or eighty-six years old.

41. Mount Gṛdhrakūṭa, located in the northeastern part of the ancient country of Maghada in central India. It is so named because the shape of its peak resembles a vulture.

42. Lived 665–760. He was known for his great compassion.

6. Taking Refuge in the Three Treasures

1. The speaker is probably the Buddha Śākyamuni, but the text is not clear on this point.

2. The five merits are (1) the precepts, (2) *samādhi* (total absorption), (3) Wisdom, (4) freedom from desire, and (5) self-awareness of enlightenment.

3. In Mahāyāna Buddhism there is the belief that the Buddha Śākyamuni simplified many of his teachings, particularly the earlier ones, in order that people of various capacities could understand them and eventually be led to the final doctrine. These simplified teachings are thought to have only a provisional nature.

4. The eight divisions are (1) correct views, (2) correct thinking, (3) correct speech, (4) correct action, (5) correct livelihood, (6) correct endeavor, (7) correct remembrance, and (8) correct meditation.

5. Nothing more about this *sūtra* is known; its Chinese pronunciation is used here because the Sanskrit original has been lost.

6. This *sūtra* consists of fifty sections divided into fifty-two chapters. It is said to have been first translated into Chinese by the Indian monk Dharmanandi in 384.

7. The five marks of decay are (1) his robes becoming dirty, (2) his hair-flowers fading, (3) his body smelling bad, (4) sweating under his arms, and (5) not enjoying his original status.

8. Nothing more about this Buddha is known.

9. Nothing more about this *sūtra* is known; its Chinese pronunciation is used here because the Sanskrit original has been lost.

10. A tall tropical tree with thick foliage.

11. This refers to a layman who receives each of the five lay precepts on a separate occasion rather than all five at the same time.

12. This *sūtra* consists of two sections divided into thirty-nine chapters. It was composed by Dharmatrāta and translated into Chinese by Vighnal during the Wu dynasty (A.D. 222–80). A collection of moral teachings, its main stress is on good conduct stabilized by concentration and strengthened by perfect Wisdom.

13. In the first of the four stages to Arhathood one is freed from attachment to the three delusive worlds. (See "Deep Belief in Causality," note 7.)

14. Nothing more about this *sūtra* is known; its Chinese pronunciation is used here because the Sanskrit original has been lost.

15. Nothing more about this ancient Indian country is known.

7. Deep Belief in Causality

1. Lived 720–814. He was the Buddhist heir of Ma-tsu Tao-i and is famous for having written the first set of regulations for a Zen monastery. These regulations, known as the *Pai-chang Ch'ing-kuei*, are no longer extant.

2. In Sanskrit this monk is known as the

karmadana, a title that originally designated the person in charge of the general affairs of a monastery or temple. In Zen monasteries, however, this title, pronounced *ino* or *ina* in Japanese, designates the monk who is in charge of the meditation hall and general monastic discipline.

3. Died 850. Huai-hai's most prominent disciple, he was noted for his strong sense of irony and strict teaching methods.

4. In China all foreigners were known as "barbarians" (*hu*) and were believed to have red facial and body hair. In this instance, Huai-hai is comparing the enlightened Huang-po to his Indian predecessor, Bodhidharma.

5. A thirty-section work recording the lineage of the Zen sect from ancient times through the Sung period (960–1279).

6. Born in northern India at the end of the third century A.D.

7. The four stages to Arhathood, in ascending order, are (1) *Srotāpanna,* the stage in which one has entered into the stream of sanctification, abandoning all false views in the three worlds; (2) *Sakṛdāgāmin,* the stage in which one has only one rebirth left before realizing enlightenment; (3) *Anāgāmin,* the stage in which one will never again return to the world of desire; and (4) Arhat, the stage before Buddhahood, in which one is free from all craving, rebirth, and other defilements.

8. He is considered to be the eighth patriarch of the Chinese T'ien-t'ai sect.

9. Lived 1091–1157. He was the Buddhist heir of Tan-hsia Tsu-ch'un and is said to have had more than twelve hundred disciples.

10. The lowest four of the six realms of existence. (See "The Meaning of Practice-Enlightenment," note 2.)

11. Lived 1063–1135. A Lin-chi (Rinzai) Zen monk who is famous for his comments on a collection of *kōan* known as the *Pi-yen-lu (Hekigan-roku).*

12. Lived 1089–1163. A Lin-chi (Rinzai) Zen monk who entered the monkhood at the age of seventeen and realized enlightenment under the guidance of Zen Master Yüan. He is said to have had more than two thousand disciples.

13. An eccentric Chinese Zen monk who lived during the latter part of the T'ang dynasty. He had the reputation of being an excellent fortuneteller and is worshiped in Japan as Hotei, one of the seven gods of good fortune.

14. In this statement Dōgen departs from the usual Mahāyāna exposition of causality to assert that from the standpoint of undifferentiated reality (enlightenment), freedom from the law of causality is not, in fact, its denial, just as subjection to it is not its affirmation.

8. Karmic Retribution in the Three Stages of Time

1. Nothing more about this monk is known.

2. The lowest class within the Indian caste system. Its members are fishermen, jailers, slaughterers, and so on.

3. Although usually translated as "meditation" or "concentration," this Sanskrit term has a wide variety of meanings. Here it is used to describe a meditative state of heightened awareness in which the practitioner is able to "view" the three stages of time. This *samādhi* is very different from that which Dōgen taught with regard to the practice of zazen.

4. Said to have been the third important king of the Kuṣāṇa dynasty of northern India, he is thought to have lived in the latter half of the first century or the first half of the second century. He was a great patron of Buddhism and Buddhist art, and built temples, dispatched missionaries, and had commentaries compiled.

5. An ancient country in northern India, located north of the present-day Punjab and northeast of Kashmir.

6. Nothing more about this monk is known; the Chinese pronunciation of his name is used here because the original Sanskrit has been lost.

7. The son of King Bimbisāra of Magadha. When he was the crown prince, he killed his father and imprisoned his mother at the instigation of Devadatta. After ascending the throne he conquered central India, becoming the mightiest Indian monarch of his day. He died twenty-four years after the Buddha.

8. His name means "the unconquerable," but nothing more about him is known. He is not to be confused with the Bodhisattva Maitreya, who is also sometimes known as Ajita.

9. The present Brahmayoni, located one

mile west of the city of Gayā in central India.

10. The five false teachings are that monks should (1) wear discarded cloth, (2) beg for food, (3) eat only one meal a day, (4) do zazen in the open, and (5) not eat meat.

11. The source of this quotation is unknown.

12. In Buddhism hell, the lowest of the six realms of existence, is divided into eight different categories. Avīci hell, the hell of incessant suffering, is the lowest and worst of the eight. It is thought to be located beneath the continent of Jambudvīpa. Those who are reborn in this hell are always crying out because of the heat of fire.

13. Here "one *kalpa*" is used to indicate an infinitely long period of time.

14. Nothing more about this monk is known.

15. The last of the four stages of life, that is, the intermediate existence after death and before rebirth in another realm of existence. It is generally considered to last for forty-nine days, after which one's past karma determines in which of the six realms of existence one will be reborn. The first three stages of life are birth, living, and death.

16. A *yojana* is an Indian unit of distance equivalent to either 20 or 27 kilometers (12 or 16 miles).

17. The capital of the ancient Indian country of Kośala.

18. Nothing more about this monk is known.

19. Little more about him is known other than that he was said to be remarkably intelligent, which earned him the nickname of Ts'en Ta Ch'ung (Ts'ên the Tiger).

20. The twenty-fourth patriarch, born in central India in the sixth century. He propagated Buddhism in the ancient northern Indian country of Kaśmīra (present-day Kashmir). He was executed by the king of Kaśmīra after having been falsely accused by an influential non-Buddhist.

21. Lived 748–834. He was the Buddhist heir of Ma-tsu. He entered the monkhood at nineteen; realizing enlightenment under Ma-tsu, he established a Zen monastery when he was forty-eight. He is famous for the *kōan* known as "Nan-ch'üan's cat-killing."

22. The three moral natures are good, evil, and neutral (neither good nor evil).

23. The stage in which one enters the "last body," that is, one's last body in the transmigratory world of the six realms of existence. Those in this stage will enter Nirvāṇa at death.

24. The first three kinds of karma indicate the three time-periods in which karmic retribution occurs. The fourth and fifth indicate karmic retribution whose content (good or bad) is either fixed or unfixed. The sixth and seventh indicate karmic retribution whose time of occurrence is either fixed or unfixed. The eighth indicates karmic retribution in which neither the content nor the time of occurrence is fixed.

9. The Four Horses

1. The one great vehicle of the Buddha. Its teachings, which enable all beings to attain Buddhahood, are thought to be superior to those of both the three and the five vehicles. "One" means being only one and nondual; "vehicle" refers to the means of attaining enlightenment.

2. One of the four *Āgamas* (early collections of the teachings of the Buddha). It consists of fifty sections and was translated by the Indian monk Guṇabhadra.

3. The length of one *ch'ih,* a Chinese unit of measurement, has varied in different periods. In Dōgen's time it was 30.7 centimeters (11.8 inches.)

10. A Monk at the Fourth Stage of Meditation

1. Śāriputra had refused to allow Punyavadharna to enter the monkhood because of his advanced age. The Buddha, however, accepted him as his disciple, and he eventually realized Arhathood.

2. These six religious philosophers lived in central India at the time of the Buddha. They were Purāṇa-kāśyapa, who held a negative attitude toward morality by denying good and evil; Maskarī-gosālīputra, a fatalist; Sañjaya-vairattīputra, a skeptic; Ajitakesakambala, a materialist; Kakuda-kātyāyana, who explained the universe in terms of seven elemental factors; and Nirgrantha-jñātaputra, the founder of Jainism, who believed in the relativity of all things.

3. The Buddhist heir of Tao-chang; he was affiliated with the Yün-mên school of Zen.

4. A thirty-section work consisting of biographies of Chinese monks, nuns, noblemen, and distinguished commoners.

5. Nothing more about him is known.

6. A one-section work recording Huinêng's teachings. *T'an* refers to the platform from which he expounded the Law.

7. A Chinese philosopher famous for having developed Taoist thought, particularly the concept of *wu-wei* (nonaction).

8. A Chinese *sūtra,* its origin is unknown.

9. Lived 521–490 B.C. He was one of Confucius' leading disciples.

10. Nothing more about him is known.

11. Nothing more about him is known; the Chinese pronunciation of his name is used here because the original Sanskrit has been lost.

12. This refers to Chih-i; here Dōgen quotes from his *Mo-ho-chih-kuan.*

13. Lived 1118?–1051? B.C. The fourth son of Emperor Wên of the Chou dynasty (c. 1123–256 B.C.), he is famous for having raised the cultural level of China. Confucius later used him as an example of the ideal ruler.

14. Legendary Chinese emperors who are said to have developed farming, animal husbandry, and cooking.

15. Legendary Chinese emperors who are thought to have possessed superior political and administrative skills.

16. Composed in approximately 1000 B.C. to praise the virtues of various Hindu deities, including Brahma, the creator god of the universe; Agni, the god of fire; Varuṇa, the god of water; and others. In addition, there are sections dealing with the proper rituals and festivals for worshiping these deities, as well as the curing of illness through the use of incantations. They consist of the *Ṛg-veda, Sāma-veda, Yajur-veda,* and *Atharva-veda.*

17. The four illusions are (1) *nitya-viparyāsa,* the illusion that the phenomenal world is permanent; (2) *sukha-viparyāsa,* the illusion that the world is a source of pleasure; (3) *śuci-viparyāsa,* the illusion that the phenomenal world is pure; and (4) *ātma-viparyāsa,* the illusion that there exists a real ego.

18. The three poisons are greed, anger, and ignorance.

19. Lived 499–569. He was a monk from western India who went to China in 546 at the invitation of Emperor Wu of the Liang dynasty. He translated numerous Buddhist scriptures and is regarded as the founder of the Shê-lun sect in China.

20. Chih-i.

21. Philosophical treatises dealing with various aspects of Buddhist doctrine.

22. The three worlds are subdivided into nine realms in the following manner: the world of desire is equivalent to one realm, the world of form to four realms, and the formless world to four realms.

23. A contemporary of Chuang-tzŭ. He was a government official in the Liang dynasty.

24. The T'ien-t'ai sect teaches that a phenomenon can be viewed in three different ways within the same instant. First, because a phenomenon is produced by various causes, its essence is devoid of any permanent existence, that is, is "empty." Second, nevertheless it does have a real, if only temporary, immediate existence. Third, since a phenomenon is thus a blending of both ultimate emptiness and temporary existence, it should be seen as occupying a position midway between the two poles.

25. A Taoist work recording the biographies of Lao-tzŭ and his disciples.

26. A Taoist work purported to have been written by Lao-tzŭ. It attempts to show the superiority of his teachings to those of the Buddha.

27. Present-day Kansu and Hsia-hsi provinces in western China.

28. A thirty-section work composed by the Chinese monk Tao-hsüan in 1004. It contains the biographies of 1,701 Indian and Chinese Zen masters.

29. Located in present-day Honan Province, central China, at the foot of Mount Sung.

30. A twenty-section work by Chih-i that explains the various aspects of meditation from the standpoint of the T'ien-t'ai sect.

31. Nothing more about him is known; the Chinese pronunciation of his name is used here because the original Sanskrit has been lost.

32. An inhabitant of the ancient Indian country of Kośala. After losing a debate with the Buddha he became his disciple.

33. One of the Buddha's ten leading disciples, and uncle of Śāriputra. He was known for his skill in debate.

34. Before becoming the Buddha's dis-

ciple he had taught that man's self (soul) is eternal.

11. One Hundred and Eight Ways to Enlightenment

1. The name of this *sūtra* is unknown, though it is probably the Chinese *T'ien-shêng Kuang-têng-lu,* not actually a *sūtra.*

2. Nothing more about this Bodhisattva is known; the Chinese pronunciation of his name is used here because the original Sanskrit has been lost.

3. An elevated dais; the mightiness of a Bodhisattva is thought to be analogous to that of a lion.

4. The four kinds of right effort are (1) to prevent faults from arising, (2) to abandon faults when arisen, (3) to produce merit, and (4) to increase merit when produced.

5. The four bases of supernatural power are will, exertion, thoughts, and investigation.

6. One is the extreme view of existence, which erroneously holds that all phenomena are real; the other is the extreme view of nonexistence, which holds that all phenomena are totally nonexistent and void.

7. *Pāramitā* refers to the crossing over from this shore of birth and decay to the other shore of Nirvāṇa. Here the term is used to designate one of the practices leading to this objective.

8. The four ways of leading sentient beings to enlightenment are (1) offerings, both spiritual and material, (2) loving words, (3) benevolence, and (4) identification (of self with others).

9. The ten powers of a Bodhisattva are (1) devotion to the Buddha's teachings and no attachment to anything, (2) increasing one's devotion, (3) the expedient ability to instruct people and alter their conduct, (4) understanding what people think, (5) satisfying people with what they want, (6) no cessation of exertion, (7) including all vehicles without abandoning the Mahāyāna, (8) the mysterious power of showing the appearance of the Buddhas in every world in each pore of the body, (9) making people turn toward the Buddha's teachings and leading them to perfection, and (10) satisfying all kinds of people with even a single phrase.

10. Nothing more about him is known.

12. The Eight Aspects of Enlightenment

1. The traditional date of the Buddha's death is 485 B.C., though there are differing opinions on this point.

2. The northern of the four continents of traditional Indian geography, Uttarakuru, is omitted from consideration here because its inhabitants do not know the teaching of the Buddha.

Glossary

ABBREVIATIONS USED: Skt. (Sanskrit); Ch. (Chinese); J. (Japanese)

Ābhāsvara Heaven J., Kōon-ten. The third and highest of the three heavens comprising the second group of heavens in the world of form.

Abhidharma One of the three sections of the Tripiṭaka, or Buddhist canon. It consists of works called *śāstras*, attributed to the Buddha's disciples or great Buddhist scholars, that attempt to state or interpret Buddhist doctrines systematically.

Āgama-sūtras J., *Agon-kyō*. See *Mādhyam-āgama-sūtra*.

Ajātaśatru J., Ajase-ō. The son of King Bimbisāra. When he was the crown prince, he killed his father and imprisoned his mother at the instigation of Devadatta, a cousin of the Buddha Śākyamuni. After ascending the throne he conquered central India, becoming the mightiest Indian monarch of his day. He died twenty-four years after the Buddha.

Ajita J., Aitta. Nothing more about this disciple of the Buddha, whose name means "the unconquerable," is known. He is not to be confused with the Bodhisattva Maitreya, who is also sometimes known as Ajita.

Ajñāta-kauṇḍinya J., Annya-kyōjinnyo. *See* five monks.

āmra J., *anra*. A variety of mango tree.

Ānanda J., Anan. A cousin of the Buddha and one of his ten great disciples. He accompanied the Buddha for more than twenty years and was famed for his excellent memory.

Anavatapta J., Anokudatchi. A pond, said to be located north of Mount Sumeru, where one of the eight Dragon Kings lives.

Aniruddha J., Anaritsu. A cousin of the Buddha and one of his ten great disciples. Having once fallen asleep in the Buddha's presence, he vowed that he would never sleep again. He eventually lost his eyesight but acquired the "miraculous eye" that enabled him to see intuitively.

antimadeha J., *saigo-shin*. The stage in which one enters the "last body," that is, one's last body in the transmigratory world of the six realms of existence. Those in this stage will enter Nirvāṇa at death.

Arhat J., *arakan*. *See* Mahāyāna.

Avalokiteśvara J., Kanzeon, Kannon. The Bodhisattva who personifies great compassion, mercy, and love. He had vowed to save all beings through great compassion.

Avīci hell J., Abi-jigoku. In Buddhism hell, the lowest of the six realms of existence, is divided into eight categories. Avīci hell, the hell of incessant suffering, is the lowest and worst of the eight. It is thought to be located beneath the continent of Jambudvīpa, the southern of the four continents according to traditional Indian geography. Those reborn in this hell are always crying out because of the heat.

Bhadrika J., Batsudai. Originally one of the five monks attending Śākyamuni before his enlightenment. After the Buddha's enlightenment he became one of the first disciples. *See also* five monks.

Bhagavat J., Seson. An honorific title of the Buddha Śākyamuni, literally meaning "the world-honored one," that is, one worthy of being honored because he has destroyed all illusions and rid himself of all defilements.

bhikṣu J., *biku*. A monk who is a full-fledged member of the Buddhist community.

bhikṣuṇī J., *bikuni*. A nun who is a full-fledged member of the Buddhist community.

Bodhidharma J., Bodaidaruma. An Indian monk who went to China and is traditionally said to have arrived there on September 21, A.D. 519. After meeting Emperor Wu of the Liang dynasty (502–57) he crossed the Yangtze River and resided at Shao-lin temple, where he did zazen for nine years facing a wall. He is revered as the twenty-eighth patriarch in line from the Buddha and the first Zen patriarch in China.

Bodhi-mind Skt., *bodhi-citta*; J., *bodai-shin*. The aspiration to realize Bodhi-wisdom, that is, perfect enlightenment. In some instances this term is used synonymously with perfect enlightenment itself. *See also* Bodhi-wisdom.

Bodhisattva J., *bosatsu*. One who practices the teaching of Buddhism in both religious and secular ways. He vows to compassionately save all beings before realizing final enlightenment for himself. A Bodhisattva of the highest level of attainment (J., *isshō-fusho*) is said to be destined to be born as a Buddha in his next existence.

Bodhisattva precepts J., *bosatsu-kai*. The sixteen precepts that a Bodhisattva is expected to observe. These, consisting of the three refuges, the three pure precepts, and the ten grave prohibitions, are enumerated in "Receiving the Precepts."

Bodhi-wisdom Skt., *bodhi*; J., *bodai*. The wisdom of the Buddha's enlightenment, acquired as the result of cutting off the two hindrances, passion and illusory conceptions. The Sanskrit term *bodhi* itself is frequently translated simply as "wisdom," but in this book the two words are used together in order to distinguish Bodhi-wisdom from both secular wisdom and *prajñā* (Wisdom). *See also* Wisdom.

Book of Regulations for Zen Monasteries Ch., *Ch'an-yüan Ch'ing-kuei*; J., *Zen'en Shingi*. Written by the famous Chinese Zen master Tsu-chiao in 1101, this work, consisting of ten sections, is the oldest extant book of regulations for a Zen monastery.

Brahma Heaven J., Bon-ten. The first and lowest of the four meditation-heavens in the world of form. Its inhabitants are said to be without sexual desire.

Brāhman J., *baramon*. A Hindu belonging to the highest of the four castes of India. Male members of this caste have traditionally been responsible for conducting religious ceremonies.

Buddha J., *butsu, hotoke*. Originally this term meant anyone who is awakened or enlightened to the true nature of existence. In present usage, however, it often refers to the historical founder of Buddhism, Gautama Siddhārtha, the Buddha Śākyamuni, who was born around the year 565 B.C. to Śuddhodana, king of Kapilavastu, located in what is now Nepal. At the age of twenty-nine he left his father's palace and his wife and infant son in search of the meaning of existence. One morning at the age of thirty-five he realized enlightenment while practicing zazen seated beneath the so-called Bodhi tree. He spent the next forty-five years, until his death at the age of eighty, expounding such teachings as the Middle Path, the Four Noble Truths, and the Eightfold Noble Path in order that all sentient beings might realize the same enlightenment that he had.

Buddhabhạra J., Batsudabara. A monk born in northern India and well versed in the Zen rules of discipline. He went to Ch'ang-an in 406 and transmitted the Way to the Chinese monk Sêng-chao.

Buddhagarbha-sūtra J., *Butsuzō-kyō*. A *sūtra* composed of either three or four sections. Translated into Chinese by Kumārajīva, it emphasizes the need for Bodhisattvas to train apart from Śrāvakas.

Buddha-mind seal J., *busshin-in*. A sign of the correct transmission of the Law from a Zen master to his disciple.

Buddha-nature J., *busshō*. The potential to realize enlightenment innate in all things.

Buddhist community. *See Saṃgha.*

caitya J., *seita*. A type of Buddhist monument similar to a *stūpa* and containing *sūtras*. See also *stūpa*.

Cakravarti, King J., Tenrin Jō-ō. The Wheel-Rolling King. He is said to have thirty-two distinguishing marks and to rule the world by rolling the wheels bestowed on him at his enthronement by a heavenly deity. He manifests himself in four ways. As the Gold-Wheel-Rolling King he rules the four continents; as the Silver-Wheel-Rolling King, the eastern, western, and southern ones; as the Copper-Wheel-Rolling King, the eastern and southern ones; and as the Iron-Wheel-Rolling King, the southern one. *See also* four continents.

caṇḍāla J., *sendara*. The lowest class in the Indian caste system, beneath even the lowest of the four formal castes. Its members are fishermen, jailers, slaughterers, and so on.

Candrasūryapradīpa, Buddha J., Nichigatsu-tōmyō-butsu. A Buddha mentioned in the *Saddharma-puṇḍarīka-sūtra*. According to this work, the Buddha Candrasūryapradīpa expounded the same *sūtra* innumerable *kalpas* ago. He is said to be as brilliant as the sun and the moon, for which he is named.

Chandaka J., Kandaka. A servant of Prince Siddhārtha. He led the white horse Kaṇthaka, on whose back the prince was riding on the night of his renunciation of the world. Later Chandaka became a disciple of the Buddha.

Ch'an-yüan Ch'ing-kuei J., *Zen'en Shingi*. See *Book of Regulations for Zen Monasteries*.

Chao-chou J., Jōshū. 778–897. Buddhist heir of Nan-ch'üan. He is famous for the *kōan* concerning the Buddha-nature known as "Chao-chou's *wu*." In this *kōan* Chao-chou answers with a negative *wu* when asked by a monk whether a dog has the Buddha-nature. Later, however, he gives an affirmative reply to another monk who asks the same question. Through these seemingly contradictory answers, Chao-chou expresses the fact that the Buddha-nature is not to be grasped conceptually.

ch'ih J., *shaku*. A Chinese unit of measurement whose length has varied in different periods. In Dōgen's time, that is, the Southern Sung dynasty (1127–1279), it was 30.7 centimeters (11.8 inches).

Chih-i J., Chigi: 531–97. The third patriarch in the lineage of the Chinese T'ien-t'ai sect of Buddhism. He is the author of a number of important works on Buddhism.

Ching-tê-ch'uan-têng-lu J., *Keitoku Dentō-roku*. A thirty-section work composed by the Chinese monk Tao-hsüan in 1004. It contains the biographies of 1,701 Indian and Chinese Zen masters.

Ching-ts'ên of Mount Chang-sha J., Chōsha Keishin. Little is known about this Chinese Zen monk other than that he was said to be remarkably intelligent, earning for him the nickname of Ts'ên Ta Ch'ung (Ts'ên the Tiger).

Ch'ing-yüan J., Seigen. Died 740. One of the prominent disciples of Hui-nêng, the sixth Chinese Zen patriarch.

degenerate Buddhism J., *mappō*. According to traditional Buddhist belief, Buddhism will pass through three stages or periods after the Buddha's death. During the first period, that of the right or true Law, the Buddha's teachings, practice, and enlightenment exist. In the second period, that of the formal Law, the Buddha's teachings and practice exist, while in the third period, that of the degenerate Law, only the Buddha's teachings remain. Although it is generally agreed that the third period will last for ten thousand years, there are various views on the duration of the first two periods, some believing that each period is only five hundred years long and others that each is one thousand years long.

deliverance robe J., *gedappuku*. Another name for *kaśāya*, so called because the wearing of a *kaśāya* is thought to enable one to be delivered from illusion and realize enlightenment.

Devadatta J., Daibadatta, Daiba. A cousin of the Buddha Śākyamuni. At first he was a follower of the Buddha but later left him and even attempted to kill him. He sent a maddened elephant against the Buddha, but the Buddha "overcame it with love" and it became calm.

Dhammapada-sūtra J., *Hokku-kyō*. A *sūtra* consisting of two sections and divided into thirty-nine chapters. Composed by Dharmatrāta, it was translated into Chinese by Vighnal during the Wu dynasty (A.D. 222–80). A collection of moral teachings, it stresses good conduct stabilized by concentration and strengthened by perfect Wisdom.

Dharma J., *hō*. In its literal meaning this word refers to something that maintains a certain character constantly and becomes a standard of things. In Buddhist teaching it signifies the universal norms or laws that govern human eixstence and is variously translated as "Law" or "Truth."

Dharmākara J., Hōzō. The name of the Buddha Amitābha when he was a Bodhisattva. He made forty-eight vows to bring all sentient beings to the Pure Land.

Dhitaka J., Daitaka. A monk born in the ancient Indian kingdom of Magadha. After realizing enlightenment, he spread Buddhism throughout central India. He is the fifth Indian patriarch, the Buddhist heir of Upagupta.

dhyāna J., *zen*. *See* zazen.

Dīpaṃkara, Buddha J., Nentō-butsu. A Buddha of the past who assured Śākyamuni in a previous life that he would ultimately achieve enlightenment.

Dragon King J., *ryū-ō*. A guardian deity of Buddhism. There are eight Dragon Kings, inhabiting various waters.

eight difficult realms J., *hachi-nanjo*. The realms of (1) hell, (2) animals, (3) hungry spirits, (4) the heaven of long life, (5) remote places, (6) the state of being blind, deaf, or otherwise handicapped, (7) secular prejudice, and (8) the period of the absence of the Buddha.

eighteen heavens J., *jūhatten*. The first, second, and third meditation-heavens in the world of form are said to consist of three heavens each, or nine in all; the fourth meditation-heaven consists of nine heavens, making a total of eighteen.

Eightfold Noble Path J., *hasshōdō*. (1) Correct views, (2) correct thinking, (3) correct speech, (4) correct action, (5) correct livelihood, (6) correct endeavor, (7) correct remembrance, and (8) correct meditation.

eight kinds of suffering J., *hakku.* (1) The suffering of birth, (2) the suffering of old age, (3) the suffering of sickness, (4) the suffering of death, (5) the suffering that comes from being apart from those whom one loves, (6) the suffering that comes from being with those whom one hates, (7) the suffering that comes from the fact that one cannot have what one wants, and (8) the suffering that comes from the fact that one is attached to the five elemental aggregates (*skandhas*) of which one's body, mind, and environment are composed.

Ekkotara-āgama-sūtra. J., *Zō-ichi-agon-kyō.* One of the four *Āgama-sūtras* (early collections of the teachings of the Buddha). It consists of fifty sections and is divided into fifty-two chapters. It is said to have been first translated into Chinese by the Indian monk Dharmanandi in A.D. 384.

esoteric teachings, exoteric teachings J., *mikkyō, kengyō.* The esoteric teachings of Buddhism are found in the Shingon and Tendai sects in Japan and refer to those doctrines and rituals, deeply influenced by Hinduism, that developed in India during the seventh and eighth centuries. These teachings, having magical properties, can only be revealed to those who have been properly initiated. The exoteric teachings include all Buddhist teachings other than the above.

Fa-hsien J., Hokken. A Chinese monk of the Eastern Chin dynasty (317–420). In 399 he left China for India, finally arriving there after six years of hard travel. After studying Sanskrit and obtaining many Sanskrit texts of the Tripiṭaka (Buddhist canon), he returned to China by sea in 414. After his return he not only translated these texts but also wrote a record of his travels. He died when either eighty-two or eighty-six years old.

Fa-hua-ch'an-fa J., *Hokke-sempō.* "The Methods for Practicing the *Samādhi* of the *Saddharma-puṇḍarīka-sūtra,*" a one-section work compiled by Chih-i.

Fa-jung J., Hōyū. 594–657. A Chinese Zen monk said to have been well versed in the *sūtras* and Buddhist history by the age of nineteen. He was the collateral Buddhist heir of Ta-i Tao-hsin.

five aggregates J., *go-un.* In Buddhist philosophy, all physical, mental, and other elements in this phenomenal world are classified into five kinds of aggregates (Skt., *skandhas*): (1) *rūpa-skandha,* a generic term for all forms of matter; (2) *vedanā-skandha,* perception; (3) *samjñā-skandha,* mental conceptions and ideas; (4) *samskāra-skandha,* volition; and (5) *vijñāna-skandha,* consciousness of mind. In the case of man, the *rūpa-skandha* is the body, the *vijñāna-skandha* is the totality of the mind, and the other three *skandhas* are mental functions. Thus the five skandhas comprise the body and mind of all sentient beings in the world of desire and the world of form, but those sentient beings in the formless world of pure spirit have no material elements.

five deadly wrongs J., *go-gyakuzai.* (1) Killing one's father, (2) killing one's mother, (3) killing an Arhat, (4) injuring the body of a Buddha, and (5) causing disunity in the Buddhist community.

five delusions J., *go-ketsu.* (1) Avarice, (2) anger, (3) pride, (4) jealousy, and (5) stinginess.

five desires J., *go-yoku.* The desires for (1) property, (2) sexual love, (3) food and drink, (4) fame, and (5) sleep.

five false teachings of Devadatta J., *Daiba go-ja-no-hō.* Monks should (1) wear discarded cloth, (2) beg for food, (3) eat only one meal a day, (4) do zazen in the open, and (5) not eat meat.

five marks of decay J., *tennin-no-go-sui.* These pertain to a celestial being: (1) one's robes becoming dirty, (2) one's hair-flowers fading, (3) one's body smelling bad, (4) sweating under one's arms, and (5) not enjoying one's original status.

five mistaken views J., *go-ken.* (1) To be attached to self and to other people and things, (2) to believe either that the self is eternal or that it is noneternal, (3) to deny causality, (4) to hold mistaken views like the above to be the Truth, and (5) to regard adherence to the precepts as the way to enlightenment.

five monks J., *go-biku.* When Prince Siddhārtha (Śākyamuni) forsook the world and entered the monkhood, his father, King Śuddhodana, ordered five men to accompany him. They practiced asceticism with Śākyamuni but left him when he abandoned such practices. Later, when Śākyamuni realized Buddhahood, they joined him in the Deer Park near Benares and became his disciples. The monks were Ajñāta-kauṇḍinya, Aśvajit, Bhadrika, Mahānāman, and Daśabala-kāśyapa.

five moral powers J., *go-riki.* (1) Faith, (2) exertion, (3) mindfulness, (4) meditation, and (5) Wisdom.

five patriarchs The patriarchs of the five Zen schools in China are Yün-mên, Wei-yang, Ts'ao-tung, Lin-chi, and Fa-yen.

five vehicles J., *go-jō.* The five divisions of the teachings of the Buddha. In Mahāyāna Buddhism they are (1) the vehicle (Skt., *yāna;* J., *jō*) for laymen, in which one rightly receives the five lay precepts and upon rebirth becomes a celestial being; (2) the vehicle for celestial beings, in which one rightly practices the ten good deeds and *samādhi,* ensuring rebirth in a higher heavenly realm; (3) the Śrāvakayāna or Hīnayāna, in which one rightly understands the Four Noble Truths and becomes an Arhat; (4) the Pratyekabuddhayāna or Mādhyamyāna, in which one rightly understands the twelve links of causation and becomes a Pratyekabuddha; and (5) the Bodhisattvayāna or Mahāyāna, in which one becomes a Bodhisattva as a result of religious practice over innumerable years.

Fo-pên-hsing-chi sūtra J., *Butsu-hongyō-jikkyō.* A sixty-section biography of the Buddha and his disciples compiled in India and translated into Chinese by Jñānagupta. The Sanskrit original has been lost.

formal Law J., *zōhō. See* degenerate Buddhism.

four bases of supernatural power J., *shi-nyoi-soku.* Will, exertion, thought, and investigation.

four classes of Buddhists J., *shi-shū.* Monks, nuns, laymen, and laywomen.

four continents J., *shi-shū.* According to ancient Indian geography, the world consists of four continents in the ocean surrounding Mount Sumeru: Jambudvīpa in the south, Pūrvavideha in the east, Aparagodānīya in the west, and Uttarakuru in the north.

four elements J., *shi-dai.* (1) Earth, which has hardness as its nature and can support things; (2) water, which has moisture as its nature and can contain things; (3) fire, which has heat as its nature and can bring things to perfection; and (4) wind, which has motion as its nature and can cause things to mature.

four forms of life J., *shi-shō.* Womb-born, egg-born, moisture-born, and metamorphically born.

four heavens J., *shi-ten.* The heavens of (1) boundless knowledge, (2) infinite emptiness, (3) nonattachment to either knowledge or emptiness, and (4) nonthought and non-nonthought.

four illusions J., *shi-tendō.* (1) *Nitya-viparyāsa,* the illusion that the phenomenal world is permanent; (2) *sukha-viparyāsa,* the illusion that the world is a source of pleasure; (3) *śuci-viparyāsa,* the illusion that the phenomenal world is pure; and (4) *ātma-viparyāsa,* the illusion that there exists a real ego.

four insights J., *shi-nenjū, shi-nenjō.* The insights that (1) the world is transient, (2) the body is impure, (3) perception leads to suffering, and (4) the mind is impermanent.

four kinds of right effort J., *shi-shōgon.* These are the effort (1) to prevent faults from arising, (2) to abandon faults when arisen, (3) to produce merit, and (4) to increase merit when produced.

Four Noble Truths J., *shi-tai.* A basic Buddhist teaching, which explains the cause of suffering and the means of deliverance therefrom. This was one of the first doctrines taught by the Buddha after his enlightenment. The truths are that (1) all existence entails suffering; (2) suffering is caused by ignorance, which gives rise to desire and illusion; (3) there is an end to suffering, and this state of no suffering is called Nirvāṇa; and (4) the way to end suffering is through the practice of the Eightfold Noble Path.

Four-Quarter Kings J., *shi-tennō.* Four mythical kings said to live halfway down Mount Sumeru. They protect the eastern, southern, western, and northern continents of traditional Indian geography.

four stages of meditation J., *shi-zenjō.* These enable one to remove delusions and attain bliss in the world of form. In the first stage, five states of mind—investigation, reflection, joyfulness, bliss, and a concentrated state of mind—are realized. They are accompanied by eight kinds of feelings and the ten virtues. In the second stage there are four states of mind: serenity of mind, joyfulness, bliss, and a concentrated state of mind. The third stage is characterized by five states of mind: equanimity, remembrance, wisdom, bliss, and a concentrated state of mind. The fourth state has four states of mind: neither suffering nor joy, equanimity, remembrance, and a concentrated state of mind.

four stages to Arhathood J., *shi-ka.* In ascending order, these are (1) *Srotāpanna,* the stage in which one has entered into the stream of sanctification, abandoning all false views in the three worlds; (2) *Sakṛdāgāmin,* the stage in which one has only one rebirth left before realizing enlightenment; (3) *Anāgāmin,* the stage in which one will never again return to the world of desire; and (4) Arhat, the stage before Buddhahood in which one is free from all craving, rebirth, and other defilements.

four ways of leading sentient beings J., *shi-shōbō.* These ways of leading beings to enlightenment are (1) offerings, both spiritual and material, (2) loving words, (3) benevolence, and (4) identification (of self with others).

Gandhāra J., Kendara. An ancient country in northern India, located north of the present-day Punjab and northeast of Kashmir.

gandharva J., *kendatsuba.* A deity of celestial music.

garuḍa J., *karura.* A mythical gigantic golden-winged bird that is said to eat dragons.

gasshō Skt., *añjali.* A gesture of reverence, symbolizing the unity of body and mind, in which the hands are joined palm to palm, fingers extended, and placed near the breast.

gāthā J., *ge.* A verse praising the Buddha or restating succinctly major points of Buddhist doctrine.

gāthā of the whole world J., *shishikai-bon.* This verse is contained in the *Chao-jih-ming-san-mei-ching,* a *sūtra* extant only in Chinese: "The world around us is as vast as the sky, / As pure as lotus flowers rising from muddy water. / My mind is pure and beyond the ordinary world. / I pay homage to the most excellent Buddha."

Gayā, Mount J., Gaya-sen. The present Mount Brahmayoni, located one mile west of the city of Gayā in central India.

Greater Vehicle J., *daijō*. *See* Mahāyāna.

hasta J., *chū*. An Indian unit of measurement equivalent to 45.7 centimeters (18 inches).

Heaven of Pure Abode J., Jōgo-ten. The highest of the four heavens in the world of form. Beings in this heaven have only the faculty of mind and the sensation of freedom from pain and pleasure.

Hīnayāna J., *shōjō*. *See* Mahāyāna.

Hōnen 1133–1212. Founder of the Jōdo (Pure Land) sect of Buddhism in Japan. He taught that anyone, rich or poor, wise or foolish, can achieve rebirth in the Pure Land by sincerely invoking the name of the Buddha Amitābha (J., Amida) as expressed in the formula *Namu Amida-butsu* (Homage to the Buddha Amitābha).

hsieh-yeh-i J., *detchō-e*. A type of *kaśāya* made by sewing together large uncut pieces of cloth.

Hsing-ssŭ of Mount Ch'ing-yüan J., Seigen Gyōshi·*See* Ch'ing-yüan

Hsi-shih J., Seishi. A woman who, together with Mao-ch'ang, is said to have been one of the most beautiful courtesans in ancient China.

Hsüan-chüeh J., Gengaku. 665–713. A Chinese monk famous for having written the "Song of Enlightenment" (*Chêng-tao-ko*).

Huai-hai of Mount Pai-chang J., Hyakujō Ekai. 720–814. The Buddhist heir of Ma-tsu Tao-i. He is famous for having written the first set of regulations for a Zen monastery. This work, known as the *Pai-chang Ch'ing-kuei*, is not extant.

Huai-jang of Mount Nan-yüeh J., Nangaku Ejō. *See* Nan-yüeh.

Huang-po J., Ōbaku. Died 850. Huai-hai's most prominent disciple, noted for his strong sense of irony and strict teaching methods.

Hui-k'o J., Eka. 487–593. The Buddhist heir of Bodhidharma, and the second Chinese Zen patriarch. He is said to have cut off an arm to show Bodhidharma how earnestly he wished to become his disciple.

Hui-nêng J., Enō. 637–712. The Buddhist heir of Hung-jên, and the sixth Chinese Zen patriarch. He is said to have realized enlightenment when pounding rice while training on Mount Huang-mei.

Hui-ssŭ of Mount Nan-yüeh J., Nangaku Eshi. 514 or 515 to 577. A Chinese monk considered to be the second patriarch of the Chinese T'ien-t'ai sect. After having trained under Hui-wêng's guidance, in 570 he moved to Mount Nan-yüeh, where he later died. He is famous for having written a number of important works on Buddhism.

Hung-chih J., Wanshi. 1091–1157. The Buddhist heir of Tan-hsia Tsu-ch'un. He is said to have had more than twelve hundred disciples.

intermediate world J., *chū-u, chū-in*. The last of the four stages of life, that is, the intermediate existence after death and before rebirth in another realm of existence. It is generally considered to last for forty-nine days, after which one's past karma determines in which of the six realms of existence one will be reborn. The first three stages of life are birth, living, and death.

Jambudvīpa *See* four continents.

Jetavana Garden J., Gion-shōja. A garden donated by the rich merchant Sudatta to the Buddha Śākyamuni and his disciples as a place to pursue religious training; it was located in the city of Śrāvasti.

kalavinka J., *karyōbinga*. A mythical Indian bird said to have a beautiful voice even before it has hatched.

kalpa J., *kō*. The period of time required for a celestial woman to wear away a ten-mile-cubic stone if she brushes it with her garments once every three years, that is, an infinitely long period of time.

Kañcipura J., Kōshi. An ancient country in southern India.

Kaniṣka, King J., Kanishika-ō. Said to have been the third major king of the Kuṣāṇa dynasty of northern India, he is thought to have lived in the latter half of the first century or the first half of the second century. He was a great patron of Buddhism and Buddhist art, and built temples, dispatched missionaries, and had Buddhist commentaries compiled.

Kao of Mount Yüeh J., Kō Shami. A novice Zen monk who pursued the Way under Wei-yen (751–834). Nothing more about him is known.

Kapilavastu *See* Buddha.

karma J., *gō*. Deeds that are produced by the action of the mind, good deeds producing good results and bad deeds producing bad results at some time in the future. In common usage, "to produce karma" means to commit bad actions.

kaśāya J., *kesa*. A Buddhist monk's outer robe. There are three major types of *kaśāya*, consisting of five, seven, or nine strips of cloth. See "The Merit of a *Kaśāya*" for a detailed discussion of these robes and their use.

Kāśyapa J., Kashō. Also known as Mahākāśyapa, "Great Kāśyapa." One of the ten great disciples of the Buddha. He became a disciple about three years after the Buddha attained enlightenment and is said to have become an Arhat after being with the Buddha for only eight days. He is regarded as the first patriarch of Zen Buddhism.

Kāśyapa, Buddha J., Kashō-butsu. The sixth of the seven past Buddhas, and the Buddha immediately preceding Śākyamuni. *See also* seven past Buddhas.

Kiṃnara J., Kinnara. An Indian god of music.

kōan Ch., *kung-an*. Sometimes translated as "Zen riddle," *kōan* originally meant a public notice issued by the Chinese government, but it now refers to the statements, including answers to questions, made by famous ancient Zen masters. These statements are used as objects of meditation by novices in Zen monasteries of the Rinzai sect as a means of transcending the realm of duality, such as the subject-object split. In the Sōtō sect, however, they are studied only as reference points for one's own practice. In Sōtō Zen, daily life itself is seen as the ultimate *kōan*, that is, the manifestation of the Truth.

ko-chi-i J., *kassetsu-e*. A type of *kaśāya* made by sewing together small precut pieces of cloth.

Kośala J., Kyōsara. One of the sixteen major countries in India during the Buddha's time; present-day Oude in the Gogra Valley.

kṣaṇa J., *setsuna*. An instant; an Indian unit of time said to equal one sixty-fifth of a second.

ksānti J., *nimpō*. The stage at which monks progressively realize the Four Noble Truths within themselves.

Kumārajīva J., Kumarajū. 344–413. Born in Kucha in central Asia to an Indian father and the sister of the king of Kucha, Kumārajīva went to China in 401 as a Buddhist missionary. From that time until his death he was responsible for the translation of a large number of important *sūtras* including the *Saddharma-puṇḍarīka-sūtra* and is known as one of the greatest translators into Chinese.

Kumāralabdha J., Kumarata. The nineteenth Indian patriarch. He was born in northern India at the end of the third century A.D.

kumbhāṇḍa J., *kuhanda*. An earthly demon who sucks human blood and eats human flesh.

Law *See Dharma.*

Law-body Skt., *Dharmakāya;* J., *hosshin.* The absolute nature of the Buddha-mind, which transcends personality and is identical with the Truth. It is considered to be the highest aspect of the threefold body of the Buddha. *See also* threefold body of the Buddha.

Law-body of five merits J., *go-bun hosshin.* These merits are (1) the precepts, (2) *samādhi* (concentration), (3) Wisdom, (4) freedom from desire, and (5) self-awareness of enlightenment.

Lesser Vehicle Skt., Hīnayāna; J., *shōjō. See* Mahāyāna.

li J., *ri.* A Chinese unit of distance equivalent to about 666 meters (0.4 mile).

liang J., *ryō.* A Chinese weight equal to approximately 15 grams (0.5 ounce).

Lokavid J., Sekenge. One of the ten epithets of the Buddha, denoting "one who understands the world."

Lotus *Sūtra* See *Saddharma-puṇḍarīka-sūtra.*

Lu J., Ro. The family name of Hui-nêng. *See* Hui-nêng.

Mādhyam-āgama-sūtra J., *Chū-agon-kyō.* One of the four *Āgama-sūtras* (early collections of the teachings of the Buddha). It sets forth such teachings as the Four Noble Truths and the twelve links in the chain of causation. It also contains much material dealing with the origin of Buddhism, parables, and the lives of the Buddha and his disciples.

Mahābhijñājñānabhibhū, Buddha J., Daitsū-chishō-butsu. A Buddha mentioned in the *Saddharma-puṇḍarīka-sūtra.* He is said to have attained enlightenment three thousand "dust-atom" *kalpas* ago.

Mahānāma J., Makanan. One of the Buddha's cousins. He is noted for having made venerative offerings to the Buddhist community while still a layman as an expression of his deep faith.

Mahāparinirvāṇa-sūtra J., *Daihatsu-nehan-gyō.* Often abbreviated to *Nirvāṇa-sūtra* (J., *Nehan-gyō*). A Mahāyāna *sūtra* that claims to be the last sermon of the Buddha. It has been preserved in Chinese versions alone, the Sanskrit original having been lost.

Mahāprajñāpāramitā treatise J., *Daichido-ron.* A hundred-section philosophical commentary on the *Mahāprajñāpāramitā-sūtra* (J., *Daihannya-haramitta-kyō*), attributed to Nāgārjuna and translated into Chinese by Kumārajīva. It stresses the doctrine of "emptiness" (Skt., *śūnyatā;* J., *kū*).

Mahāsaṃghikā-vinaya J., *Makasōgi-ritsu.* A forty-section treatise on the Buddhist rules of discipline (Skt., *vinaya;* J., *ritsu*) for monks and nuns. It was translated into Chinese during the Ch'in dynasty (221–207 B.C.) by Buddhabhadra and Fa-hsien.

Mahāyāna J., *daijō.* Literally, "Greater Vehicle." The northern of the two main branches of Buddhism. The southern branch, designated by Mahāyāna Buddhists as Hīnayāna, or "Lesser Vehicle," arose in southern India, whence it spread to Ceylon, Burma, Thailand, and Cambodia. (Hīnayāna adherents themselves prefer the term Theravāda, "Way of the Elders," as the designation for their form of Buddhism.) In Hīnayāna Buddhism one strives to become an Arhat, that is, a person who has gained liberation by single-heartedly overcoming passion and ego. The Mahāyāna branch of Buddhism, on the other hand, spread from northern India to Tibet, Mongolia, China, Korea, and Japan. In contrast to Hīnayāna Buddhism, which tended to remain conservative and rigid, the Mahāyāna adapted itself to the needs of peoples of diverse racial and cultural backgrounds and varying levels of understanding. Its ideal became the Bodhisattva, one who is ever ready to sacrifice himself in the interest of those lost in ignorance and despair even at the cost of his own supreme enlightenment.

mahoraga J., *magoraga*. A deity with a snakelike head.

Maitreya, Bodhisattva J., Miroku-bosatsu. A Bodhisattva believed to be living in Tuṣita Heaven, the fourth of the six heavens in the world of desire, awaiting the time when he will descend to this world to succeed the Buddha Śākyamuni. It is held that he will appear in this world 5,670 million years after the death of Śākyamuni.

mani jewels J., *mani-ju*. Fabulous gems capable of responding to every wish and dispelling evil. These jewels are obtained from the Dragon King in the ocean.

Mañjuśri, Bodhisattva J., Monju-bosatsu. A Bodhisattva regarded as the idealization or personification of the Buddha's Wisdom, which is embodied in the practice of zazen.

Mao-ch'ang J., Mōshō. A woman who, together with Hsi-shih, is said to have been one of the most beautiful courtesans in ancient China.

Maudgalyāyana J., Mokkenren, Mokuren. One of the ten great disciples of the Buddha. He is said to have possessed supernatural powers.

Middle Path J., *chūdō*. One of the most basic teachings of Buddhism, this is the doctrine of the path between, or the Wisdom beyond, extremes, such as suffering and happiness.

Mo-ho-chih-kuan J., *Maka-shikan*. A twenty-section work by Chih-i explaining the various aspects of meditation from the standpoint of the Chinese T'ien-t'ai sect.

Nāgārjuna J., Ryūju. Born into a Brāhman family in southern India in the second or third century A.D., he became one of the chief philosophers of Mahāyāna Buddhism and is considered to be the fourteenth Indian patriarch in the lineage of the transmission of the Law. He advocated the theory that all phenomena are relative, having no independent existence of their own.

Nanda J., Nanda. The son of Mahāprajāpati, Śākyamuni's aunt and foster mother.

Nan-yüeh J., Nangaku. 677–744. One of the prominent disciples of Hui-nêng. He is considered to be the seventh Chinese Zen patriarch.

Nichiren 1222–82. The founder of the Japanese sect bearing his name. He believed that the *Saddharma-puṇḍarīka-sūtra* contained the ultimate teachings of the Buddha and taught that to attain salvation one should invoke the title of that *sūtra* with the formula *Namu Myōhō-renge-kyō* (Homage to the *Sūtra* of the Lotus of the Supreme Law).

nine realms J., *ku-ji*. The three worlds are divided into nine realms in the following manner: the world of desire is equivalent to one realm, the world of form to four realms, and the formless world to four realms.

Nirvāṇa J., *nehan*. Literally, "extinction." Originally, this referred to the state of enlightenment attained by the Buddha Śākyamuni. Accordingly, it means the state that can be reached by extinguishing all illusions and destroying all karma, which is the cause of rebirth. In Mahāyāna Buddhism it further denotes that state which is beyond birth and decay, and is equated with Wisdom and the ultimate Truth.

nyagrodha J., *nikuda*. A variety of tall tropical tree with thick foliage.

one billion worlds J., *sanzen-(daisen-)sekai*. The universe in its entirety.

one vehicle J., *ichijō*. The one great vehicle of the Buddha. Its teachings, which enable all beings to attain Buddhahood, are thought to be superior to those of both the three and the five vehicles. "One" means being only one and nondual, and refers to the means of attaining enlightenment.

pāmsūla J., *funzō-e*. Literally, "excreta-sweeping robe," this is a type of *kaśāya*. See "The Merit of a *Kaśāya*" for a detailed discussion of the *pāmsūla*.

P'ang, lay disciple J., Hō-*koji*. 740–803. A Chinese lay disciple of Zen Buddhism who is said to have thrown all his property into a river. He practiced the Way under the guidance of Shih-t'ou and Ma-tsu, eventually realizing enlightenment.

Paññatara J., Hannyatara. A monk born in eastern India. The Buddhist heir of the twenty-sixth Indian patriarch, Punyamitra, and the twenty-seventh patriarch. He is said to have commissioned Bodhidharma (the twenty-eighth patriarch) to introduce the Law to China.

Pao-lin temple J., Hōrin-ji. A temple on Mount Ts'ao-ch'i where Hui-nêng lived for a time.

Pāpīyas J., Ma-ō. An evil spirit who, it is popularly believed, is the lord of the highest of the six heavens in the world of desire. Together with his followers, Pāpīyas hinders people from adhering to Buddhism.

Paramārtha J., Shintai. 499–569. A monk from western India who went to China in 546 at the invitation of Emperor Wu of the Liang dynasty (502–57). He translated many *sūtras* and other Buddhist works into Chinese and is regarded as the founder of the Shê-lun (J., Shōron) sect.

pāramitā J., *haramitsu*. This word refers to the crossing over from this shore of birth and decay to the other shore of Nirvāṇa. Hence the term is used to designate the practices leading to this objective.

pata J., *man-e*. A type of *kaśāya*.

piśāca J., *bishaja*. A heavenly demon who sucks human blood and eats human flesh.

Prasenajit, King J., Hashinoku-ō. King of the countries of Kośala and Kāśi in central India. He was the same age as the Buddha and ascended the throne the same year that the latter attained enlightenment. Together with his wife and son, he became a devout follower of the Buddha.

Pratyekabuddha J., *engaku*. One who has realized enlightenment through independent study, without the guidance of a master. Like the Arhat, he does not attempt to save others.

precepts J., *kairitsu*. The rules of conduct and discipline established by the Buddha.

precepts for laymen Traditionally, laymen should observe five precepts: (1) not to take life, (2) not to take what is not given to one, (3) not to engage in improper sexual conduct, (4) not to lie, and (5) not to drink intoxicants.

precepts for monks The Mahāyāna precepts for monks consist of ten major and forty-eight minor items of morality. The ten major precepts are (1) not to kill, (2) not to steal, (3) not to engage in sexual relations, (4) not to lie, (5) not to drink or deal in intoxicants, (6) not to speak of the faults of others, whether they be laymen or monks, (7) not to be too proud to praise others, (8) not to covet either the Law or property, (9) not to give way to anger, and (10) not to disparage the Three Treasures (the Buddha, the Law, and the Buddhist community).

precepts for nuns Nuns must observe 348 precepts, including the ten major precepts for monks. *See also* precepts for monks.

provisional teachings J., *hōben.* In Mahāyāna Buddhism it is believed that the Buddha Śākyamuni simplified many of his teachings, particularly the earlier ones, in order that people of various capacities could understand them and eventually be led to the final doctrine. These simplified teachings are thought to have only a provisional nature.

Punyamitra J., Funyomitta. The twenty-sixth Indian patriarch.

Pure Land J., *jōdo.* A spiritual realm where the Buddhas and Bodhisattvas are said to live in eternal bliss.

Pu-tai J., Hotei. An eccentric Chinese monk who lived in the latter part of the T'ang dynasty (618–907). He had the reputation of being an excellent fortuneteller and is revered in Japan as one of the seven gods of good fortune.

P'u-têng-lu J., *Futō-roku.* A thirty-section work consisting of biographies of Chinese monks, nuns, noblemen, and distinguished commoners.

P'u-yüan of Nan-ch'üan J., Nansen Fugan. 748–834. The Buddhist heir of Ma-tsu. He is famous for the *kōan* known as "Nan-ch'üan's cat-killing." In this *kōan* Nan-ch'üan, seeing his disciples quarreling over the ownership of a cat, picked it up and said that he would kill it unless someone "spoke a word of Zen." When none of those present replied, he cut the cat in two. Later, when Nan-ch'üan recited this episode to Chao-chou, his foremost disciple, the latter put his straw sandals on his head and walked away. Nan-ch'üan, pleased with this spontaneous, nondualistic act on the part of his disciple, then stated that the cat's life would have been saved had Chao-chou been present during the original incident. This *kōan* points to the impossibility of grasping the Buddha-nature with the discriminating mind.

Rāhula J., Ragora. The son of the Buddha, born before his father's renunciation of the world. He is one of the ten great disciples of the Buddha.

reward-body Skt., *saṃbhogakāya;* J., *hōjin.* The body of a Buddha that is produced upon entering Buddhahood. It is a result of the vows taken and the religious practices undergone while a Buddha is still a Bodhisattva.

ri See *li.*

Rinzai sect The Zen Buddhist sect founded by the Chinese Zen monk Lin-chi (J., Rinzai: d. 867), Buddhist heir of Huang-po. Its teachings were transmitted to Japan by Eisai (1141–1215).

Saddharma-puṇḍarīka-sūtra J., *Myōhō-renge-kyō.* The *Sūtra* of the Lotus of the Supreme Law, commonly known as the Lotus *Sūtra.* This *sūtra,* composed of eight sections divided into twenty-seven or twenty-eight chapters, is one of the most important documents of Mahāyāna Buddhism. It teaches that perfect enlightenment was achieved by the Buddha many *kalpas* ago, and that even followers of Hīnayāna are able to attain perfect enlightenment.

Sahā J., Shaba. The world of ordinary human beings.

Śakrendra, King J., Taishaku-ten. Also called Śakra *devānām* Indra, he is one of the guardian deities of Buddhism. He lives in Sudarśana Palace on top of Mount Sumeru, ruling the Heaven of the Thirty-three Gods (Trāyastriṃśa Heaven). He hears of the moral condition of the people of the world through reports by the Four-Quarter Kings among others.

Śākyamuni, Buddha. J., Shakamuni-butsu. *See* Buddha.

samādhi J., *sammai*. Frequently translated as "meditation" or "concentration," this word denotes a state in which the mind, free from distraction, is absorbed in intense, "purposeless" concentration. With the mind thus completely absorbed in itself, the essential nature of the Self can be experienced directly. It should be noted that this concentrated state of mind can also be used for other (often magical) purposes. In Zen, however, such uses are generally held in low esteem.

Saṃgha J., *sōdan*. The Buddhist order or community, consisting of at least three monks or nuns.

Saṃyukt-āgama-sūtra J., *Zō-agon-kyō*. One of the four *Āgama-sūtras* (early collections of the teachings of the Buddha). It consists of fifty sections and was translated into Chinese by the Indian monk Guṇabhadra.

Śāṇavāsa J., Shōnawashu. Born in central India, he was the Buddhist heir of the second Indian patriarch, Ānanda, and became the third patriarch.

Śāriputra J., Sharihotsu. One of the ten great disciples of the Buddha, he is said to have been supreme in Wisdom among the disciples.

Sarvāstivāda J., *ubu*. One of the twenty Theravāda (Hīnayāna) schools of Buddhism. Its chief teaching is that time and existence are eternal.

Sāstā-deva-manuṣyānām J., Tennin-shi. One of the ten epithets of the Buddha, denoting "one who teaches gods and men."

Sêng-chao J., Sōjō. 384–414. A Chinese monk born in Ch'ang-an. He was well versed in the *sūtras*, the rules of discipline (*vinaya*), and Buddhist philosophical treatises (*śāstras*).

seven past Buddhas J., *kako-shichi-butsu*. Vipaśyin, Śikhin, Viśvabhū, Krakucchanda, Kanakamuni, Kāśyapa, and Śākyamuni.

seven precious things The same as the first series of the seven treasures. *See* seven treasures.

seven treasures J., *shippō*. (1) Gold, silver, mother-of-pearl, agate, coral, amber, and emerald; (2) fine rings, elephants, horses, jewels, beautiful court attendants, retainers gifted in financial affairs, and retainers gifted in military affairs.

shashu An expression of respect similar to the *gasshō*. The hands are joined, fingers curled, and placed on the breast.

Shên-hsiu J., Jinshū. 606–706. Founder of the Northern Zen sect in China, he was a leading disciple of Hung-jên, the fifth Chinese Zen patriarch. His understanding of the Way was highly intellectual, preventing him from realizing full enlightenment.

shê-yeh-i J., *shōyō-e*. A type of *kaṣāya*.

Shih-t'ou Wu-chi J., Sekitō Musai. 700–790. The Buddhist heir of Ch'ing-yüan, under whose guidance he is said to have realized enlightenment.

Shōmu, Emperor J., Shōmu-tennō. 701–56. The forty-fifth emperor of Japan, he reigned 724–49. Embracing Buddhism wholeheartedly, he built numerous temples throughout Japan, including the famous Central Cathedral of Tōdai-ji in Nara, the capital. Seven years before his death he abdicated and entered the monkhood.

Siddhārtha, Prince J., Shitta-taishi. The name of the Buddha before his renunciation of the world. Siddhārtha is variously translated as "he who has accomplished his aim," "he whose desire has been fulfilled," "he who has been successful in his endeavor," and so on. *See also* Buddha.

Siṃha J., Shishi. The twenty-fourth Indian patriarch. Born in central India, he propagated Buddhism in the ancient northern Indian country of Kaśmīra (present-day Kashmir). He was executed by the king of that country after having been falsely accused by an influential non-Buddhist.

Siṃhahanu, King J., Shishikyō-ō. The king of the ancient Indian kingdom of Kapilavastu, in present-day Nepal, and father of King Śuddhodana, who was the father of the Buddha Śākyamuni.

six lowest heavens J., *roku-yoku-ten*. The six heavens of the world of desire. In ascending order, these are (1) the Heaven of the Four-Quarter Kings, (2) the Heaven of the Thirty-three Gods (Trāyastriṃśa Heaven), (3) the Heaven of King Yama, (4) Tuṣita Heaven, (5) Nirmāṇarati Heaven, and (6) Paranirmita-veśavartin Heaven.

six non-Buddhist philosophers J., *roku-shi-gedō*. These six religious philosophers lived in central India in the time of the Buddha. They include (1) Purāṇa-kāśyapa, who held a negative attitude toward morality, denying good and evil; (2) Maskarī-gosāliputra, a fatalist; (3) Sañjaya-vairattīputra, a skeptic; (4) Ajita-kesakambala, a materialist; (5) Kakuda-kātyāyana, who explained the universe in terms of seven elemental factors; and (6) Nirgrantha-jñātaputra, the founder of Jainism, who believed in the relativity of all things.

six patriarchs The six Chinese Zen patriarchs, in chronological order, are Bodhidharma, Hui-k'o, Sêng-ts'an, Tao-hsin, Hung-jên, and Hui-nêng.

six powers J., *roku-zū*. (1) Free activity, (2) eyes capable of seeing everything, (3) ears capable of hearing everything, (4) insight into others' thinking, (5) remembrance of one's former existences, and (6) perfect freedom.

six realms of existence J., *roku-dō*. The six realms in which the souls of living beings are traditionally thought to transmigrate until they finally realize Nirvāṇa are, in ascending order, (1) hell, (2) hungry ghosts, (3) animals, (4) *asuras* (pugnacious devils), (5) human beings, and (6) celestial beings.

six schools The Kegon, Hossō, Ritsu, Jōjitsu, Kusha, and Sanron schools of Buddhism in Japan are commonly referred to as the six schools of the Nara period (710–94), although not all of them actually existed as independent entities.

śrāmaṇera J., *shami*. A male Buddhist novice who has vowed to observe the ten precepts for monks.

Śrāvaka J., *shōmon*. Originally this meant a disciple of the Buddha Śākyamuni. In Mahāyāna Buddhism it refers to a person in the Hīnayāna tradition who exerts himself to attain the stage of Arhat by observing 250 precepts in the case of monks and 348 precepts in the case of nuns. From the Mahāyāna point of view this is a lower stage than that of a Bodhisattva.

Śrīmālā-sūtra J., *Shōman-gyō*. This *sūtra* transmits the teachings of the one vehicle (that of the Buddha) and ultimate truth. It has fifteen sections and is addressed to a devout queen, Śrīmālā.

"staying at home, leaving home" J., *zaike, shukke*. It is a traditional practice in Buddhism for a novice monk or nun to undergo training in the Way as part of the Buddhist community. Hence, "staying at home" signifies living as a layman, while "leaving home" denotes one who has left home and family in order to join the Buddhist community, that is, enter the monkhood.

stūpa J., *sotoba, tōba*. A Buddhist monument, generally of a domelike form, originally erected over sacred relics of the Buddha or at places consecrated as the scenes of his acts. Various materials, such as clay, brick, carved stone, and wood, are used in its construction. In China and Japan the *stūpa* developed into the towerlike pagoda, in which are enshrined various objects sacred to Buddhism.

Subhadra J., Shubatsudara. A man who became the Buddha's disciple shortly before the latter's death and is therefore known as the Buddha's "last disciple." Subhadra realized Arhathood immediately after hearing the Buddha's last sermon.

sudden enlightenment, gradual enlightenment J., *tongo, zengo*. The position that enlightenment comes gradually, as a result of reading the *sūtras* and accumulated practice, was held by the Northern Zen school in China. Eventually this school died out and only the Southern Zen school, which advocated the sudden realization of enlightenment, survived.

Śuddhodana, King J., Jōbonnō. King of the ancient northern Indian kingdom of Kapilavastu (in present-day Nepal) and father of the Buddha Śākyamuni.

Sumeru, Mount J., Shumi-sen. The highest and central mountain of the world, surrounded by four continents, according to ancient Indian geography. On its peak lives King Śakrendra and on its slopes dwell the Four-Quarter Kings. *See also* four continents; Four-Quarter Kings; Śakrendra, King.

Sunaksatra J., Zensei. According to one tradition, a son of the Buddha.

sūtra J., *kyō*. One of the three sections of the Tripiṭaka (Buddhist canon). It consists of the dialogues and teachings of the Buddha Śākyamuni.

Ta-i Tao-hsin J., Dai-i Dōshin. 580–651. The fourth Chinese Zen patriarch and Buddhist heir of Sêng-ts'an, the third patriarch.

Ta-man J., Daiman. 602–75. A Buddhist heir of Ta-i Tao-hsin.

Tan-hsia J., Tanka. 739–834. A man who first studied Confucianism but later entered the Buddhist monkhood and became one of the Buddhist heirs of Shih-t'ou.

Tathāgata J., Nyorai. A title of the Buddha Śākyamuni. It signifies a person who has arrived from and gone to *tathatā* (J., *shinnyo, nyo*), that is, the absolute reality that transcends the multitude of forms in the phenomenal world.

ten fields of knowledge J., *jū-riki*. The ten fields of knowledge of a Buddha are (1) distinguishing right and wrong, (2) knowing the relation between karma and its result, (3) comprehending various kinds of meditation, (4) judging the inferiority or superiority of people's capacities, (5) seeing into what people understand, (6) knowing people's lineage, (7) understanding the law of rebirth, (8) remembering the past, (9) knowing the births and deaths of people throughout the three periods of time (past, present, and future), and (10) rightly knowing how to extinguish every affliction in oneself and others.

ten good deeds J., *jū-zengo-dō*. The opposite of the ten wrong acts. *See* ten wrong acts.

ten great disciples The ten chief direct disciples of the Buddha Śākyamuni were Ānanda, Aniruddha, Kāśyapa, Kātyāyana, Maudgalyāyana, Pūrna, Rāhula, Śāriputra, Subhūti, and Upāli.

ten powers J., *jū-riki*. The ten powers of a Bodhisattva are (1) devotion to the Buddha's teaching and no attachment to anything, (2) increasing one's devotion, (3) the expedient ability to instruct people and alter their conduct, (4) understanding what people think, (5) satisfying people with what they want, (6) no cessation of exertion, (7) including all vehicles without abandoning the Mahāyāna, (8) the mysterious power of showing the appearance of the Buddhas in every world in each pore of the body, (9) making people turn toward the Buddha's teachings and leading them to perfection, and (10) satisfying all kinds of people with even a single phrase.

ten stages J., *jū-ji*. The ten stages of developing Bodhi-wisdom are (1) joy at benefiting oneself and others, (2) freedom from all possible defilement, (3) the emission of the light of Wisdom, (4) glowing Wisdom, (5) overcoming the utmost difficulties, (6) the realization of Wisdom, (7) proceeding far, (8) the attainment of immobility, (9) the attainment of expedient Wisdom, and (10) the ability to spread the teachings over the *Dharmadhātu* (the whole universe) as clouds overspread the sky.

ten wrong acts J., *jū-aku.* (1) To kill living things, (2) to steal others' belongings, (3) to engage in improper sexual conduct, (4) to lie, (5) to deceive others, (6) to be two-faced, (7) to speak ill of others, (8) to be greedy, (9) to become angry, and (10) to hold false views.

Theravāda *See* Mahāyāna.

thirty-two distinguishing marks J., *sanjū-ni-sō.* The body of a Buddha is said to be marked by the following distinctive features: (1) flat soles, (2) the *Dharmacakra* (wheel of the Law) on the soles, (3) slender fingers, (4) supple limbs, (5) webbed fingers and toes, (6) rounded heels, (7) long legs, (8) slender legs like those of a deer, (9) arms extending below the knees, (10) a concealed penis, (11) an armspan equal to the height of the body, (12) light radiating from the pores, (13) curly body hair, (14) a golden-hued body, (15) light radiating from the body ten feet in each direction, (16) supple shins, (17) legs, palms, shoulders, and neck harmoniously proportioned, (18) swollen armpits, (19) a dignified body like that of a lion, (20), an erect body, (21) full shoulders, (22) forty teeth, (23) firm white teeth, (24) four white canine teeth, (25) full cheeks like those of a lion, (26) flavored saliva, (27) a long slender tongue, (28) a beautiful voice, (29) blue eyes, (30) eyes shaped like those of a bull, (31) a bump between the eyes, and (32) a bump on the top of the head.

three evil worlds J., *san-akudō.* The three lowest of the six realms of existence in which the souls of living beings are traditionally thought to transmigrate until they finally realize Nirvāṇa. In ascending order, these are the realms of hell, hungry ghosts, and animals. *See also* six realms of existence.

threefold body of the Buddha Skt., *trayaḥ kāyāḥ;* J., *san-shin.* The Law-body (Skt., *Dharmakāya;* J., *hosshin*), the reward-body (Skt., *Saṃbhogakāya;* J., *hōjin*), and the manifestation-body (Skt., *Nirmāṇakāya;* J., *hōjin*). *See also* Law-body; reward body.

three poisons J., *san-doku.* Greed, anger, and ignorance.

three stages of time J., *san-ze.* Past, present, and future.

three sufferings J., *san-netsu.* The three sufferings of a dragon are (1) having its body scorched by a hot wind, (2) having its precious robe carried away by an evil wind, and (3) being attacked by a *garuḍa.*

Three Treasures Skt., *ratnatraya;* J., *sambō.* The Buddha, the Law, and the Buddhist community.

three types of superior Wisdom J., *sammyō.* The second, fifth, and sixth of the six powers of saving sentient beings. *See* six powers.

three vehicles J., *san-jō.* The three divisions of the teachings of the Buddha. In Mahāyāna Buddhism these are (1) Śrāvakayāna or Hīnayāna, in which one rightly understands the Four Noble Truths and becomes an Arhat; (2) Pratyekabuddhayāna or Mādhyamyāna, in which one rightly understands the twelve links of causation and becomes a Pratyekabuddha; and (3) Bodhisattvayāna or Mahāyāna, in which one becomes a Bodhisattva as a result of religious practice over innumerable years.

three viewpoints J., *isshin-sangai.* The Chinese T'ien-t'ai sect teaches that a phenomenon can be viewed in three different ways within the same instant. First, because a phenomenon is produced by various causes, its essence is devoid of any permanent existence, that is, is "empty." Second, nevertheless it does have a real, if only temporary, immediate existence. Third, since a phenomenon is thus a blending of both ultimate emptiness and temporary existence, it should be seen as occupying a position midway between the two poles.

three worlds J., *sangai*. The celestial world of unenlightened people, which is divided into three: (1) the world of desire, whose inhabitants have appetite and sexual desire; (2) the world of form, whose inhabitants have neither appetite nor sexual desire; and (3) the formless world, whose inhabitants have no physical form.

T'ien-shêng Kuang-têng-lu J., *Tenshō Kōtō-roku*. A thirty-section work, compiled by Li Fu-ma, recording the lineage of the Zen sect from ancient times down through the Sung dynasty (960–1279) in China.

Trāyastriṃśa Heaven J., Tōri-ten. The second of the six heavens of the world of desire, also called the Heaven of the Thirty-three Gods. It is located on top of Mount Sumeru and is ruled by King Śakrendra.

Tripiṭaka J., Sanzō. The Buddhist canon, consisting of *sūtras*, the *vinaya* (rules of discipline), and *śāstras*, commentaries on Buddhist doctrines.

true Law J., *shōbō*. *See* degenerate Buddhism.

Truth *See Dharma.*

Ts'ao-ch'i, Mount J., Sōkei-zan. A mountain located in present-day Hsinchou, Kwangtung Province. The sixth Chinese Zen patriarch, Hui-nêng, lived there in Pao-lin temple.

ts'un J., *sun*. A Chinese unit of measure equivalent to approximately 3 centimeters (1.2 inches).

Ts'ung-kao of Mount Ching J., Dai-e Shūkō. 1089–1163. A Lin-chi (Rinzai) Zen monk who entered the monkhood at the age of seventeen and realized enlightenment under the guidance of Zen Master Yüan. He is said to have had more than two thousand disciples.

Tuṣita Heaven J., Tosotsu-ten. The fourth of the six heavens in the world of desire, where the Bodhisattva Maitreya lives waiting to descend to this world to succeed the Buddha Śākyamuni.

two vehicles J., *ni-jō*. The teachings for Śrāvakas and Pratyekabuddhas.

uḍumbara flower J., *udon-ge*. A mythical Indian flower said to bloom only once every three thousand years. For this reason it is often used as an illustration of how difficult it is to come into contact with the true Law.

Upagupta J., Ubakikuta. A monk born in the Indian kingdom of Mātaṅgā. The fourth Indian patriarch, he was the Buddhist heir of Śāṇavāsa, the third patriarch, and is famous for having encouraged the construction of more than 84,000 *stūpas* in India.

Upāli J., Upari. One of the ten great disciples of the Buddha. He became a monk together with Ānanda and was very strict in his observance of the precepts.

Utpala, Utpalavarnā J., Uhatsurage. A woman born to a noble family in the city of Rājagṛha in ancient India. When she discovered that her husband had committed adultery with her mother, she left him. Later, after remarrying, she was shocked to find that the mistress of her second husband was her own daughter by her first marriage. This discovery drove her to such despair that she left her second husband and became a prostitute. Still later, she became a nun under the guidance of Maudgalyāyana.

Uttarakuru J., Hokuosu-tandai. The northern of the four continents of traditional Indian geography. Its inhabitants are said to live to be a thousand years of age and to enjoy constant happiness. They do not know the teaching of the Buddha.

Vedas J., *beida*. Hindu scriptures, composed around 1000 B.C., praising the virtues of various Hindu deities, such as Brahma, the creator god of the universe; Agni, the god of fire; and Varuṇa, the god of water. In addition, they contain sections dealing with the proper rituals and festivals for worshiping these deities, as well as the curing of illness through the use of incantations. They consist of the *Ṛg-veda, Sāma-veda, Yajur-veda,* and *Atharva-veda.*

Vulture Peak Skt., Gṛdhrakūṭa; J., Ryōju-sen. A mountain located in the northeastern part of the ancient country of Magadha in central India. It is so named because its peak resembles a vulture in shape.

wheel of the Law J., *hōrin*. The preaching of a Buddha. The Law is likened to a wheel because it crushes all illusions.

Wisdom Skt., *prajñā;* J., *e, chie*. The function of the mind that makes decisions and eliminates doubts. It also enables the mind to gain a correct understanding of phenomena and is therefore closely associated with enlightenment itself. Wisdom is not to be confused with Bodhi-wisdom. *See also* Bodhi-wisdom.

Wu, Emperor J., Bu-tei. 464–549. A Chinese emperor of the Liang dynasty (502–57) and a devout Buddhist. In his later life he is said to have been more devoted to Buddhism than to government administration.

wu J., *mu*. Absolute being, which is beyond the relative concepts of being and nonbeing.

yakṣa J., *yasha*. One of the eight kinds of demons, and sometimes regarded as a protector of Buddhism.

Yama J., Emma. The king of the world of the dead. Yama judges the dead to determine whether they have committed any wrongdoing during their lifetime. He reigns over the realm of the dead because he was the first human being to die.

yojana J., *yujun*. An Indian unit of distance equivalent to either 20 or 27 kilometers (12 or 16 miles).

Yüan-wu of Mount Chia J., Kassan Engo. 1063–1135. A Lin-chi (Rinzai) monk who is famous for his comments on a collection of *kōan* known as the *Pi-yen-lu* (J., *Hekigan-roku*).

zazen Sitting in meditation (Skt., *dhyāna;* J., *zen*) in either the full or the half lotus position. *Dhyāna* is usually translated as "meditation," although it actually refers to a state in which discriminatory thinking has ceased and reality, the Truth, is experienced directly. See "A Universal Recommendation for Zazen" for a more detailed description.

zenji Ch., *ch'an-shih*. An honorific title used in Zen Buddhism that literally means Zen master or teacher. In Japan, this honorific title is always added to the name of a noted Zen monk as a siga of respect.

The "weathermark" identifies this book as a production of John Weatherhill, Inc., publishers of fine books on Asia and the Pacific. Supervising editor: Suzanne Trumbull. Book design and typography: Rebecca Davis. Production supervisor: Yutaka Shimoji. Composition, printing, and binding: Kwangmyong Printing Company, Seoul. The typeface used is Monotype Baskerville, with hand-set Baskerville for display.

天福元年中元日

書于觀音導利院